Amazing Grace for Those Who Suffer

Amazing Grace for Those Who Suffer

10 Life-Changing Stories of Hope and Healing

Jeff Cavins and Matthew Pinto

ASCENSION
PRESS

Acknowledgments

Many thanks to . . .

- Maria Ruiz Scaperlanda for her tireless effort in assisting the editors and contributors with her editing expertise. This book would have taken another six months without you.

- Kinsey Caruth for his professionalism in producing the cover design.

- Mark Brumley and Tom Nash for their theological assistance.

- Tracy Moran, Lucy Scholand, Lisa Lynch, Elena Perri, and Jim Bofenkamp for their proofreading expertise.

- John O'Rourke of Loyola Graphics for, once again, delivering excellent typesetting services in an upbeat and professional manner.

- And, most importantly, to the ten contributors who shared their hearts as they shared their personal experiences. It is our great hope that your leap of faith in sharing your story will bless countless souls with the healing grace given by Jesus Christ. You have all become good friends. We are delighted to have had the chance to work with you.

—Jeff Cavins and Matthew Pinto

Contents

To all the families of missing children.

— Jeff Cavins

To my parents, Albert and Barbara Pinto, for all the sacrifices they made for my six siblings and me. Only in heaven will we know all that you have done for us. Thank you.

— Matthew Pinto

Introduction

How many times in the past year have you said, "My life is perfect"?

If you're like most people, you may not have said it at all. Our lives, no matter how good, are often interrupted and complicated by difficulties. For some of us the suffering is minor; for others, intense suffering accompanies every heartbeat of every day. Suffering can be visible and dramatic, or it can go unnoticed by all around us as we valiantly try to cope. One thing is for sure: Any type of suffering can take a person to the breaking point.

We human beings have always gone to great lengths to avoid suffering. Many of our attempts only lead to more suffering. How many lives have become more problematic, for example, from the supposed "quick fix" of substance abuse or abortion? Understanding suffering and its meaning can help us respond to it in a healthy, constructive, and life-affirming manner.

Most of us do not give serious thought to the subject of suffering until we are in the midst of it. And in the midst of suffering we often lack proper perspective. Stuck in the quicksand of our pain, we are distracted, even panicked, and we feel that the answers are just out of reach. It is then that we are most likely to turn to God for understanding.

The question we most often ask in the midst of suffering is *Why?* Why is this thing happening to me? As you will see through the stories told in this book and the concluding chapter, our *why?* finds its answer in the larger question, Why did God come to earth to suffer as a Man? How does God help us understand suffering in a world where drudgery coexists with delight, brokenness with bliss?

Where the suffering of humanity and the suffering of God intersect, we find profound meaning. As Pope John Paul II has said: "The springs of divine power gush forth precisely in the midst of human weakness. Those who share in the sufferings of Christ preserve in their own sufferings a very special particle of the infinite treasure of the world's Redemption, and can share this treasure with others" (*Salvifici Doloris,* 27).

When our lives are joined with Christ, we change. Every aspect of our life is changed, even our suffering. The suffering actually becomes redemptive, and we participate with Christ in redeeming the world. Once we discover meaning in our suffering, we gain a key to spiritual treasures, both in our earthly life and in the life to come. We obtain a wisdom that enables us not only to survive but to *thrive*, even while adversity continues.

Since you have taken up this book to read, you no doubt recognize a need to invest some time in reflection on this matter—and such reflection is a critical prerequisite to understanding the mystery of suffering. Perhaps you are suffering, or perhaps you know someone who needs answers. This book may be a lifesaver, thrown to you in the nick of time, or it may fortify you for future ordeals.

Amazing Grace for Those Who Suffer looks into the lives of ten ordinary people who have endured extraordinary pain. These Christians, at various places along their spiritual journeys, could not have foreseen the course of events that would lead to such adversity. Nevertheless, they found grace to discover in their ordeals that God was there to meet them and bring meaning to what the world would consider senseless circumstances. We trust you will discover, as we did, the treasures they gained in the midst of their pain.

Here you'll meet:

- **Carl Cleveland**, a dedicated Catholic deacon and successful New Orleans attorney who was falsely accused of fraud and spent two and one-half years in prison;
- **Janet Moylan**, who looked on helplessly as her husband and daughter were swept out to sea;
- **Debbie Harding**, a former New England Patriots cheerleader whose fairy tale life turned into a simultaneous battle against breast cancer and her husband's drug addiction;
- **Joan Ulicny**, who suffered a near-fatal head-on collision with an eighteen-wheeler;
- **the Clarey family**, whose eleven-year-old daughter was murdered on her paper route;
- **Grace MacKinnon**, who was born with a severe handicap and faces a lifetime of serious disability;
- **Peggy Stoks**, who suffered the deep pain of sexual abuse at the hands of a family member;
- **Dr. Kim Hardey**, a successful Ob-Gyn who came face-to-face with his own sin following the tragic death of his son;
- **Tom Howard**, the renowned Catholic convert and author, who has suffered quietly for more than thirty years with debilitating migraines;
- **Deb Headworth**, who lost nine children through miscarriage and has endured numerous other physical maladies.

It is our sincere hope that you will learn more about the mystery of suffering by watching the passion, death, and resurrection of Christ lived out daily in the lives of these ten remarkable people. And we hope as well that you will experience a transformation in spirit.

We must all take to heart the words of Pope John Paul II, a man acquainted with great personal suffering: "It is suffering, more than anything else, which clears the way for the grace which transforms human souls" (*Salvifici Doloris*, 26).

Are you experiencing sorrow and trouble in your life? You are not alone. Others have been where you are. More importantly, *Jesus* has been where you are. Open yourself to experience the transformation we ourselves experienced in bringing you this book. Discover the source of power for all who believe: God's grace, His *amazing grace*.

In Christ,

Jeff Cavins and *Matthew Pinto*

I Choose God

Janet Moylan

August 1, 1996.

That date, indelibly carved in my memory, divides my life in two: before Tim's and Jenni's deaths and after. It is the day my life was changed forever.

In 1996 my husband Tim and I had been married eighteen years and were the parents of five wonderful children. Tim was a successful businessman and entrepreneur. Among his career accomplishments, Tim had developed a gas marketing company; built a community swimming pool for families in our area of Omaha; and built a double-rink ice-plex in partnership with the city of Omaha. Tim served on the boards of businesses and charities. He truly used his God-given talents to make this world a better place.

My parents, Jack and Virginia Neneman, celebrated their fiftieth wedding anniversary that summer. In a continuation of the golden celebration, we invited them to join us on our summer vacation to Cabo San Lucas, Mexico. Several other family members also joined us: my brother Jack and his wife, Joan; my brother Rick, his wife, Jane; and their three children.

We arrived on July 31. My parents were staying at the beach house with us, and my brothers and their families at a nearby hotel. On the first morning, Tim got up early and went into town to buy groceries to fix us a big breakfast. The children were eager to go outside to the beach and quickly dressed in their swimsuits. We told the children that they would need to wear life jackets when they played in the water. They quickly put them on.

Tim went out on the beach with our four oldest children. When he realized how strong the surf was, he told them they could not swim. The weather that day was beautiful and sunny, but the water was rough. Hurricane Douglas, still far out in the Pacific Ocean, was definitely stirring up the waves on the coast. I sat high up on the beach with eighteen-month-old Ann Marie as she played in the sand. Our oldest, fifteen-year-old Michaela, came to sit nearby, enjoying the sunny day with me and my parents.

Nothing could have prepared us for what happened next.

Tim and our middle children—Amy, fourteen, Jenni, ten, and Daniel, nine—were walking along the beach when a towering wave came up on the shore, pulling the children forcefully into the ocean. Amy saw the wave coming and was able to crouch down and remain firmly grounded. She was not dragged out as far as the others and was able to get out of the water on her own. Tim immediately ran into the water to rescue Jenni and Daniel, who were being dragged out by the current's force.

The immense wave reminded me of a ferris wheel. From where we were we could see Tim, Jenni, and Daniel rise up at the crest of the wave, then crash down into the ocean and out of our sight, only to be pulled up to the top of the wave again. This circular motion continued, yet it did not pull them out to sea. I could see that Tim had Jenni in his arms, but I could also tell there was no way he could swim out of that monstrous wave.

Within seconds of hearing their screams, I ran down the beach to the water's edge, where a man stopped me, yelling at me not to go in after them. As I helplessly watched them trapped in the wave, I prayed. I prayed harder on that beach than I have ever prayed in my life. I begged God to save them, and I had strong faith that He would do it. Even when there seemed to be no chance of their survival, I did not give up my hope and faith. I knew God could instantly put them on a rock on the shore if He willed it. And I believed He would give them back to me.

After being trapped in the wave for what seemed like an eternity, Daniel was thrust out, landing in shallow water. The man on the beach helped me carry him out of the water and up to higher ground. Our son was exhausted but still conscious. He had swallowed a lot of water and sand. My first thought was to thank God for saving Daniel, and then I immediately returned to praying for Tim and Jenni to be rescued. Minutes later Jenni's life jacket washed up on shore, but we could not see her or Tim any more.

In mere minutes life was forever changed. One moment I was sitting on a beautiful beach with my parents, Michaela, and Ann Marie. The next minute I was frantically praying for my husband and children to be spared a horrible death.

Somebody from a nearby house brought out a big comforter to wrap around Daniel to keep him warm. About fifteen minutes later an ambulance came to take him to the hospital. I knew Daniel needed me with him, and I realized the only thing I could do for Tim and Jenni now was to continue to pray. Even then, I never stopped believing that God could give us a miracle and save them. I knew Daniel's survival was already a miracle.

Daniel was taken to the Clínica Levy, a small hospital with only a few rooms. When he was able to speak, Daniel looked up at me from his bed.

"Mom," he said, "two things saved me: my life jacket and God. I prayed to God, 'Please save my life,' and I begged Him for mercy for anything I'd ever done wrong. The next thing I knew, I was on the beach."

I was amazed at Daniel's prayer—and at the depth of my nine-year-old's faith. At the hour of my own death, I hope that I have the presence of mind to pray for forgiveness the way Daniel did.

We had not been at the hospital long when the physician taking care of Daniel, Dr. Najar, called me out of the room. I looked intently at his face as he informed me that they had found Tim's body. He was dead. Although they had not found Jenni's body yet, he said, they assumed she was dead too. I cried out loud, falling onto the waiting room couch. My world had collapsed.

There are no words to describe that moment. I was grief-stricken. But I had to be strong. I had a weak little boy waiting for me in the hospital room. I felt so grateful that Daniel's life had been spared, and I needed to be with him.

I did not want Daniel to know about his dad and sister yet. I was afraid that if he cried too hard it would jeopardize the condition of his lungs. In answer to the prayer of my heart and totally by God's grace, I was able to stop my tears and calmly return to Daniel's room. As devastated as I was, I tried to focus on the fact that Daniel was alive and that I needed to help him recover.

The first time Daniel asked about his dad and sister, I told him we did not know anything for certain yet, which was true at that moment. Later in the afternoon Dr. Najar examined Daniel again and then talked to me in the hall.

"I think he knows," Dr. Najar said. "Daniel is very sad."

Daniel was showing improvement, and the doctor thought it was time for me to tell him about Tim and Jenni. I agreed. But first, I prayed to the Holy Spirit for the strength to tell Daniel calmly. And I prayed for Daniel to have the strength to hear what I had to say.

As I reflect back on this moment, it is obvious to me that Daniel and I were, indeed, filled with the Holy Spirit. I do not remember the exact words I used to tell Daniel that his dad and sister had died. I just remember we were both at peace as we talked about Daddy and Jenni being with God.

Daniel said, "At least we know they are okay now."

We also talked about their seeing Grandpa Moylan and Daddy's two sisters, Barbara and Molly, in heaven.

"And," Daniel added, "they get to see our baby!"

He was referring to our baby whom I had miscarried in 1984. Once again I was amazed at this wonderful son of mine. I was also thankful that Daniel offered me such a comforting thought, as I imagined Tim and Jenni meeting and holding our little baby.

Having family with us in Mexico was such a blessing. I can't imagine what it would have been like without their love and support. My parents were with the girls when I went with Daniel to the hospital. My brothers, Jack and Rick, were called at their hotel, and they immediately went to the beach house to be with my daughters too. Later, they carried Tim's body off the beach and made the official identification required by the police. Rick and Jane stayed with Daniel so I could go see Tim.

When I insisted that seeing Tim was extremely important to me, the officials consented, cautioning me to remember Tim as he had been. I am glad I insisted. I think I always would have regretted not seeing him. My mind may have tricked me into believing that it really had not been Tim's body.

Tim lay on a table surrounded by curtains on three sides. When I was allowed to see him, I hugged my husband of eighteen years, kissed him for the last time, and told him good-bye. I thanked Tim, telling him what a good husband and father he had been and how much I loved him.

I was devastated, but I needed to get back to Daniel. Being

in a foreign country, with my daughters at the beach house and Daniel at the hospital, I could not allow myself much time to grieve. I needed to take care of my children and try to get our family back home.

I went back to the beach house that evening to see my daughters. They had suffered this great loss too, and I had not been able to be with them that fateful day. We sat in the bedroom, talking and crying. I then gathered a few personal things so that I could spend the night with Daniel at the hospital.

When I arrived at the hospital, Rick and Jane told me that Daniel had gotten sick to his stomach and spit up sand. His I.V. had come out, and he had been bleeding on the bed. Yet Daniel stayed calm.

Just forty-eight hours earlier our family had been in Omaha preparing for our vacation. Now my husband and daughter were both dead, and my son was lying in a hospital bed. At this point Jenni still had not been found. Because the ocean was so rough, boats had not been able to go search for her.

I needed so much help and strength from God. I prayed the rosary and other prayers throughout the night. I believe that God was holding me and helping me to get through the worst night of my life.

During the night Daniel awoke and told me he was bleeding. His I.V. had come out a second time. There was a puddle of blood on the floor and a lot of blood on Daniel's bed. I stepped outside the room after the nurse fixed his I.V. and cleaned up the mess. On my way back to the room, I saw a group of men come into the hospital and walk toward the front desk. Since it was about 2:30 A.M. and the only people in this tiny hospital were Daniel, the nurse, an elderly woman across the hall, and me, I felt nervous. I could not imagine what anyone would want at that time of night, and I prayed for our protection.

The nurse called me over to talk to the men. One introduced himself as the mayor of Cabo San Lucas. Because he could not speak English, he called his wife on the phone to translate. The mayor expressed his sympathy and said that he would help our family in any way that he could. I found out later that a friend from the states, Howard Buffett, had called the Mexican governor, who in turn must have called the mayor of Cabo to ask him to do everything possible to recover Jenni's body.

Jack and Joan came to the hospital early the next morning with food for Daniel. Jack told me that our parish church, Saint Wenceslaus, had held a rosary prayer service the night before for our family and that the church had been full. I wept. Knowing that there were so many people praying for us was very comforting. I believe that the prayers of so many helped in Daniel's return to health and in the eventual finding of Jenni's body.

Later I went back to the beach house to shower and to see Michaela, Amy, Ann Marie, and my parents. While I was there, my other brother, Roy, called from Omaha. I told him I was praying that we would recover Jenni's body before we had to go home.

Roy started crying. He said my prayers were already answered. He had just received a call from Rick Dunning, our friend in Oklahoma City who owned the house where we were staying. Rick's crew from the marina had found Jenni, and they had her on the boat.

I yelled the news to the family. Everyone started crying and hugging each other. I do not know how I could have left Mexico without Jenni, yet we needed to get Daniel home to a better-equipped hospital.

That afternoon I went to the police station to sign papers regarding the accident. Rick, without my knowing, went to identify Jenni. Once again, the officials were trying to protect me, but I just had to see my little girl one more time.

I told Rick that I feared the worst, that Jenni had been dismembered by sharks. But he assured me that her body was only very bruised. My sweet Jennifer had entered this world with a bruised face, and she left it with a bruised face. She was such a big baby—ten pounds, three ounces—that her face was bruised during the delivery. I prayed that this final bruising happened after her death. I prayed that she and Tim had not suffered long. It must have been so frightening for them. I like to think that they died at the same moment and that Jesus took them to heaven together.

Now that we had Jenni back, we could go home. Pat Lenaghan, a friend who works at Methodist Hospital in Omaha, arranged for a direct Med-Evac flight to bring Daniel, Ann Marie, and me home on August 2. The plane was too small for Michaela and Amy to join us, so they traveled home with my parents and Rick's family. Jack and Joan stayed one more night to make sure that Tim's and Jenni's bodies were flown home the next day. Back in Omaha my sister, Susie, and my brother, Roy, took care of many details and communications.

When we arrived in Omaha, Susie and her husband, Rick, met us at the airport and took Ann Marie home. I rode in the ambulance with Daniel to Children's Hospital, where we were met by our pastor, Father Frank Dvorak, our pediatrician, Dr. Mary Lou Flearl, and a group of dear friends. Daniel was examined and x-rayed. He checked out fine, and I was able to take him home. As we drove into our neighborhood of Pacific Hallow, we were welcomed by yellow ribbons lining the streets, placed there by our neighbors.

Over the next few days countless people came to our home to be with us, bring us food, grieve with us, and love us. God's compassion and love poured out on our family through our relatives, friends, and parish community. It gave us strength in our tremendous sorrow.

During those early days I was in constant prayer, asking the Holy Spirit to please help me through each difficult task that arose. I remember clearly how direction was given to me when I had to select the cemetery plots. I also felt Tim with me through this heartbreaking chore.

Still, I did not know how I would make it through the rosary wake service, greeting the hundreds of people who came. I prayed so hard for strength.

By the time the service started, I knew God was holding me. As each person came up to me in line, I seemed to know his or her name immediately. (Even in the best of circumstances, I have trouble remembering names.) Although people would have understood if I had just sat and cried, I wanted to acknowledge and thank each person.

The morning of the funeral I was exhausted, as I had been unable to sleep. The sorrow was overwhelming. I was dreading the final act—the funeral Mass and taking my child and husband to the cemetery. I needed to be strong for my children, but I felt weak. Again I prayed for the Holy Spirit to hold me up and help me through the day. And I also prayed to Tim, asking him for his intercession.

There was a huge crowd at our church. Father Frank Dvorak was the celebrant, and Archbishop Elden Curtiss and several other priests concelebrated. I thought it was important for my children and me to be the ones who covered the caskets with the palls, but that moment was heart-wrenching. It was also important to me to be fully aware in this Mass, which was so significant for our family. I knew this was an important day, the most important Mass our family would ever attend. We were sending Tim and Jenni to God.

God did not let me down. He gave me the grace, and He carried me through these immensely difficult events and days.

The day after the funeral was my fortieth birthday. It was the first day since Tim and Jenni died that we could sleep late. We did not have to be anywhere at a certain time. We were exhausted and needed a quiet day. My sister and brother-in-law invited us over for dinner, and though I had no desire to celebrate my birthday, it was comforting to get out of the house and eat a meal with loved ones.

Ten days after Jenni died was her eleventh birthday. She had been looking forward to this day and had mailed party invitations before we left on our vacation. Although I knew it would be painful, I wanted to have the party and see Jenni's friends again. I wanted to celebrate my wonderful daughter's life and the loving, beautiful child that she was. My friend Mary Eileen hosted the party, and we invited the mothers of Jenni's friends. The girls brought gifts for children at the Catholic Charities Women's Shelter in Omaha. During the party they sang "Happy Birthday" to Jenni and released helium balloons to the sky.

A few weeks later school began. This helped our family to focus on moving on with our lives, yet it was indescribably sad. Jenni would not begin the sixth grade, and Tim was not there to share the special first day with our children. I drove Daniel to Saint Wenceslaus, and as I sat in my car watching Jenni's classmates walk into the building, my tears came in a flood.

Little Ann Marie was too young to understand the sorrow that we felt. Her innocent joy and laughter were a big help in our family's healing. In the midst of our sadness, she could make us laugh and play. New life brings great joy into families. On our sixteenth wedding anniversary we had told our children the happy news that we were expecting a new baby (Ann Marie). Jenni had told us that every year when she blew out her birthday candles, she had wished for a baby sister! It is interesting to watch Ann Marie, now seven years old, who so resembles Jenni in her looks, interests, spirit, and laughter. How I wish that Tim and Jenni were with us still and that Ann Marie could know them. Jenni loved her little sister dearly and would have enjoyed growing up with her. Still, I am confident that Jenni and her daddy are watching over us.

Ordinary things become difficult when loved ones are no longer with you. It was so hard to sign birthday cards from our family, because it seemed wrong not to write "Tim" and "Jenni" with the rest of our names. Our parish was compiling a new directory that would include photos of each family. A family picture without Tim and Jenni felt incomplete, yet it would have been unfair to my children to avoid the photo. Every "first" that we experienced without Tim and Jenni was tough. We celebrated birthdays and holidays with smiles on our faces but with sorrow in our hearts.

When my husband and daughter died, I lost two people with whom I had the deepest of loving relationships. Usually we lose and mourn one beloved person at a time, but I had lost two—and the depth of the pain was at times more than I could bear. Sometimes I wept for Tim, sometimes for Jenni. But most of the time I wept for the loss of both of them.

The following summer I wanted to take the children on a vacation, yet I did not want to go to an ocean or even a lake. The mountains seemed to promise a good change for us, so we planned a trip to Colorado. I also wanted to be home on August 1 to go to Mass and visit the cemetery on the first anniversary of Tim's and Jenni's deaths. And I wanted to be home to attend Mass and the cemetery on Jenni's twelfth birthday, August 11. The rest of the summer was open for our trip.

I called my friend Jeannie to inquire about renting her family's condominium in Frisco, Colorado, for a week. She said they were booked but she would call me if there were any cancellations. On June 4, Tim's birthday, Jeannie called to say there was a cancellation and that the condo was available from August 2 to August 8. Some may look at this as coincidental, but I believe this was a grace from heaven. We received a special present on Tim's birthday! I think Tim helped to make this happen.

The month of July was very difficult. As the one-year anniversary of the deaths of Tim and Jenni approached, I found myself remembering all the things we did together during those last weeks of their lives. I began to dread August 1.

As always, God was very good to me. During this tough time He blessed me with a dream that gave me great comfort. In the dream I sensed that there was a distance between Tim and me, and this really saddened me. I perceived we were not getting along and had not spent much time together. I was determined to get back together with Tim. I felt that if we could talk, everything would be okay.

I had just started making small talk with him when I noticed he was wearing a magnificent robe that reached to his ankles. There was a pattern on most of the robe, a gold design on a white background, with the edges trimmed in gold cloth. It was unlike anything Tim ever would have worn on earth.

He asked me, "Do you like my robe?"

I was puzzled as to why he would buy a robe like that, but I answered, "You look like royalty."

Tim was smiling and being like his old self, and I felt that everything was right between us again. Then I realized this was a heavenly robe. It was a sign that he was going to die. In my dream I had already suffered some sort of a tragedy, but I did not think of it as Tim's and Jenni's deaths. I was struck with the thought that Tim was going to die and I was going to lose him.

In my dream, I started crying and went to my room. Tim followed me. He wanted to know why I was crying, but I could not tell him that he was going to die. Yet he was my husband, the one person to whom I could tell my most personal thoughts. I had to tell someone. But if not Tim, then who? This dilemma kept me crying.

I woke up crying. In my half-awake state I realized Tim had already died. My tears became tears of joy as I remembered how I had just seen and talked to Tim in his heavenly robe! I knew this was an important dream, and I never wanted to forget it. I immediately took out my notebook to record it.

As I wrote the day's date, 7-11-97, I realized the significance of those numbers. Jenni and I celebrate our birthdays in August. Mine is on the seventh and hers is on the eleventh. Jenni once told me that seven and eleven are our special numbers. Again, the date of this dream may seem coincidental, but to me it was another grace from heaven.

I see this dream as a gift from God. Jenni had been in the dream briefly, at the beginning. I was happy to see her again. God gave me a glimpse of Tim and Jenni to comfort me and to reassure me that they are in heaven.

In November of 1997 I received a great grace from the Bible. I had been diagnosed with bladder cancer two years earlier and had to be checked every three months. Just before Thanksgiving my doctor discovered another tumor in my bladder. He told me that I would need surgery.

When I left his office, I drove down the street to the cemetery where Tim and Jenni are buried. I sat in my car near their graves and cried for a while. I was sad about the surgery, but I was more sad about facing it without Tim's support. I was also missing Jenni.

When I left the cemetery, I went to Saint Wenceslaus Church for my hour of eucharistic adoration. I opened the Bible to the New Testament, where I read: "My brothers, count it pure joy when you are involved in every sort of trial. Realize that when your faith is tested this makes for endurance. Let endurance come to its perfection so that you may be fully mature and lacking in nothing" (James 1:2–4).

Reading that Scripture passage at this time of deep sadness lifted me up, filling my heart with great joy. I felt God's presence, speaking to me through His Word. Yes, this was a time of trial, but with God's grace I would endure. I knew I was not alone. God was with me, and He would carry me through another one of life's trials.

Several months after Tim and Jenni died, I heard Dr. James Dobson on the radio talking about how people deal with tragedy in their lives. Dr. Dobson pointed out that you either choose God or despair. I thought emphatically that I had chosen God and that I would continue to do so. I was crushed, full of sorrow, but I would not despair. God was my rock, and I was holding on to Him for dear life. I had faith and trust that God would help me, and He did. And He still does.

One of my great comforts as I reflect on the time before Tim's death is the awareness of the many ways God was working in both his life and mine. I can see how God was strengthening our faith and preparing us for this defining moment. A few years earlier I had become ill with influenza, developed pneumonia, and needed to be hospitalized.

I now look upon this illness as one of my faith builders. I relied on prayer, the rosary, and reading the Bible to help me through those days. I was blessed with a great desire to read spiritual books. Secular novels lost their appeal, and I grew in my faith through the books I was reading. When our church started perpetual adoration, I signed up for one hour every week. Praying regularly before the Blessed Sacrament has been a great help to me on my spiritual journey.

When I was diagnosed with bladder cancer, Ann Marie was just nine months old. This was devastating news, and I recall thinking that I might not live to raise our children to adulthood. Tim would be doing this without me. As with the case of influenza, living with hospitalizations and surgeries pushed me again to rely on God for my help and my strength. I think God was preparing me for the hardest thing in my life, when I would lose my husband and daughter. Looking back at that time, as difficult as it was to be dealing with cancer, it was a small cross in comparison to the deaths of Tim and Jenni.

Tim's faith was also growing in the last year of his life. He had signed up for the 4:00 A.M. hour on Wednesdays for perpetual adoration, and he began to pray the rosary daily. Tim also started a spiritual journal. In his writings there is a sense of awareness that he possibly would not live much longer and of his wanting to use the time God had given him to do His will. Taking more time for his family and cutting back on new business projects became priorities in Tim's life. We began and ended each day by praying together, which helped us to grow closer to God as well as to each other. I believe that God was tugging on Tim's heart and preparing him for eternal life.

Another great comfort for me has been my children. I thank the Lord for Michaela, Amy, Daniel, and little Ann Marie, who keep me going. As their mother, I knew I had to be strong for them. I did not want my children to despair and give up on life. God would not want that, and neither would their dad and sister. The children have helped me to take the focus off my sorrow and to concentrate on them. I am so proud of each of them. They have not let this great loss destroy them. They have continued on with their lives, friendships, and education.

My extended family and friends have been very supportive. God shows His great love for us through the love and help of those close to us. A group of my neighbors formed a rosary group, and we have been meeting weekly to pray, discuss the Faith, and enjoy our friendship. As Scripture says, "We know that God makes all things work together for the good of those who love him, who have been called according to his decree" (Romans 8:28).

I thank the Lord for giving me my faith and my family. I thank Him for helping me through my suffering and for giving me hope in the midst of my sorrow. I still miss my husband and daughter greatly, but knowing that I will see them again in heaven someday eases my pain and is a wonderful comfort to me. Day by day, I continue to choose God.

The deaths of Tim and Jenni have touched the lives of every person who knew them. It has been very comforting to hear stories of renewed faith that have resulted from our loss. There are people who have found their faith or strengthened their faith directly because of this tragedy. He has spiritually healed some, emotionally healed others, and reminded me daily of His faithfulness in times of great trial. These stories have been a source of peace for me—knowing that our Lord gives when He takes. He has brought good out of bad.

My Thorn in the Flesh

Carl Cleveland

In a way, this is another "Why Do Bad Things Happen to Good People?" story. But it is also a good deal more. You see, I spent nearly two and a half years in jail—but I was innocent.

After thirty-five years of practicing law as a civil litigation trial lawyer, I learned through bitter experience that our federal system of criminal justice is badly broken and in need of an extensive overhaul. I have some ideas about the problems and possible solutions, but those are for another book.

I also learned that there is an inexplicable practical power in prayer and boundless reason for hope in all circumstances, no matter how grim or overwhelming. I was dead and have come back to life. Not only back to merely existing but to living in boundless joy and peace.

Finally, I learned firsthand that hard work, faith, and a dauntless sense of humor help immeasurably in surviving what can only be described as our own personal "dark night of the soul." I am convinced that at some point we are all challenged beyond our perceived ability to endure. Because of this common human experience, it is my hope that every reader will find something of value in reliving the ordeal my family, clients, friends, and I shared for five and a half years.

Early in the morning on a hot August day in 1995 as I was walking from my law firm's parking garage to our office, I was unaware that an army of FBI agents was watching and waiting with a search warrant that would end my life as I knew it.

My office building was a historic structure, more than 175 years old, that I had purchased and converted from a rundown, $3-per-night flophouse into the nicest law offices in downtown New Orleans. The three-story, rose-colored building had been rebuilt to its original splendor with painstaking attention to detail. My personal office on the second floor had a twenty-foot-high ceiling, mahogany doors, a fireplace, and walkthrough windows opening to an elegant wrought-iron balcony typical of the city's famous French Quarter. Library shelves surrounded my mahogany desk and conference table. The walls were covered with mementos from years of successful litigation and pictures from skiing, hunting, and fishing trips with my buddies.

My firm typically represented in court the powerless and downtrodden against people and institutions in positions of power. We worked on a contingent basis, getting paid and recovering our expenses only if we won. We almost always won. Although we had only ten attorneys and our firm was considered small, our reputation was much bigger. We experienced many years of beating the biggest and best law firms in Louisiana and in the large legal centers of Dallas, Atlanta, Washington, D.C., and New York.

I had started the firm almost twenty years earlier with three partners. Over the years, two younger partners and three superstar sons of my closest friends had joined us. My eldest daughter, Kitty, had also joined me, and I hoped she would come to share my love for law and its usefulness in resolving disputes and correcting grave injustices.

It is safe to say that I took pride in my office, my partners and employees, our clients, my work, and the amazing success we enjoyed. Unlike many lawyers, jaded by years of cynical combat, I loved my legal practice. Each morning I rose early and left home, eager for another day of challenges. My work was satisfying, challenging, lucrative, and personally rewarding. I planned to not retire as long as there was an interesting case or someone needing help. After more than thirty years of learning and struggling to overcome obstacles, everything seemed nearly perfect in my chosen life's work.

From a personal faith perspective, I felt equally satisfied and at peace. In 1983, my wife made me attend (much against my will) a Cursillo retreat. Cursillos are designed to form and stimulate persons to engage in evangelizing their everyday environments. I had a powerful conversion experience while on the retreat. Before long I joined a men's prayer group and began to read Scripture and pray with fervor for the first time in my life. A few years later, I began a three and one-half year deacon formation program at Notre Dame Seminary for the Archdiocese of New Orleans.

In 1989 I was ordained a permanent deacon and assigned to my home parish. I assisted at Mass, preached on a regular rotation on Sundays, administered the sacraments of baptism and matrimony, presided at funerals, and discharged other duties. With my legal training in public speaking, homiletics came naturally to me. One of my main responsibilities was providing baptismal seminars for unwed mothers who wanted Baptism for their children. This grew naturally into counseling these young mothers as they struggled with the overwhelming realities of single motherhood. I cherished all of my opportunities to share my faith journey with my congregation.

My wife, Joey, served as director of New Orleans Right to Life, a well-known pro-life group. A suburban mother of six daughters, she gave talks to teenagers at all interested high schools—public, private, and parochial—in the New Orleans metro area. I grew accustomed to Joey's interviews on the evening news and her trips to the state capital to lobby the legislature. With courage and determination, she accomplished miracles and overcame the difficulties inherent in pro-life work.

I was equally proud of each of my six daughters. Kitty, the oldest, practiced law with me. Connie is a former flight attendant who, after a conversion experience, went back to Franciscan University in Steubenville, Ohio, to get a master's degree in theology.

My third daughter, Beth, moved to New York City after college to go into business for herself. Patricia, daughter number four, worked hard to become a nurse, a field in which her gentleness and compassion serve her well.

Caroline, our fifth child, recently graduated from high school at the top of her class. Our youngest daughter, Caitlin, is nine years younger than Caroline. I was forty-six when she was born. Not surprisingly, she is everyone's favorite. She is bright and pleasant and an excellent athlete.

In short, the Cleveland family enjoyed a bountiful life. Despite the normal personality clashes, we were a close-knit family. We had financial success and good health. We shared faith, many friends, and a sense of purpose in our various ministries. We felt a real sense of belonging in our church and community, and we were accorded a gratifying amount of respect and recognition.

And then, on August 17, 1995, the FBI showed up.

Instantly I was involved in a headline-grabbing political scandal the likes of which even Louisiana, the state of wild politics, never had seen before. Although my role was minor, and the press focused primarily on elected officials, I soon grew tired of the lurid headlines and my near daily appearances on the six o'clock news. I felt sure that the prosecutors

would soon see the error of accusing my clients—and me—
of wrongdoing.

I had clients in the controversial video poker business, and
I had appeared before legislative committees drafting operating regulations. I always insisted that my clients play strictly
by the rules. I discouraged campaign contributions to members of the legislature who were involved in the regulatory
process. And I requested that my clients' contacts with leg-
islators be exclusively through reputable registered lobbyists.
I was sure my clients were following the rules.

It soon became clear that dozens of well-known senators,
representatives, lawyers, lobbyists, CPAs, and business people
had been subject to government wiretaps. Carefully orchestrated government leaks of selected portions of the wiretaps
ended the public service of many members of the Louisiana
legislature. The prosecutors promised the public multiple in-
dictments and convictions. It was hinted that the governor of
Louisiana was the ultimate prize for the investigators. Simply
being identified as the possible target of such a broad federal
investigation was devastating to dozens of public officials
who were never prosecuted. They lost re-election or simply
retired in undeserved disgrace.

The nightmare grew daily. Finally I was afforded the cour-
tesy of a meeting with the U.S. Attorney. I was confident that
my ordeal would soon end. I had an offer for them: I wouldn't
seek any form of immunity. On the contrary, I offered to answer any question on any topic under the penalty of perjury.
If the attorney-client privilege would prevent my answering,
I was certain I could get the consent of my clients to waive
the privilege so that I could respond fully and freely. All I
asked in return was a good-faith gentlemen's agreement that
I would not be prosecuted if I was successful in convincing
the prosecutors that I was innocent. The government had

nothing to lose, and as far as I knew, they were interested in the truth, not just convictions at any cost.

I was not ready for the response.

Upon hearing my offer, the ranking prosecutor in the district flung my files to the floor and, shouting profanity, left the room. I was shocked, confused, and speechless. My offer was fair and a no-lose deal for the government. It was rejected in emphatic terms.

But then the assistants to the lead prosecutor began to hint that another deal was possible. I could get a slap on the wrist for pleading guilty to some lesser charge (this guilty plea would supposedly buttress my credibility when I testified against others targeted by the prosecutors) if I would "cooperate" by providing the government with damaging testimony against any of several public officials whose names I was given. When I said I had no such knowledge or information, they persisted nonetheless. They emphasized that I only had to say what they "needed to hear." It was stressed that as a lawyer I should know what that meant.

I was confused at first, then stunned. They were inviting me to commit perjury to avoid prosecution; at least that was my strong impression. As they emphasized what a believable witness I would make, I felt nauseated. I resisted their proposal, and then they pointed out that my career would be ruined if I did not "cooperate" with the government. I resolved on the spot that, no matter what the cost, I would never sell my soul. I would not destroy someone else's life by buying a deal for myself with perjury.

Once my proposal was rejected, I did not speak to the prosecutors again until I took the witness stand in my own defense. I could not understand why they pursued me with such vengeance. I had not refused to cooperate; I had refused to lie! Most painful were the direct or implied threats made against my partners, my employees, my daughter, Kitty, and the young lawyers who worked with me—my fellow "unindicted co-conspirators."

After long delays, during which I continued to hope against hope that my offer to answer questions would be accepted, I was indicted. Once again the media circus camped out in my life. Also charged were an old client, his daughter, his CPA, and two prominent state senators. The trial was scheduled for May of 1997. Then, the week before the trial, mystical experiences and an unexpected spiritual transformation began in earnest.

A few days before the trial began in May, Connie graduated from Franciscan University. Joey and I attended the graduation with a pall of gloom hanging over the joyful occasion.

At a post-graduation luncheon at a local restaurant, we ran into Patti and Al Mansfield, whose son was also getting his master's degree. Patti is known to Catholic charismatics around the world as Patti Gallagher, the college student whose experiences and books ignited the worldwide charismatic renewal in the Catholic Church in the 1960s. Aware of my trial, she asked if she could pray with me. I accepted eagerly, and Patti said that she was moved to share a passage from Scripture. It was 2 Corinthians 12. I was only dimly aware of the passage, but after that day I read and reread it repeatedly. From the first time I read the passage, a cold sense of dread crept deep into my soul.

> But [the Lord] said to me, "My grace is enough for you, for in weakness power reaches perfection." And so I willingly boast of my weakness instead, that the power of Christ may rest upon me. Therefore, I am content with weakness, with mistreatment, with distress, with persecutions, and difficulties for the sake of Christ; for when I am powerless, it is then that I am strong [2 Corinthians 12:9–10].

In the chapter Saint Paul also talks of a mystical experience a man, presumably he, had had fourteen years before. My adult conversion experience at the Cursillo retreat had been fourteen years earlier. Saint Paul talked about a thorn in his flesh that tormented him for four years. My public disgrace and persecution were a thorn in my side that I could hardly endure. For my pain to last for four years, I would have to lose my trial and my appeal. At the time that seemed unthinkable.

Saint Paul admitted that when his suffering came, he prayed three times for it to pass, and God said, "No." Just as Saint Paul begged the Lord to be saved from his thorn, my family, fellow parishioners, and I were praying day and night for deliverance from my ordeal. The Lord's response to Saint Paul was that the grace of God showered upon him was all that he would need to endure, "for in weakness power reaches perfection."

I began the trial with an intense sense of foreboding. If I was to share in Saint Paul's ordeal, I was obviously not going to win. But, ironically, the trial went spectacularly well. Even the press began to question why I was being prosecuted.

"Shadow jurors" were hired by my lawyers to mirror the experience of the actual jurors. They sat in the courtroom audience believing they were working for the government. Each day their belief in my innocence grew and was revealed in their daily debriefings. Witnesses called by the government supported my side of the case rather than the government's. Each day optimism grew, and acquittal seemed more certain. I wondered about 2 Corinthians 12 and its relevance if I was to be acquitted.

Finally the day came for me to take the stand in my own defense. Although I testified for what seemed an eternity, the government attorney's cross-examination was painfully inept and made no apparent damaging impression on the jury. Optimism continued to grow; even the prosecutors appeared deflated and discouraged.

The very day the jury was to consider my part of the case, 2 Corinthians 12 reappeared as the second reading at daily Mass. (For those of you who are not Catholic, the readings at daily Mass rotate in cycles every three years, which means there is an approximate one-in-a-thousand chance of this coincidence.) Yet I found myself asking, How could my ordeal be just starting? I was already far beyond the limits of my personal strength, financial resources, and spiritual endurance.

After weeks of delay and nine days of deliberations, the jury returned. It was now July of 1997. My case was the first of the six cases consolidated for trial to be reported by the jury foreman. The first count was read, and the verdict was announced.

Guilty!

Pandemonium broke out. My daughters sobbed uncontrollably. I felt as though I would never breathe again. The verdict went on. There were acquittals on some charges but other guilty verdicts. Even though I was a lawyer, I did not know exactly what it all meant.

When a TV newsman stuck a microphone in my face as I left the courthouse, I was coherent enough to tell him the verdict was a virtual death sentence for me. My life was over! Little did I know how true my first reaction was. The phrase "My God, my God, why have you forsaken me?" ran in a continuous tape through my mind. All that I could cling to for hope was the Scripture promise that we are never challenged beyond our ability to endure, if we are open to God's bountiful graces.

In a matter of days I was ordered to forfeit more than $3 million in assets to the government. My law firm was declared a criminal enterprise, and I was named the leader. Even though we were considered first offenders, my client and I both received sentences of ten years and one month —without benefit of parole. Two other defendants were acquitted, and two received relatively light sentences. My devastation was complete, but I was determined to appeal and pursue a reversal of this inexplicable and unjust verdict.

I was ordered to report to prison even while my case was on appeal, and I did so on December 29, 1997. My service as a deacon was over. My law firm was dismantled. I agreed to suspend my law license. My clients were lost. My assets not consumed in the legal battle would soon be turned over to the gleeful prosecutors. My family was crushed.

I became the poster boy for what happens to witnesses who do not "cooperate" with federal prosecutors. No more moments of glory and justice in the courtroom. No more watching with pride as my young protégés battled it out in front of spellbound jurors. No more cooking for or ministering to unwed mothers. No more "dad adventures" with my daughters. No more living, except in the technical sense that I still breathed and my heart was beating.

I found little consolation in reading a newspaper interview with a juror who admitted he was not sure exactly what my crime was but felt I must have been guilty of something. In his simplistic view the government wouldn't have spent so much time and money trying to get me unless I had done something illegal. There is no "innocent until proven guilty" mind-set in jurors who are afraid of street crime and think that all lawyers and politicians are crooks. The principle I had heard so often in law school, that it is better to free one hundred guilty defendants rather than convict one innocent defendant, no longer had meaning.

My only consolation was that my stay in jail would be brief

and bearable. Surely the court of appeals would reverse my conviction. Or so I thought.

My arrival at prison as a voluntary "self-surrender" was the worst day of my life. It was too much for my wife to bear, so an old friend dropped me off. As I entered the prison compound at a Pensacola Navy base, everyone stared at the "new fish." Within minutes I was stripped naked, processed, and issued a fluorescent orange, one-piece, pocketless jump suit and oversized slip-on canvas shoes. No underwear. No belt. No shoelaces or socks. None of my belongings were permitted except a rosary, my glasses, and my wedding band.

After several hours in an isolation cell, I was assigned a bunk and dumped into the general population, a dazed, glow-in-the-dark, forlorn human pumpkin. As a middle-aged, white, overweight lawyer, I stuck out like a sore thumb among the mainly young, tattooed, black and Hispanic drug dealers who made up 85 percent of the prison population.

I could hardly breathe, much less think, react, or comprehend the utter sense of loss that overwhelmed me. My life was over, and I was surrounded by hostility and violence, rather than compassion.

The first letter I received in prison was from Father Frank Montalbano, a seminary professor who taught Scripture courses in the diaconate formation program. He said the real challenge of mature Christianity is to bear our crosses bravely, in faith. We need only surrender in faith and patiently and prayerfully await the moment when God will reveal Himself to us more fully. As part of the ongoing prophetic glimpses of my future, he too quoted 2 Corinthians 12. This was the third appearance of that passage in my descending spiral of despair.

After a week in prison I wrote home to describe my experience. I asked my wife to send my "newsletter" to any

family members, clients, and friends who she thought might
be interested. Each month after that I wrote a newsletter,
which was then sent to a rapidly expanding list of readers.

Prison regulations forbid diaries or journals by prison inmates, but my newsletters describing my efforts to cope with
my new, strange existence were somehow permitted. I am
not sure how many got my messages each month, but I received thousands of responses.

My most basic survival mechanisms were to forget what
happened immediately, to try to laugh at the often-bungling
antics of my keepers and fellow felons, and to try to avoid
dwelling on my pain. What started as therapy for me became
an indispensable tool, without which I could not accurately
reconstruct what had happened. It also served as a reminder
of how God's grace always equaled what I needed for the
day.

A sample from my first newsletter home gives a feel for
my day-to-day reflections:

Dear Family and Friends:
As of 11:00 A.M. today, I have been here for one full week.
What a week! For the first 48 hours I truly experienced
the "dark night of the soul." For the first time in my life
I felt a deep sense of sadness and despair.

Over and over I asked myself and my God how this could
have happened to me. The legal system I have devoted 32
years to serving faithfully, fully believing in its fairness,
has obviously let me down. I am puzzled and perplexed at
what could possibly have led the FBI, the U.S. attorneys,
the judge, and the jury to utterly and mercilessly destroy
everything in my life that is precious to me. They all seemed
to pursue me with a vengeance that is not merited by my
alleged "crimes," or by my life in and service to our community.

Countless times two passages from Mark's Gospel have

come to mind. First, the Agony in the Garden when Jesus Himself confessed to Peter, James, and John that "my heart is filled with sorrow to the point of death" (Mark 14:34). Never before have those words so totally described exactly how I feel! The second passage is Jesus' cry from the cross shortly before He died, "Eloi, Eloi, lama sabachthani," which means, "My God, my God, why have you forsaken me?" (Mark 15:34). Jesus Himself prayed fervently to His Father, with the power to do all things, to let the cup of His crucifixion pass from Him.

Hundreds of faithful family and friends have joined their passionate plea to our loving God, with the power to do all things, to let the "cup" of public humiliation, professional ruin, separation from family, friends, and the joys of day-to-day life, and ten years of incarceration pass from my lips. God's response was "No" to His beloved and faithful Son. For God's plan for the salvation of mankind to come to fruition, it was necessary for Jesus to be unjustly tried, convicted, and executed so that God's power could be revealed in the Resurrection; and Jesus' message of love, peace, hope, and joy would be remembered and spread throughout the world. God has now also said "No" to me.

As my thoughts became dark, desperate, and bordering on despair, I read the first few psalms. The first psalm promises that God will "watch over the way of the just." The third psalm speaks of trust in God during times of danger, despair, and injustice. The fourth psalm desperately asks (as I do), "Men of rank, how long will you be dull of heart? Why do you love what is vain and seek after falsehood?" The psalmist urges trust in God and promises that those who do trust God when suffering intensely will each day lie down and "fall peacefully asleep." Miraculously I can usually sleep peacefully in the midst of the chaos, which is a fact of life here.

Psalm 5 is an ardent prayer for God's help from someone in a desperate situation. The psalmist's tormentors are described in a way that my prosecutors might also be described: "In their mouth there is no sincerity; their hearts teem with treacheries. Their throat is an open grave. But God protects the just man with the shield of his good will."

The sixth psalm is a prayer for help in a time of deep distress. The writer described himself as "chastised by God" and as "languishing." His body and soul were in "utter terror" at what was happening to him. He begged God to "return his life to him" and described how he "flooded his bed at night with weeping" and "drenched his couch with tears." His eyes were dimmed with sorrow and his body aged by distress. After a lifetime of manly absence of tears, I now for the first time find myself crying often when I am alone.

As I read, it occurred to me that these ancient Hebrews were describing my pain and my recent life experiences passionately and eloquently. What a helpful insight—we all suffer! My next thought was whether there could be a significant purpose in seemingly unjust suffering.

The seventh psalm is a plea for divine help by David as he was pursued. He feared he would be torn to pieces like a lion's prey with no one to rescue him. He begged God for justice because he was an innocent and just man. He vowed to sing God's praise if he was rescued.

At this point in my reading I picked up the *Barclay Commentary on the Psalms* and began to read with great interest. These ancient expressions of sadness and despair on the one hand, and joy and justice on the other, had suddenly become intensely relevant to my life. About forty pages into the commentary, the author discusses the seventh psalm. He poses the question: Why should just people who believe in and serve a loving God have to suffer unjustly? Saint Paul observed that all of humanity and all of nature must suffer (Romans 8:22). He [Barclay] observed that Jesus willingly suffered and concluded that it is a "sheer impertinence" for any true believer to ever cry out, "Why should this happen to me?"

Then there was a remarkable punch line (the ultimate answer for me): "Of course, it is out of suffering and pain that the kingdom of God arrives." In other words, we eventually find God, and might lead others to God by example, i.e., suffering without whimpering and self-pity. It is unequivocally promised that in the end our suffering ends, our lives are resurrected, and boundless joy returns.

The realization that there is a purpose in my suffering, perhaps even a great and as yet unseen purpose, has empowered me to take heart. Hope has returned. Faith is rekindled. Some brief moments of joy peek out through the dark clouds.

In closing, remember that you need not cry for me. My suffering is a natural part of life that I will embrace. God must love me a lot.

—Carl

After about six months of writing newsletters, a newspaper editor who stumbled upon an issue requested that I write a newspaper column entitled "Faithwalk." This too became a source of spiritual therapy, as each month, out of my pain and sadness, topics and insights sprang into my consciousness without deliberate planning on my part. I simply sat down each month and began to type. I was convinced the Holy Spirit inspired the words that flowed in a torrent. When the warden discovered I was writing "Faithwalk," I received his specific permission to continue, with the requirement that I never disclose that I was a federal inmate or refer to the prison in any way.

Until I was an adult, I had never experienced real suffering, and I had never grappled with the reasons that suffering exists in the world at all. The old explanation that penance is offered in atonement for sins has theological validity. After all, we are all sinners.

However, I believe there is another very real and compelling reason for practicing ritual penance. It prepares us for suffering. Sooner or later real suffering will come to each of our lives. It may be physical, emotional, spiritual, financial, or other. But it comes. Not only do these experiences come, but they are also an essential part of our personal discovery and experience of God. Without them we can know God intellectually, but we do not really experience Him until He bears us up on the wings of angels and brings us through difficulties that are beyond our own strength.

Surprisingly, within the minimum security institution there was considerable freedom of movement, but everything was crowded, noisy, and uncomfortable. The state was using a former Navy base as a prison, and we lived eight-to-ten men in dorm rooms designed for two Navy flight cadets during the Second World War. The rooms were furnished wall-to-wall with double-deck bunks. No personal possessions were permitted except for basic toiletries and a few books, plus several items that could be purchased in the prison commissary.

The original heating and air conditioning were still in use. The system permitted no fresh air circulation. It heated or slightly cooled the same stale air in a room and recirculated it endlessly. Doors and windows could not be opened due to some senseless bureaucratic rule. Restrooms were always crowded and filthy. The food was at best edible and at worst disgusting. Most dishes were single ingredients baked, boiled, or deep-fried without seasoning.

Eighty-five percent of the inmates were drug dealers, and one-third of the men were "snitches." The noise level was unbelievably intrusive, and the talk almost always senselessly profane. The taunting, cruelty, macho posturing, and selfishness were difficult for me to accept as an inevitable fact of life.

A few years earlier Rush Limbaugh and Barbara Walters had reported that this particular facility was like a "Club Med vacation," calling it "Club Fed." But I can assure you that those two would go crazy after a week there.

Medical care was a real problem. Everyone seemed to have perpetual colds, allergies, and bronchitis. I developed an excruciatingly painful abscessed tooth. For thirteen months I literally begged for treatment, going repeatedly to the prison dental office. During each visit, I sat on the floor in the hallway, waiting for a turn. Each time I was processed, I was turned away without seeing the dentist. It was too late or too early. My file was lost. My x-rays were lost. The drain in the sink was stopped up. Either I was an emergency case on a non-emergency day, or vice versa.

When I was finally allowed to see the elusive dentist, he chastised me for not taking care of my teeth. I accepted the loss of my tooth and the months of agony without complaint. He casually pulled out the rotten tooth from my decaying jawbone with little effort. Tossing it into the trash, he admonished me to do better in the future. The only response I could offer without harsh consequences was to thank him for his time.

Others with serious medical problems fared much worse. One of my roommates was unmedicated, untested, and untreated for a full day after an extremely painful abdominal aneurysm. A fellow inmate and I finally carried him to the infirmary, from which he had been turned away several times during the day, and stuck our necks out by demanding that he be helped. A few hours later we heard that he had died in the ambulance on the way to the hospital. We were devastated, but the medical staff was unconcerned. His reputation as a hard worker in the prison bakery, his history as a heart patient, and his obvious agony were casually ignored.

This was standard operating procedure for the Bureau of Prisons (BOP). Lesson learned: Do not get sick in prison. To avoid the chronic respiratory illnesses prisoners suffered from, I began washing my hands frequently and gargling with mouthwash compulsively.

The prison rules were confusing, contradictory, and senseless. This confusion gave the guards total power over the inmates. Whatever the closest guard said or demanded was law. Logic, reason, fairness, and simple decency were irrelevant.

Shakedowns and searches were frequent. Accusatory questions were a daily event. Alcohol and drug testing occurred at all hours of the day and night. Being awakened by a bright flashlight in the face for needless bed checks every two hours during the night was routine.

The "hacks" (an acronym for Hard-Ass Carrying Keys) had free access to my prison file. With ten years to serve without benefit of parole, my sentence was the longest of any inmate there. A few used the absurd pain and injustice of my much-publicized conviction and long sentence to torment me.

Our prison supplied laborers of all types to seven Navy bases in the area. For most inmates, regardless of age and physical condition, work was a full day of weed whacking at some Navy base. The Navy paid minimum wage for our services, with the BOP keeping most of the proceeds of the near slave labor arrangement. The inmates received a mere $5 to $20 per month to buy toilet articles and junk food from the prison commissary. The day before I was to have reported to the "landscape detail" to become an upside-down helicopter pilot (weed-eater operator), I received a mysterious call to report to the prison safety office.

The chief clerk in the safety office was a former neighbor, a bank officer, who was serving a relatively short sentence for charges pressed against him in the savings and loan meltdown. Recognizing my state of numbed shock, he went to bat for me and convinced his boss that I was an expert on OSHA (Occupational Safety and Health Administration) and Navy safety regulations. My unusual job became reviewing safety programs at the prison and bringing them into compliance with all safety regulations.

In my former life I never would have considered wasting my time on such trivia. In prison the job was a godsend. My job helped pass the time, but more importantly, it got me away from most of the other inmates and the hacks. I was able to operate all the heavy equipment, such as tractors, back-loaders, and forklifts, and since I prepared operator licenses for inmates, I licensed myself for everything.

Prison sports were another revelation. I wanted to play everything in a belated effort to get back into some kind of physical shape. To my horror, I soon learned that all prison sports are played by "jungle rules," with grudges and conflicts resolved under the guise of aggressive play. The result was barely controlled mayhem.

Instead I opted for workout programs operated by inmates. We had "abs class" several times each week. We also practiced yoga, flexibility and toning exercises, and high-energy step aerobics. I walked and eventually began jogging for miles each day. I lost fifty pounds in six months and experienced muscle aches during my entire incarceration. But I got in the best physical shape I had been in since my college football days. More importantly, the hard physical labor all day, each day, and the intense workouts left me exhausted for the nights when chaos broke loose in the dorms. Without earplugs and exhaustion, sleep would have been impossible.

To my surprise, there were few participants in prison chapel activities. Most of the inmates were young drug dealers serving fairly short sentences, and they had not reached the level of loss that turns us naturally to God. Instead they longed for their return to the streets, drug deals, and lure of quick money that landed most of them in prison in the first place. They had not fallen far enough to realize that happiness is found in faith, not in the heady rush and sense of power they hoped to find in the drug world.

Chapel attendees were often ridiculed by the "real" men, but I found a nightly prayer group that did not care about the mockery. We met for about thirty minutes each evening to pray. Once a month a group from a nearby Catholic church came to pray with us. The group was a godsend.

My wife, daughters, son-in-law, mother-in-law, and a family friend were occasionally permitted to sing at Sunday Mass when they came for visits. They were sensational. Attendance at Sunday Mass always shot up when they came. At times they were even advertised on the prison bulletin boards as the "Von Cleveland Family Singers." The toughest looking inmates, covered with tattoos, scarred from knife and bullet wounds, and sporting shaved heads and scowls, cried openly when my daughters sang.

The joy of family visits was bittersweet, reminding me of the life I had once taken for granted and now missed so much. Each visit left me depressed. I consciously thought that my life was so hopeless that I would gladly have accepted death. I was not suicidal, but for the first time in my life, living was so painful that *any* alternative would have been okay.

At the same time I was amazingly at peace. I felt wrapped in a cocoon of love by an acutely present God who revealed Himself in new and wondrous ways each day. I gradually surrendered my life, accepting my loneliness and powerlessness as normal parts of my existence. "Surrender" became my daily mantra.

I had never before seen any particular value in suffering, and I felt it should be avoided if possible. But then I began to think about one of the great paradoxes of Christianity. Though Christ is the resurrected and victorious Lord, Christians are called to selfless lives of sacrifice, good works, endurance, faith, and courage. These acts of faith can be difficult and, at times, seemingly impossible.

Saint John of the Cross' description of his "dark night of the soul" really hit home with me. Saint John, a Carmelite priest, is one of the Church's greatest mystical theologians. He was imprisoned by his own religious order. He said real peace came to him in prison only after he willingly gave up all the normal pleasures and distractions of life that were available to him. Since I had been deprived of most of what I treasured in my life, it made sense to me to follow his example by consciously giving up the few simple pleasures available to me in prison.

In place of all other activities except hard work and strenuous workouts, which were pure misery for me, I substituted praying, meditating, and reading. I read everything sent to me. I became a modern-day ascetic, giving up coffee, newspapers, TV, occasional freezer-burned chicken leg quarters, all sweets, salad dressing, snacks, and all drinks except water. I decided that instead of being angry with God about my fate, I would embrace it fully, in total surrender to whatever His will might be for my family and me. At times this was overwhelmingly difficult.

My worst recollection of total despair comes from the first family visit. We had a grand time playing ball in the visiting yard, much like our "practices" at home each night. At eight years old, Caitlin was already becoming a star athlete in every sport. I loved our time together, although it made it impossible for me to keep my thoughts from wandering to all I had lost, especially my family.

When it was time for my family to leave, I walked with them to the visiting area. They left through one door to go home. I was to leave through another door, where I would then be embarrassingly strip-searched to be sure I had not received any contraband from my sinister visitors.

As I took one last glance at my departing family, however, I saw my usually obedient "baby" defy her mother. She sat on the ground just outside the door to the visiting center. Crying uncontrollably, my precious Caitlin wailed pitifully, "I won't leave my daddy!" She had to be carried to the car. For days I was haunted by the desperate sound of her useless protest. It appeared certain that my family and I would be apart until Caitlin was out of high school—unless I won my appeal.

My pain at the loss of my older daughters and wife was alleviated by their letters and visits. With my former lawyering, diaconal ministries, and hobbies, I always had been too rushed, impatient, and distracted to be closely involved in their lives. In prison, their letters became my lifeblood. Remarkably, I entered the lives of those I loved on a deeper and much more satisfying level through our frequent correspondence. What an unexpected blessing!

Then I heard that the unthinkable had happened. A year and a half after my original verdict, I lost every issue in the court of appeals! The three-judge panel rubber-stamped my conviction and sentence without really addressing the many legal and factual issues raised on appeal. My innocence and the absurdity of the charges against me were brushed aside.

More than ever before in my life, I felt the desolation of God's apparent abandonment. For days I was in a trance-like state. Prayer was impossible for me. Just breathing was difficult. The daily torments and dehumanization continued with new fervor from some of the hacks and from a few inmates who found perverse satisfaction in my misery. Eventually I resigned myself to prison for eight more years.

One month became two, then three. While I busied myself trying to ignore the difficult prospect of long-term life in prison, my attorneys still had great hope in an appeal to the United States Supreme Court. But I knew that the odds of even getting a hearing were only about one in eighty thousand. As I saw it, my choices were either to despair or to surrender even more fully to God's incomprehensible plan for me. Somehow, through the prayers of hundreds of faithful family members and friends and even strangers, I was able to survive the shock of my situation. I surrendered even more.

At work the safety manager gave me a new challenge. I was asked to negotiate a contract with the Navy to turn over to the prison the recycling program on the Navy base where the prison is located. I was also asked to implement the program and make it successful.

My rewards were spectacular. I was given a small recycling office as far away from the prison compound as was possible. Better yet, I planted a small vegetable garden with tomatoes, garlic, peppers, squash, cucumbers, cantaloupe, and an orange tree. Even though the garden was a violation of prison regulations, it was far removed from the prison compound and for some reason was tolerated by the hacks. Like my own spiritual harvest, my garden flourished, and its daily growth gave me something tangible to look forward to.

My prayer evolved from desperate pleas for a miraculous

rescue to calm requests for acceptance and peace, no matter what came. I read and thought and allowed God to totally embrace me in my misery and isolation. In the midst of chaos, suffering, and despair, I was inexplicably at peace. What an illuminating miracle! Just as God provided for the birds of the air and the lilies of the field, He provided abundantly for me when my personal resources and strength were exhausted.

And then, a miracle happened.

Out of the blue I was called to a prison secretary's office. A garbled message, written phonetically, was indecipherable. Then it dawned on me! The message said, "The Supreme Court granted a writ of *certiorari* today."

The United States Supreme Court had agreed to hear my case. My one chance in eighty thousand had hit! Getting a hearing usually indicates at least four of the nine judges want to reverse a decision. From hopeless underdog I was now an odds-on favorite to get a reversal. I was overcome with joy. I went out to the track and shouted to the sky. I laughed and cried. I called home and, for the first time in months, felt a real surge of renewed hope. Then I settled in to wait once again, afraid to believe that I might actually go home. It could still be months before anything happened.

But then came a stunning and unexpected event! The trial judge who had ruled against me in every controversy in my case, both large and small, ordered that I be released from prison *immediately*! At 3:30 P.M. on April 27, 2000, I was BOP prisoner No. 25306-034. At 3:45 I was, at least temporarily, Carl W. Cleveland, a free man.

After 840 days in hell, I took nothing with me except the workout shorts and T-shirt I was wearing. My family and I embraced and shouted and cried in exultation! Our first stop was at McDonald's to satisfy my craving for a hamburger and fries. No $50 steak had ever tasted as good. Within hours of the announcement, I was home, in my own bed, with my precious wife. I awoke the next morning at sunrise, numb. I felt as if I were in the Garden of Eden as I stood on the patio of my home, where spring was in full bloom.

My final newsletter, announcing a party to celebrate my release, went into the mail almost immediately. I went to Mass to thank God for restoring my life from the ashes of pain, loneliness, and oblivion. Everything was joyfully fun, even the things that ordinarily would have been an unwelcome pain.

Ever since that first day back home, I have gleefully cooked every meal. I also do most of the grocery shopping, ironing, laundry, and housework. Once onerous tasks are now pure delights. Most of the time I am in a dazed state of disbelief. I was dead, and now I am alive again! Praise God! Praise God! Praise God!

My case was argued in the United States Supreme Court on October 10, 2000, days before the controversial Bush/Gore presidential election. My optimism surged when the court seemed sympathetic in its questions to my attorneys, but I could not help feeling anxious. I committed the impertinent blasphemy of explaining to God that I simply could not go back to prison. I was ashamed that my faith should fade so fast, and I struggled to regain my sense of surrender to God's will and my willingness to go in faith wherever He might send me.

A decision was expected in three to nine months. To pass the interminable time, I offered to help a rice-farming friend with some tractor work. With the new mental discipline I had learned in prison, I put the case out of my mind and worked to the point of physical exhaustion each day.

On Election Day, November 7, 2000—a mere twenty-eight

days after my release—the wife of a wonderful Christian missionary friend drove up to the edge of the rice field where I was driving a tractor. With tears in her eyes, she read me a note scrawled on a napkin. At first I was confused by her unexpected visit and feared bad news. Then she handed me the note. I read, "The Supreme Court *unanimously* reversed your conviction."

The United States Supreme Court had decided my case in the quickest decision in U.S. history, but more significantly, it had unanimously set aside my conviction. The court reasoned that what I was charged with was not a crime at all (except in the minds of the overzealous prosecutors). I would have been more gratified had the court concluded that I was not guilty of committing the alleged criminal acts themselves, but the victory was total nonetheless.

On Valentine's Day 2001, my case finally made its way back to the trial court for formal implementation of the Supreme Court's decision. The prosecutors proposed another deal. If I would abandon my appeal on two minor tax conspiracy charges that were not involved in the appeal to the Supreme Court, they would agree not to attempt to pursue me any further. If I refused, they threatened to pursue me for years and to seek to re-indict me and retry me for anything they could dream up. After a family meeting I agreed to the proposal, even though IRS audits of all my tax returns while I was in prison had validated every detail of my innocence of the tax offenses.

My personal agony in the garden, scourging at the pillar, crowning with thorns, and crucifixion formally ended almost exactly four years after my trial began in May 1997. Once again my thoughts were drawn to 2 Corinthians 12.

As Saint Paul suggested, it is through suffering that we truly discover God and His miraculous powers. We need only surrender totally to His divine mercy and will. Each person's unique life challenge is to trust God's plan and to serve Him as best we can despite our anxieties and pain. Without an intense boot camp of personal suffering, most of us are simply not ready for personal redemption and eternal union with Him.

There is one more story to share in this faith journey. Of the thousands of letters I received in prison, there was one from an unexpected source. The intercessory prayer group at Second Ponce de Leon Baptist Church in Atlanta, Georgia, was praying for me daily and writing to me several times each week. I was deeply moved that total strangers would do this and often wrote back to thank them for their inspirational faith in the power of prayer.

This group became so involved in my situation that they invited my wife to give her testimony at their 2000 Praise Fest, while I was still in prison. Even before the final decision in my case a year later, they requested that my family and I go to Atlanta to participate in their 2001 Praise Fest. The visit became a family affair, which included my daughters Kitty, Caroline, and Caitlin, my wife, and my mother-in-law.

Kitty sang beautifully at the contemporary Sunday morning service and at the traditional service, which was televised. Between Baptist services, she went to Mass at the Catholic cathedral next door. She came back to report to me in wonder that 2 Corinthians 12 was the passage used as the scriptural basis for the homily. This was the fourth time the passage had presented itself in my life, and I concluded that that was to be the topic of my talk at the Praise Fest.

I shared our story and the awesome way that God had protected and guided me through the process of surrendering my life to Him. Kitty sang the title song of her new

Christian CD, "Surrender," a song about my ordeal. The people laughed and cried and exulted with us as we relived so much of our painful journey.

I presented a sampling of our many blessings. Two daughters had gotten married during my confinement. I regained the physical health and vigor of a young man. Our family finances worked out so I could not only pay my deserving attorneys but also support my large clan. Our first grandchild, Abigail, arrived soon after my release, and a second, Adeline, has since been born. Months of family therapy and shared prayers of thanksgiving built a special new bond among us all. We learned to appreciate passionately our countless daily blessings, taken for granted until we lost them. And I have been welcomed back to my life by family, friends, neighbors, and clients with a level of enthusiasm and support I would not have believed possible. I also hope to be reassigned to my diaconal duties in the future. In the meantime, I am volunteering at a nearby Catholic high school, helping the students come to know more about Jesus and the Church. As to whether I will renew my law license, my family and I are prayerfully discerning this question now. The idea of my focusing on full-time ministry is certainly appealing and would present many exciting challenges.

I realize that the story is not over. What is it that God has prepared me to do in His plan for the salvation of all people? What is it that I am called to do? King David, Saint Paul, and Jesus submitted willingly to the crosses they had to bear in God's plan for the salvation of humankind. All remind us that we will each get our turn at crossbearing.

If we accept suffering in faith and turn to God without recrimination, salvation is truly ours. When all appeared lost, I was rescued and returned to my family and friends and to a life even more abundant than the one I had left behind. I experienced God's loving embrace in my powerlessness and despair in a way I had never imagined possible.

When overwhelming difficulty makes its way into your life, surrender your anxiety and your fears to our loving God, who will bless your faith abundantly. After you have experienced Him totally and learned to trust Him completely, He will restore you to abundant life. This is not possible without learning the lessons of 2 Corinthians 12. God's grace is enough for us in all of life's trials, for it is in accepting and embracing powerlessness that we become truly strong.

It Stops Here

Peggy Stoks

It was raining lightly by the time I reached the rural cemetery where many of my forebears had been laid to rest. After parking the car, I walked through the gate and sought the shelter of an enormous fir tree. I had brought my journal, for I had come to take care of some long overdue business.

Surprisingly, it was dry under the tree. I sat cross-legged on the ground, staring at the grave I knew I had to visit. A few birds made their presence known, and a soft wind rustled the leaves of the mature oak and elm trees standing as silent sentinels to the few hundred tombstones.

At first I felt foolish, but this soon faded as I traveled back to the past and began writing. The rain picked up, and drops of moisture began to penetrate the thick canopy. The dreariness of the summer evening was a fitting backdrop to my undertaking as well as for my return to the locale I had once sworn I would never revisit.

After some time a man's voice startled me, causing me to clasp my book against my chest.

"I live across the road, ma'am," said a gentleman in his sixties, "and I saw you here doing your homework. I thought you might be getting wet, so I brought you this. You can just leave it under the tree when you are done." He smiled, extended a blanket, and quickly excused himself.

How kind, I thought, gratefully accepting the blanket. I watched him return to the house across the country lane from the cemetery. *There is still some goodness in the world.*

The mosquitoes were beginning to become a problem, and I was glad for the added protection as I wrapped myself in the blanket and returned to my musings.

At some point I concluded that I had done enough writing and that it was time to stand before the grave. I prayed God would give me the courage I needed to face the name of the person who had injured me so deeply. I emerged from beneath the tree, going from damp to soaking wet in half a dozen steps.

When I reached the upright granite marker, I wondered how many other lives this "pillar of society" had devastated. But that was not why I had come. I was there to stand up to all the times and ways I had been defiled by a man whose role was to love me, to enrich my life, and to safeguard me from evil. But my maternal grandfather had not been that kind of man. With skill and cunning he had preyed upon me to feed his depraved sexual desires.

As I spoke his offenses aloud, I also acknowledged that there was no way I could offer him forgiveness on my own. Could any human? Although I was a believing Christian, all I could present to Jesus was a heart that *wanted* to obey His command to forgive others as He forgave us. I had to trust Him to do the work inside me that I could not do on my own. And so I prayed for Christ's forgiveness to flow through me so that I could forgive my grandfather, at the same time beseeching the Lord to heal me from the deep wounds I had carried since childhood.

This was not the movies. Nothing momentous happened in this private time, unless you consider a thirty-something woman standing in the rain talking to God and to a dead man a momentous event. Yet somehow I knew something important had taken place and that it was time to leave. As I began to walk to the car, however, I decided the least I could do was to return the blanket to the generous-hearted man across the road. While I walked away from that grave, I thought more about the journey that had brought me to this point in my life.

I had grown up in a typical nuclear family of the 1960s: dad, mom, one daughter, one son. We occupied a three-bedroom, ranch-style home in a safe, middle-class neighborhood of a small suburb. My father was a machinist who, during my childhood years, started and established a successful business of his own. My mother was the kind of homemaker who faithfully provided her family with meat-and-potato meals, homemade pies, and line-dried sheets.

As a young girl I was high-spirited and inquisitive. I loved playing outdoors and could think of no finer way to spend a day than swimming. Reading was my second favorite way to pass time.

Both sets of grandparents lived near us, as did almost all of my aunts, uncles, and cousins. We regularly got together with relatives, even outside of the holidays, and I recall many happy memories spent with family from my father's side in particular.

When did I first realize that something was very, very wrong on my mother's side of the family? As an adult I have scrutinized my memories, searching for evidence of the malignancy that smothered the Meyer[1] family before it entangled me in its grasp. My first certain memory is from 1969, when I was eight years old and my brother and I had been left in my grandparents' care.

My brother and I were playing a game on the living room floor when Grandpa called me upstairs. Curious about what he wanted, I left the game and went up to meet him. When I left, my brother turned on the television and quickly became

---

[1] Name has been changed.

absorbed in a show. I thought I was in for a wonderful surprise when Grandpa put his finger over his lips, instructing me to be quiet.

Grandpa descended a few steps and peered over the banister to make sure my brother was occupied, then led me to the top of the stairs and down the hall to the furthest bedroom. I remember noticing that he quietly locked the door and wondering why he did.

He then sexually molested me.

I still can recall vividly the colors of the plaid bedspread, the stale smell of this seldom-used upstairs bedroom, the loud ticking of the travel clock at the bedside. When it was over, I was sent back downstairs to finish the game with my brother. And numbly, I did just that, not knowing what to make of the events that had just transpired. Though my brother was not aware of anything different about me, in the ten minutes we had been apart I had been forever changed. Grandpa's imperative words—*Don't tell anyone*—rang in my head, and I clearly understood that I must keep what had happened upstairs a secret.

I did not tell, nor did I even cry. For the rest of the day I tried to carry on as if nothing were out of the ordinary. I apparently succeeded, because no one—not my grandmother, mother, father, or brother—asked me if anything was the matter.

Though I did not understand what had happened to me, I knew it was bad. Dirty. Did Grandpa Meyer do those things to other little girls, or was I the only one? In the days and weeks, then months and years, to come I wondered, *Why me?*

Yet even with those questions in my mind, I knew there was no one I could ask, because I was not supposed to tell.

As I look back, I have no doubt that my grandfather counted on my obedience. Most certainly he exploited it. Even at the age of eight I realized that my grandfather's affection came with a terrible price, a price I did not know how to avoid paying. I will spare you a catalogue of my grandfather's sins against me. Who could ever believe the things he continued to do, oftentimes with people as near as the next room? They were horrible, made even more horrible by their premeditation. He was relentless in his pursuit of me.

Adding to that was our family's unspoken standard: *Don't ever talk about anything real.* A heavy, smothering silence engulfed our home and the homes of my mother's relatives when it came to anything but superficial subjects. Underneath the surface, however, roiled unspoken moods, emotions, and occurrences. Children and outsiders learned quickly never to ask questions.

I suffered physically, mentally, and spiritually. I quickly came to believe that my involvement in my grandfather's wicked designs made me every bit as guilty as he. This consciousness of guilt translated into feelings of shame. As a child growing up in the 1960s, I was too young to be cognizant of the then-contemporary young adult slogan "Trust no one over thirty." But even so, I took the philosophy a step further: "Trust no one." I reasoned that if a blood relative could violate me in such a way, then who on earth *could* be trusted? Early on I learned I could count only on myself.

I hungered as a child for things of faith, wishing our family could be regular churchgoers. I wanted to know more about God and His Son, Jesus, but religion was another prickly, uncomfortable subject in our home. I tried reading the Bible on my own but never got much beyond the first or second chapter of Exodus. When I was in fourth grade, my mother took my brother and me to Methodist Sunday school, which I loved. But we attended only one year.

I think my devout Catholic paternal grandmother knew of my yearnings, and during my childhood she took me to Mass as often as she dared. *Catholic* had always been worse than a swear word in our home, and my mother took every opportunity to malign the Church and its practices. "Confession? It is something Catholics do on Saturday afternoon so they can go out that night and do any old thing they please. Catholics are nothing but a bunch of hypocrites." My father was far less vitriolic, but to him, one word summed up the Catholic Church of his youth: *superstition.*

Because my mother's father was my abuser, and because she and her family lacked the courage, desire, or fortitude to look into a problem they desperately did not want to find, things were always strained between my mother and me, more so the older I became. After the abuse had gone on for about three years, I recall some faint hearted queries from my mother: "Is Grandpa . . . ah . . . bothering you?"

By that time, however, I was bound so deeply by guilt and shame that I would have died rather than admit the truth. Ironically, the lack of straightforward communication in our home and on the Meyer side of the family outraged and frustrated me. So when my mother began asking questions about Grandpa, rather than answering I set out to force her to talk in plain language. If she would only *really* talk to me! How I yearned to break past the stilted, strangled communication style of our home.

"'Bothering' me? What does that mean?" I would ask.

"Ah . . . well . . . you know . . . has he ever *bothered* you? Acted funny?"

"What do you mean by funny? Telling jokes?"

And so the conversation would continue for a few more

rounds, with my acting more obtuse as she became ever more evasive, and then it was over. No ground gained, none given. After those conversations I experienced equal amounts of disappointment and relief and, though I did not realize it at the time, a great deal of anger.

People thought my maternal grandfather was the most wonderful man in the county. He was known for his kindness and charm, his sense of humor, and his generosity. He was a business owner, an active member of many social organizations, and the caretaker of the local cemetery. Toward children his manner was jovial, fun-loving, conspiratorial. Making chocolate malted milks was his specialty, and he was forever telling jokes and giving away quarters. This type of behavior, mixed with the other, was enough to keep me off balance and confused.

Whenever Grandpa was charming a group of children or telling a humorous story that made everyone in the room laugh, I would tell myself, *Maybe he is not as bad as you think. See how everyone loves him? You're supposed to love him, too. He's your grandfather, after all. Mom says he has a drinking problem and that he's just not himself when he drinks. Maybe he does those things to you when he's drinking . . . or maybe you're exaggerating in your mind what has really happened.*

But then he would maneuver me into being alone with him, if only for a few minutes, always taking maximum advantage of every opportunity. He never threatened me with physical violence; he did not have to. Once I had been trapped in his evil web, I felt powerless to free myself. Finally, when I was thirteen or fourteen, the abuse stopped for good. I suspect he had started to prey upon my younger cousins.

Many times as a teen I acted out in rebellion. Behind my tough-girl façade, however, many of my growing-up years I was uncomfortable, confused, and lonely. On the surface I am sure that my teenage self-esteem woes appeared typical, but in my heart, deep pain coexisted with self-hatred. I was convinced I was ugly of both face and form and that the deepest part of me had been permanently ruined.

Being a flaming redhead with freckles did not help matters any either, as peers made fun of my coloring. The experiences I had with boys only served to reinforce my belief that the male gender cared about only one thing. In high school one kind boy fell in love with me, undoing a little bit of the damage done by the opposite sex. Yet when I was placed in the position of having to thwart a pass made by our beloved family doctor during an office visit, I began to wonder if I wore an invisible sign: *All perverts, stop here.*

I was eighteen when I finally told my mother about the abuse. Grandpa had cancer, and he was dying. Then a college freshman, I was a tangle of confused emotions. Though I'd tried distancing myself as much as possible from him, I had never known anyone who had died, much less anyone to whom I was related. What was I supposed to feel? What *did* I feel? Did I love him or hate him?

I did not know.

To my regret, the timing of my revelation was very difficult for my mom to handle. One evening after supper I asked her into my room and told her that Grandpa had, indeed, abused me. Her reaction was one of shock, horror, and deep pain. Yet the pain seemed to be more for herself than for me, and much of my hope for having a closer relationship with her died that night.

A few days before he died my grandfather asked to see me. All alone, I walked down the hall to the first-floor bedroom of his home, hearing the hiss of the oxygen tank grow louder as I neared. I was filled with dread, feeling as though I were walking to my doom. I did not want to see him or talk to him, yet at the same time my heart was wrenched with agony at the knowledge that he was dying. When I entered the room, he turned his head and motioned with his fingers for me to come near. Pale and emaciated, he was propped up in bed, laboring for every breath.

"I'm sorry," he rasped, taking my hand and squeezing it with surprising strength. "I'm real sorry about things."

Sorry for what? Robbing my innocence? For the filthy notes you used to slip into my pockets? The explicit phone calls you made to me while my mother stood nearby, cooking something on the stove? The Polaroids you've hidden only God knows where?

Mumbling something absurd like, "That's okay," I fled the room. I had learned how to turn off my feelings, and I found it expedient to do so at this time. *Am I supposed to love him or hate him?* I wondered again on that day—and for many years to come.

After high school graduation I sprinted through a two-year registered nursing program at our local community college. I passed the state boards and began working as a graduate nurse at the age of nineteen. Presenting an image of strength and success had become very important to me, perhaps to prove to myself and to the world that I was just fine, thank you very much. As ludicrous as this sounds, I even believed that the abuse had made me a tougher person, giving me an edge over others in coping with adversity.

On a spiritual level, one thing I had done after graduating from high school was to enroll in the Catholic Church's rite of initiation for people who wish to become Catholic (RCIA). While it had thrilled my Catholic grandmother, it had devastated my mother. Another act of rebellion on my part perhaps? After completing the RCIA program, I entered the Church and received the sacraments of baptism, reconciliation, Communion, and confirmation. However, I soon opted for the pleasures of the world rather than pursuing the sweet sacramental life to which I had been briefly exposed.

By this time my first boyfriend and I had parted company. While visiting a girlfriend's college, I met a handsome young Catholic man who thought I was something special. Jeff and I dated, and just before my twenty-first birthday, we married. Not long afterward we bought our first house, and within a few years we were the parents of two daughters. I continued working, finding self-worth and satisfaction in the fast-paced, high-risk obstetrical unit where I practiced. Six years later we built a bigger house. Life, on the surface, looked good.

Up to that point in my life I never doubted God's existence, but I did not know how that related to a person's life in practical terms. My lapsed Catholic father and inactive Methodist mother had decided it would be best for my brother and me if they allowed us to grow up to make our own choices about what we wanted to believe. Dad and Mom were "good, decent people" who came from "good, decent people." To them, being well-mannered, honorable, and respectable was of far greater value than being religious.

After Grandpa's death, stories began to filter in about my younger female cousins, confirming that they had also suffered the same exploitation. This information was never disseminated clearly but in tiny, indirect parcels. The unspoken Meyer Family Mantra remained in effect: *Don't ever talk about anything real.* Weather, gardens, and songbirds were safe topics about which to converse, but woe to anyone who dared to tackle something deeper.

My husband, on the other hand, comes from an extended family of energetic, candid talkers and, thankfully, is an empathetic listener. Both of us were frustrated by the manner in which my family communicated, not to mention outraged by the cover-up and excuse-making that prevailed regarding my grandfather's perversions. Together Jeff and I coined a phrase: "It stops here." Grandpa was dead, so we need not fear for our daughters' safety. And together we vowed to raise our children in a home of openness and honesty.

Life went on until 1993, when things for me turned sideways, then upside down. Unbidden "God thoughts" began bombarding my mind at all times of the day and night, making me wonder what was happening to my sanity. *Who was God?* I found myself asking. *What did He want of people? Did He hear those who prayed? With all the religions in the world, which one was the right one?*

I also began to wonder what it meant to be a Christian.

After becoming a mother I had begun going to Mass again, but it seemed to me that people were just going through the motions. *I* was just going through the motions. *Is this all there is?* I wondered many times. An Evangelical Christian girlfriend came to mind as these "God thoughts" continued dogging me over a period of weeks, then months. Since she was forever talking about Jesus, I thought she would not laugh or think I was crazy if I told her how my mind seemed to be consumed by God.

I called her and asked if we could get together. She spent a whole day illuminating the gospel message in a way I had never heard. Jesus Christ was both God and a real Person to her, and it was obvious that her relationship with Him was genuine. With the discipleship and influence of this woman and a few other godly women, I realized I too wanted to have that kind of personal relationship with Jesus.

In my first fumbling attempts at prayer and listening to God, I sensed He was asking the question, *Peggy, are you going to live for Me or not?* Casting aside my fears about being different, I chose to submit my life and will to the Lord.

My cradle Catholic husband thought I had taken leave of my senses. He was dismayed that I had become one of those "grinning, wild-eyed, crazy Christians" who bothered him so greatly. That conflict notwithstanding, the next several months were a spiritual honeymoon of the sweetest sort. I devoured Scripture and devotional readings, awakening every morning with delight at the idea that I could pray intimately to Jesus. With great sorrow I reflected on the many sins of my life, repenting of them and begging forgiveness. I wanted to change. I wanted with my whole heart the new life that I was promised as a sincere believer.

It never occurred to me to ask God to heal me from the abuse of my past. The past was just that—the past—and I tried to think of it as little as possible. The Grandpa Meyer episodes were packed and tucked away in a neat little compartment that I seldom retrieved or opened. If anyone would have suggested that I had been harmed by being molested, I would have heartily disagreed.

During this time, and to our great surprise, Jeff and I found ourselves expecting another baby. After a period of adjustment, tensions between us eased as we anticipated the birth of our new child. Jeff began to accept the fact that this "Jesus thing" was more than a passing phase in my life. Though an inactive parishioner for many years, he balked at leaving the Catholic Church. He grudgingly accompanied me as we shopped around for a church that would feed my ravenous hunger for the Word of God and satisfy his requirements—basically that the church would require little of him.

In the midst of this quest, in February of 1994, our youngest daughter joined the family. For a short time everything was rosy, but then came a period of personal tribulation I never could have imagined. With breathtaking swiftness, a postpartum depression descended upon me. Days turned into weeks as I withdrew from my husband and others into a world of bleakness and despair. I cared for my children and my household, but nothing brought me joy. I did not live but merely existed. Though I did not actively contemplate suicide, I wished I could be dead.

Not once did I consider that the abuse of my childhood could have anything to do with the present. While other people might have such problems, I stubbornly and proudly believed my constitution was too strong to allow the past to take me down.

I manifested signs of clinical depression: sleeplessness, lack of appetite, and bouts of terrifying anxiety. Three months after delivery I was fifteen pounds below my pre-pregnancy weight and so weak I could barely walk down the stairs in the morning. Getting through each day became a dreadful thing, for the hands of the clock never seemed to move. What did I have to look forward to?

One day when I lashed out at Jeff in rage, he expressed concern that something was very wrong with me. Something in me clicked. The next morning I called the office of a well-known Christian psychologist whose name had been mentioned some time before by a friend. To my astonishment, there was an opening that very afternoon. And so began a new chapter of my life that was infinitely painful yet, in the end, contributed enormously to my formation as a Christian.

A cheerful-looking poster in the reception area of the doctor's office greeted me: "THE TRUTH WILL SET YOU FREE, BUT FIRST IT WILL MAKE YOU MISERABLE." *What's that supposed to mean?* I wondered. I quickly found out just how accurate the statement was. Through Dr. William Backus, author of such titles as *Telling Yourself the Truth* and *The Hidden Rift With God*, I began to learn about identifying and rooting out wrong thinking, replacing my misbeliefs with truth.

An overarching truth became apparent to me during my weeks of therapy. God was using this experience of depression to teach me something about trust. It took a situation that I could not control, no matter how hard I tried, to learn what it means to be dependent on Him. Despite all my striving, I could not make the tears stop. I could not banish the feelings of hopelessness, reverse my weight loss, or find the solace of sleep.

My prayers were filled with pitiful pleas to be restored, to no longer be weak and helpless. When those prayers went unanswered, I turned to Jeff to make me feel better, to be my sole source of comfort. That is a burden no man can bear, and obviously, it was no more successful than any of my failed attempts to get myself together. Late one night as I lay, sleepless, a still, small voice whispered in my heart, *Put your trust in Me, not in Jeff.*

Figuratively and spiritually speaking, the lights went on. Though I professed faith in God, I was still trying to find ways to manage my problems on my own. That night the focus of my prayers changed. Instead of begging to be returned to normal as quickly as possible, I told God that I trusted Him to supply me with the necessary graces to carry me through my present journey.

Not long afterward, to my great joy, the gospel message penetrated Jeff's heart, and he surrendered his life to Christ. We visited a Catholic parish a few towns to the north of our home that was known for its clear Catholic teaching and charismatic worship. From the moment Jeff and I walked through the doors, we knew this was our spiritual home.

Yet while so much was beginning to go right, much remained wrong. At times Jeff and I excitedly shared matters of faith, but we still related to each other warily, lacking complete trust in the other. I did not like things this way. I wanted more out of our marriage, so I reverted to subtle means of control and manipulation to try to change matters.

My attempts went over like a lead balloon. Tensions between us grew thicker. I began having outbursts of anger, even fury, when things did not go the way I thought they should. I used terrible language, broke things, and wounded my husband with demeaning words. After such episodes I felt like a fraud, beating myself up for days. I dared to call myself a Christian?

My childhood pattern of withdrawing emotionally made me feel somewhat better, but I could no longer sustain my detachment for any length of time. God, the master electrician, had disabled the turn-off-your-feelings switch that I had once been able to throw so easily and for as long as I wished. And I had come too far in my Christian journey to believe that numbing one's heart was anything God desired. During a fight one evening, Jeff insisted that the root of all my problems was the "Grandpa issue." He demanded to know when I was going to deal with it.

Deal with it?

The contemporary, psychobabble term raised my hackles. What did "deal with it" really mean, anyway? I did not have split personalities or repressed memories. I recalled every rotten thing Grandpa had done to me and, despite it all, had managed to become a responsible adult and productive member of society.

I sought Dr. Backus' opinion about the matter, and he said he would be happy to help me, if that was what I wanted. His next words, however, struck terror in my heart.

"It's going to be a walk through a painful and very dark valley," he warned. "In fact, it most likely will be so bad that you'll think you are not going to make it." After pausing, he went on gently, "But you will make it, Peggy, and much good will come of such a journey. Pray about it. Ask God if He would have you do this thing right now."

Even before I returned home, I knew in my heart that the Lord wanted to heal me of the damage that had been done. Though the feeling grew within me as the week passed, I began to fear that the process would be too difficult for me.

Indeed, the journey was every bit as awful as Dr. Truth-Seeker had promised. As I began looking—*really looking* —at what had been done to me, I alternated between two dominant emotions: fury and hopelessness. Not even God Almighty was exempt from my outbursts.

If you have seen the movie *Forrest Gump,* which I happened to view during this period of my life, recall the scene where Forrest and Jenny return to her old, abandoned house. Jenny, who was abused by her father, picks up a rock and flings it at the house. Soon she is pelting the house with rocks just as fast as she can pick them up, wildly, fiercely, and when she has exhausted the supply of stones in her vicinity, she hurls handfuls of dirt until she finally collapses, sobbing. Forrest observes that sometimes there just aren't enough rocks. That is how I felt.

There were many days that I hung on to life—to the hope of healing—by the most slender of threads. I barely functioned as a wife and mother. Many days I simply could not function as a nurse. I called in sick, traded away shifts, avoided my hospital friends. For days on end I experienced a physical, agonizing ache in my chest, and I cried so much that my eyelids were always swollen.

Rage, outrage, despair, and sadness were my constant companions, speaking much louder than either the promises in Scripture or Dr. Backus' quiet, confident assurances that God was faithful and that with His help and grace I would, indeed, emerge from this trial, that I would heal. "Yes, but will I ever laugh again?" I cried out to the Lord. "Feel joy? Know peace? I do not think I can do this. I'm not going to make it. I'm not strong enough."

During those months of therapy I railed against the injustice of how my innocence had been stripped from me and with it, much of my childhood. I felt rage at how, as this monstrous evil had gone on, the very ones who failed to protect me were promulgating the message: "Look at us! We're a normal, happy, well-adjusted family!"

How could that have been true? In ten minutes' time I had gone from being an innocent child, unaware that such things as incest existed, to a bewildered, shame-filled eight-year-old. I had not even been able to apply words to what had happened to me because there weren't any in my vocabulary that were relevant.

It seemed so hideously unfair that much of my formation as a person had been strongly influenced by the perversion that invaded my early life. Yes, I had become a strong, focused woman, filled with tireless energy and blessed with many talents and accomplishments. But underlying these attributes were much uglier things: self-contempt, contempt of others, perfectionism, and a refusal to be dependent on anyone for anything. From my tender years I had learned that the only person on whom I could fully rely was myself.

If my childhood had been a lie of one sort, my adult life was a lie of another. Why did I struggle and strive the way I did? Selflessness? Altruism? Love for God and others? Oh, no. To my great dismay, the truth did indeed make me miserable. Longings for affirmation and esteem were the motivations ruling my heart, as was fear of rejection, being disliked, and discipline. I was prideful and self-protective. In none of these traits did I see anything of godliness.

Even with my new life in Christ, I realized that the greater part of my soul lay in oppression, even deadness. More awful than that was acknowledging the fact that I was the one who had killed it, in order to spare myself the pain of being vulnerable or being wounded further.

Retrospectively, I see that I was at a great crossroads in my life's journey. The wide, well-traveled road led to such destinations as complacency, justification, bitterness, and living life as a permanent victim. The slender, less-traveled track threaded its way toward healing and wholeness by a route of sorrow, repentance, humility, and genuine love.

Owning up to all my sins, whether or not I would have committed them without Grandpa's influence on my character and morals, was pivotal if I wanted to continue in my Christian walk. I realized that my armored, self-protective mechanisms would also have to go, which was both liberating and terrifying. Did I want to be free? *Yes!* Did I want to be healed? *Yes!* Did I believe it could really happen? *Sort of.* Could I imagine life any other way than what I had always known? *No.*

Walking into an unknown future was frightening. But since knowing, loving, and serving the Lord had become my deepest desires, there was no other choice for me. Seventeen years after my first sacramental confession, I made my second.

The grace that God poured out in the confessional that day washed over me like a mountain stream. My heart, aching with sorrow and repentance, was filled with purity and hope. And along with Christ's gifts of forgiveness and freedom, I felt renewed courage and a brand-new awareness of how dearly my heavenly Father loved me. From that point on I began to receive the Eucharist with an ever-increasing sense of gratitude and awe. Before long I learned to be still before the Lord in eucharistic adoration—sitting or kneeling in reverence before the exposed holy Eucharist.

With a changed heart and a return to the sacraments, I trusted that God would somehow accomplish what until then I believed to be an impossible work of restoration in my life. From Dr. Backus I received the practical tools of knowing how to handle my thoughts, feelings, and expectations. *Self-talk*, he called it. Scrutinizing the things I told myself by holding them up against the light of truth allowed me to see where lies and misbeliefs had crept into my heart, mind, and soul.

I was not ruined for life, a terrible person, or spoiled goods. My situation was not hopeless, nor would my life always be painful and unpleasant. Slowly my negative and deeply entrenched ways of thinking began to wither beneath the power of the truth.

As I persevered in prayer and in this process, I began a journal of my spiritual journey. The Lord spoke many words to me from Scripture, which during difficult moments kept me from giving up. I was also greatly blessed to receive the baptism in the Holy Spirit, a transforming experience whereby I became more fully aware of the reality and presence of Jesus Christ and of the power of His Holy Spirit. This incredible spiritual encounter released a mighty flood of God's grace and power in my life, breaking many of the strongholds of evil that had bound me.

Over time the good days began to outnumber the bad, and I experienced a true reconciliation with my past such as I never had before. Though I wished the abuse had never happened, I began to think in terms of how my experiences might one day be used to help men and women who had been similarly wounded. The purpose of my visit to Grandpa Meyer's grave was twofold: to acknowledge that I could not forgive such things on my own, and to submit to the Lord any and all vestiges of unforgiveness still inside me.

Nighttime was quickly falling as I crossed the road and walked up the driveway of the man who had brought me the blanket. He was working in his garage, and I handed him the blanket, thanking him for his kindness. He was chatty, and for a few minutes we made small talk about such things as the weather, the sweet corn, and perhaps some songbirds.

"So . . . did you have any family across there in the cemetery?" he finally asked, fingering the brim of his cap.

I nodded, finally adding the word, "Meyer."

"Joe Meyer?"

"Joe Meyer was my mother's cousin," I allowed, feeling his sharp eyes studying me and wondering if he thought I was deranged for spending nearly two hours in a deserted graveyard in the rain. I took a half step backward, preparing to leave.

Suddenly a grin covered his face. "That makes you related to *George* Meyer, then . . . his granddaughter, I'll bet! I tee a golf ball on his grave every once in a while and whack it out into the woods. Yessiree, that George was some great fellow." He went on about the marvelous man my grandfather had been.

Incredulous, I stood before him with the grace of a fence post, my journal burning a hole where I held it against my side. The man poured out his admiration for my grandfather, expressing sorrow that such a noble man was no longer with us. Finally, mercifully, he finished his tribute and I excused myself, imagining the look on his face if I told him why I had visited.

On the way back to the car I wondered if I should laugh or cry. *Heaven knows you have done enough crying,* I told myself as I put the key in the ignition and shook my head. Though I was out of the rain, water continued dripping down my face and arms. What had just happened? Had my life turned into an episode of *The Twilight Zone?* Then a wry chuckle finally escaped me, and I knew that something inside me was different. By God's grace I was healing.

Since then, healing has continued. As my relationship with the Lord deepens, He gently reveals new residue of my childhood injuries. I might become aware of an attitude of self-worthlessness or discover that I am overly critical in some way, or perhaps that I am placing undue expectations on others. It might be that I come to terms with hidden anger or a lack of forgiveness toward someone. Sometimes I fight God on these issues, sometimes I do not. And then the process is the same: I acknowledge sorrow, I repent, I choose humility and the way of genuine love.

Though this may sound simple and formulaic, I assure you it is anything but that. My issues still involve trust. There is still the occasional day when I am tempted to fall into despair over the mess my life became because of the abuse. This usually happens when I allow my feelings to dictate the level of my faith. And though I know it is not rational, my automatic response is to think *pedophile* whenever I see a bald man wearing a plaid shirt.

I wish I could say that my mother and I came to a place of peace about the abuse, but she continued to make excuses for her father until her death from cancer a few years ago. Had she been abused herself? I suspect so, though she denied my suspicion with vehemence. As her coma deepened and all my hoped-for somedays slipped away, the Holy Spirit impressed a single word upon my heart—*mercy.* Yes, with God's grace I had chosen the way of forgiveness, but now He sought something beyond that. God asked for my compassion toward my mother and her shortcomings and inabilities in this area of my life.

Again, with God's grace, or rather only because of His grace, I was able to oblige, and thus another deep work of healing took place. The evil perpetrated against me *did* stop with me because of God's mercy, poured out more abundantly than I ever could have imagined. To my three daughters I leave a legacy of faith and hope.

To you I give this testimony of amazing grace in one ordinary woman's life. If my story is in some way your story, the first place I urge you to go is to your knees. Be assured that in Christ there *is* hope, there *is* healing, even if you can see no light at the end of the tunnel. He may heal you in an instant; most likely He will not. His vehicles of grace are many and varied, perhaps including pastors, psychologists, counselors, and support groups, in addition to prayer, the sacraments, family, and friends. There is a path of Life for you; be confident of that.

Behold, the Lord will do a new thing. The same God who makes rivers in the desert longs to restore your soul and help you grow in holiness. He loves you deeply, passionately, beyond what you can think or imagine, and He promises to restore to you the years the locusts have eaten. Be assured that God is with you always.

The Mystery of Suffering

Thomas Howard

Migraines have given rise to a virtual cult. There are symposia and colloquia and conferences and even support groups on migraines. People with migraines love to exchange tales of their troubles, like codgers sitting with their feet up on the potbellied stove in the Currier and Ives country hardware store. There is a generalized notion, which is gratifying to migraine people, that these headaches hit only very brilliant people. The hard evidence for this is, to say the least, inconclusive.

As far as I can remember, my own headaches came on when I was in my thirties. My wife and I were living in New York, where I was teaching at a boys' day school—a school where the rich and famous send their boys. I should have kept some of the memos that came to my desk from the switchboard.

"Please tell Stephen A. that his *mother's* chauffeur, rather than his *father's* chauffeur, will pick him up today." That sort of thing.

One boy had to be absent because of the unveiling of the portrait of his grandfather, Harry Truman, at the White House that day. Another boy came to see me one day, in great distress over the news that his mother had eaten the entire five pounds of Beluga caviar that he had gotten for Christmas. *Alas*, I thought, *the troubles of the very rich*.

Once when we were studying American history, we came to the building of the railroads to the West Coast. When the name of one railroad tycoon came up, I heard a boy murmur, "That was my great-grandfather." The man had owned the Union Pacific, or the Southern Pacific, or one of the great transcontinental railroads.

But back to migraines. At some point during my time at the school, I began to be assailed with headaches that were obviously more than routine in their severity. I was fairly philosophical about headaches, since both my father and my mother had had perpetual trouble with them, especially my father. But that was back in the days of aspirin, and the word "migraine" was never said as far as I can remember.

The doctors finally decided that my father was allergic to milk and milk products, so my mother had to prepare meals sedulously avoiding milk, cream, butter, cheese, and so forth. This seemed to bring some relief to my father's situation, but as I recall, the relief was very far from complete.

I think in my own mind there was a continuum between my father's interior distress and his headaches. He was the editor of a Protestant weekly journal and also the head of the whole office staff. Unfortunately, he lacked what would now be called "interpersonal relationship skills." This meant that he had to sort out the squabbles among "the girls in the office" (this is how he referred to the middle-aged typists, who did, in fact, seem to constitute an extraordinarily touchy and weepy group). The sight of one of these women sniffling into a Kleenex rolled a great stone onto his spirit.

How close the cause-and-effect relationship was between such trials and his headaches, no one knew. But on the surface of things it certainly seemed plausible to assume a direct correlation.

You could say, then, that I grew up with headaches as part of the daily fabric of existence. Perhaps because of this, I have trouble recollecting both the onset of migraines in my own head and my reaction to this visitation.

Our life in New York was, to say the very least, colorful. We were raising first one child, then two. I was teaching, which brought all these impressive people into our orbit (or us into theirs would be closer to the truth). I was also finishing up a doctoral dissertation at New York University. We were great opera fans and often went to the ballet, the Philharmonic, the cinema, and fancy restaurants. Our memories of those years come to us now as a great twinkling kaleidoscope, and it is difficult to pin down any exact sequence to things.

I remember that I began to take a prescription drug called Cafergot, which came in the form of little flying-saucer-shaped tablets, a robin's egg blue in color. One pill seemed to do the trick at first.

Then one pill began to fail under the onslaught of the headaches, and a second one had to be introduced. This was the start of a melancholy sequence, which has continued until the present (I am writing this thirty-five years later). There is always brief success with such-and-such a prescription, followed by that prescription's failure to help, followed by a second nostrum, then a third, and so forth. I remember something called Fiorinal (I am not at all sure that this is a correct spelling, nor do I know whether the pill even exists any more), which helped for a while but not for long.

At some point the doctor prescribed Percodan for me. I had no idea that this was a narcotic. As far as I knew, Percodan was just another prescription for migraines. I can remember during the early days of taking this pill that, briefly, the world would seem reasonably manageable. There was even a rather thin rosy light that suffused things. I suppose that people who have experienced narcotics know what I am talking about. But fortunately, my metabolism is such that I am virtually immune to stimulants and sedatives. Hence, though I have carried Percodan in my pocket for thirty-five years, I have never had the urge to pop one in just for relief from life's rigors.

At about this time I experienced a strange and apparent answer to prayer that seemed to veer very close to the miraculous. I am not one whose life is punctuated by signs, wonders, locutions, apparitions—or even any very discernible divine interventions at all. My prayers go up daily. I trust that the Most High receives them in His gracious magnanimity and knows what He is about, whether the situation in this vale of tears changes much or not.

I had not yet been received into the Catholic Church. I was what is known as an "Anglo-Catholic." That is, the sort of Episcopalian who thinks of himself as "catholic" (*not* Protestant) and likes to speak of "the Mass" and so forth, but who does not suppose that obedient and organic union with the Apostolic See makes any difference. But God heard my prayers nonetheless, even though at that point I was among the "separated brethren."

I had been asked to speak at a weekend retreat for a group of Episcopal clerics who were meeting with their bishop in New Hampshire. Since I am a layman, it was a slightly unusual situation to be *the* speaker for a bishop and his clergy. Nonetheless, that is how it was.

The retreat center was several hours away, and as we drove (two of the retreatants took me in their car), I felt an unmistakable migraine cruising in. It immediately became clear that this was to be no mini-migraine. It was heavy artillery.

I groped in my pocket and discovered that I had not brought my pills. *Chaos*, I thought. Here were all these nice men awaiting me, and I would arrive staggering, clutching my head, and vomiting violently, quite unable to mount any sort of meditation for them. So, with very small faith, I began to implore God to intervene.

I had never experienced any such thing as "healing," nor had I known anyone who had. In fact, while I was an undergraduate at a Protestant evangelical college, I had pursued, in a desultory way, the whole question of healing, mainly out of curiosity. My friends and I went again and again to Pentecostal healing meetings in Chicago, most anxious to witness some heavenly intervention. We saw (and heard) a great deal of turbulence, shouting, waving of hands, praising of Jesus, and people falling down—apparently healed (at least if one attached importance to their own loud testimony and the high-decibel attestation of the congregation). But we never witnessed anything visible. The ailments tended to be discomfort in people's livers and similar hard-to-check disorders. I wanted most earnestly to see crutches thrown away, club feet straightened, and severed limbs restored.

I never concluded, however, that God does not heal people miraculously (He clearly does). But I had to settle for the fact that such wonders may be expected to occur in my own world only with the greatest infrequency. As we drove along toward our New Hampshire destination, my prayers grew ever more desperate and my expectations ever more slender.

We arrived at the retreat center, where everyone greeted us most cordially. I had to murmur to the bishop that I was in the throes of a migraine and would need to be excused from the cocktail hour to lie down, on the off chance that the headache might disappear—a hope, by the way, based on nothing at all but the possibility of God's intervening. I had never had a migraine simply fade away in fewer than eight hours. The bishop graciously consented, of course, and I took myself to a darkened bedroom.

The headache disappeared. That is the plain fact. And if my hesitation about asserting stoutly that "God healed me" is culpable, then I am culpable. It does not come easily to me to make such claims. But what am I to say of this instance? I have no other example, by the way, in my sixty-seven years, of any such palpable and instant divine help. So perhaps my reticence may be laid at the feet of this fact.

I must admit to a certain tension in my own inner being, not necessarily bad, between "God *can* do such and such" and "God *will* do such and such." My own makeup is much more inclined to suppose that, when it comes to asking for specific interventions, the word is more likely to be "This is a chance for you to learn quiet endurance and patience and trust," rather than "Right: here comes a miracle." This applies to efforts to find a parking space, or requests that the weather be good for a picnic, or desires that God will cheer someone whose heart has been broken.

But the headache disappeared, and I was able to give the retreat.

I have learned that there are all sorts of migraines. Besides constituting a virtual "cult" in our society, the matter may be said to constitute an industry as well. I cannot comment on the wide reaches of the topic since I have never made much of my own migraines, other than to keep myself under the care of the best doctors I could find and hence in touch with the most up-to-date prescriptions.

I do know that many migraine sufferers experience certain visual phenomena, for example, twinkling lights in their eyes. I have never experienced that. All of us, as far as I can make out, would testify to the appalling *force* of migraine pain. I often use the word "thermonuclear" to describe my own level of discomfort. Nearly everyone will tell you also that the pain settles fairly quickly in either the left or the right half of the cranium (hence the word "migraine," which means "half-cranium").

In my own case, I will awaken, say, at three or four o'clock in the morning with a pressure at the base of my skull in the back. I know what's coming. It is inexorable. There is no waving off these heralds. Once they are afoot, there is nothing to do but prepare for the siege.

First this pressure takes on the form of discomfort, and then comes the pain. The pain increases with frightening insistence and ferocity, until I am in a state that might be called torture. The pain resolves itself into what I describe as a railroad spike driven through either my right eye or my left, and then at an angle that reaches the back of my neck. Nausea ensues, and in my case this has often been the most dramatic part of the spectacle, certainly for those around me. The nausea takes an extremely violent, not to say spectacular, form, and I am often reduced to curling up in the fetal position on the floor of the bathroom. At this stage of things even a pillow is impossible to endure, and I have to clutch my head in my hands.

My doctor has had many of his patients attempt to draw or paint what a migraine feels like. These pictures hang in his waiting room. I find them utterly fascinating and oddly amusing. It is not that I lack sympathy for the suffering depicted. But the ingenuity with which his patients have depicted their pain is, well, ingenious. One has zigzag cracks running all over the head, like an egg that has been carefully and slowly cracked. Another has multiple concentric circles in the eyes. Yet another (my scene) has a spike driven into the bone of the skull. Others have wavy lines radiating out from the skull, suggesting an inferno of agony. Readers who themselves know one or another sort of pain will testify that there is a particular comfort to be derived from discovering someone else whose experience matches theirs. Indeed, misery loves company.

As I have intimated above, I am not disposed to pay much attention to these headaches in the sense of billing myself as a "migraine sufferer." I have always thought that one simply has to get on with life. This is perhaps worth mentioning, since it has affected the manner in which I have "dealt with" my "suffering." It never occurred to me to "offer it up."

For one thing, I was not yet Catholic when the migraines appeared, in my thirties. When I was received into the Church at the age of fifty, I learned about the ancient practice of recognizing one's adversities as opportunities to unite oneself with Our Lord's own self-oblation at Golgotha and hence to enter into what Saint Paul calls "the fellowship of his sufferings." Catholics who attended parochial schools in the old days often chuckle about "offering it up"—the nuns' response to hangnails, lost homework, skinned knees, and other of life's difficulties. But there is a fathomlessly deep and rich truth here, and one that changes—even "transubstantiates," in a manner of speaking—suffering into the gold of glory.

For another thing, I never thought of my headaches as anything worth offering up. That transaction, surely, applied only to the mountainous suffering of people with lifelong debilities, broken households, wayward or crippled children, terrible poverty, the dispossession of war, and so forth. I must confess that even to this day I approach the matter with the greatest diffidence. It seems almost a presumption to enter these holy precincts, in the company of those who may genuinely claim to suffer greatly, with my sparrow-sized offering. And yet I know from Scripture and from the teaching of the Church that it is a most solemn matter, not to be lightly evaded. What else is one to do with this pain?

Pain. Plain, physical, specific torture. We all know how vision and ardor fade and crumple with the onset of pain. Everything is, by necessity, concentrated on this one thing. Everything else must be set aside. For me it was often some inconsequential matter like having to forgo a few hours of correcting college term papers or writing letters or reading. I cannot pretend that my headaches have forced me to abandon very much.

Mine have been vexations, as it were, but scarcely hardships. I wonder, in fact, if they have not been harder on my wife than on me. Many is the night when she has been awakened with the unhappy news and had to dress, drive me to the emergency room, and sit there, sometimes for hours, before my "case" came up.

I remember one night when I writhed on the hospital bed while doctors chatted cheerily with some old lady who was greatly enjoying the attention being paid to her neuralgic knee, with family all gathered around, laughter, and general bonhomie. I would sometimes have to go to the washstand in the room and chafe my temples with hot washcloths as an alternative sensation to the pain, since to leave it alone became intolerable.

My oldest friend, who is a physician near Philadelphia, followed from afar my migraines, and he finally decided that enough was enough. After some research, and having canvassed all sorts of hospitals and clinics, he concluded that the best (it was also the oldest) place for me to have a major overhaul was the Diamond Headache Clinic in Chicago. I was in my mid-fifties when I went there one summer. I was immediately put to bed. This is by far the nicest sort of hospitalization, since you are not sick but you have a reason (or an excuse) to stay in bed all day and read.

They took me off all of my medicines and weighed in with their own regimen, which eschews narcotics of any sort. I strongly suspected that I was getting "kickback" headaches from the Cafergot, since I was at the point where I would have to take six or eight pills (instead of one) in one day in order to overcome a headache. This would happen approximately three times a week. When I was at the clinic, they worked exclusively with DHE-45 and something called Norgesic Forte. When I would ring for the nurse, feeling a headache creeping toward me, she would give me my choice between these two prescriptions.

I was discharged after an idyllic week there, sent away with prescriptions for both medicaments. The DHE-45 was the stronger of the two, and it entailed hypodermic needles and little ampules, which I was instructed to carry with me for the rest of my life.

As I was standing in the check-in line at the airport ready to go home, a thermonuclear attack unleashed itself on me. The pain quickly rose to the highest possible level of agony. A woman in front of me turned, looked at me, and said, "You are in terrible pain, aren't you?"

I nodded, and I instantly became the center of the most lavish kindness from bystanders. People rushed to get me to a chair. They picked up my bags and brought them to me, murmuring sympathy and encouragement. One man went off to find the airport medical facility, which luckily was very close to the check-in counter. I was accompanied into the little room by anxious fellow travelers and received by the kindest possible nurses. They, of course, could not prescribe, but they did give me a shot of something or other to alleviate the nausea.

I was packed into a taxi, which took me back to the Diamond Clinic. The staff there put me to bed again, and I stayed for another full week, again in blissful and total silence.

Upon my discharge this time I was able to make it home to Boston. There I began a sort of new phase of life. It was an immense comfort having these new, and apparently successful, prescriptions. Things worked out quite well, and my life of college teaching went on.

For several years, I depended on the DHE-45. At first I thought that stabbing myself with a needle would be an ordeal so alarming as to be impossible. But I discovered it was not all that bad.

Not being a medical person, however, I did not always aim the needle correctly (you stick yourself in the big muscle above your knee), and I had a way of hitting a blood vessel and starting a dramatic flow of blood. Or I would not get the thing deep enough into the tissue and ended with a hard lump of DHE just under the skin. This lump stubbornly refused to ease itself into my system, simply sitting there causing pain. On other occasions I am not sure what the needle struck, but I might as well have been injecting Greek fire into my leg.

Intermittently I got it right, and both the shot and the results were most gratifying. I was using the DHE four to five times a week, instead of the normal (for most people) once or twice a month. This worked for a few years. But it was a highly inconvenient business, always darting into airport rest rooms and gas stations along the interstate to administer the shot.

About six months ago at a party, a physician friend of mine, upon inquiring how I was, noticed my guarded answer and said, "Oh! There is a new pill called Zomig that works wonders!"

I leaped at the information. I checked it with my headache man, who is an eminent international migraine authority, and he gave me the green light to try out this Zomig.

So I am now on Zomig, a very nice small pink pill, which if not miraculous, is certainly the counterpart, in the realm of nature, to the grace of miracle. Who knows how long it will remain effective? Right now, and for the past year, I never have to sustain a migraine, since one pill at the onset evaporates the whole ordeal.

But of course one is set to mulling these things over. Where
has God been in all of this?¹ Were migraines ordained especially for me? Or don't we dignify the matter with that sort of
vocabulary? Has God "helped" me, ever, and if so, just how?
Certainly God has never alleviated the pain, except in that
one instance when it seems that He knew it was necessary.

I have often wondered about the martyrs. As the flames first
licked at their feet, reddened the skin, blistered it, charred it,
and finally ate their way up the shins and thighs—what sort
of help was granted from heaven? Did the fire hurt them
less than it would an ordinary criminal merely paying for
his treason? Somehow this does not seem to align itself with
our being granted the opportunity to "share" Christ's agony
at Calvary.

Or were the martyrs granted some mode of grace that,
while not lessening the pain, nevertheless allowed them to
bear it? We read of martyrs who sing and praise God through
it all, and we find this unimaginable. As the lions tore the
first gobbets of meat from breast or leg did God in any way
"help"? Surely it must be so, although again, we have difficulty getting a grip on the picture.

And what about those Catholic missionaries in places very
far from Europe who were subjected to cunning and dia-
bolically protracted suffering—over days or even weeks—
before blessed death arrived? Did the flaying or the crushing
or the disemboweling not drive them to dementia? If not,
then how could they, with their wits still in place, endure?

We do not know the answers to these questions, of course.
But the people who suffer and who happen to be Christians
can tell us something about it all. I do not say "suffer *as*
Christians," since that would imply technical martyrdom.
We are speaking of sufferings that ordinary mortal existence
visits upon us and to which anyone and everyone might be
subjected.

What about the mystery of suffering? Certainly the questions that arise are as crushing as the whole problem of evil. Sin, pain, suffering, injustice, hardship, death: This can't be right. Something is rotten in the state of Denmark, or so Hamlet and his friends would have it. Bad things happen to good people. Rabbi Harold S. Kushner felt he had to conclude that God, who must surely be good, simply is not able to control things. That can't be right.

The question has been mooted for aeons—probably even by Adam and Eve when they stumbled upon the dead body of their beloved Abel. A Catholic must hold two apparently contradictory notions in some sort of tension in his mind: God is good and hence must hate evil. But He is also omnipotent and could stop it all if He wanted to. Or so our mortal thinking runs. Job ran into the problem, besought some sort of answer from the Most High, and was never given the formula. "I am God" was, in effect, the answer he got. Saint Paul attacked the same problem and was told that the clay has no business raising its head and expostulating with the potter.

These dicta seem cold comfort to us mortals. The psalms and the prophets, not to mention the Gospels, overflow with the assurance not only that the Most High is on the side of widows, orphans, the penurious, and the suffering but that He will come to their rescue. And yet we do not see it happening.

What of the thousands of orphans in Romania, India, and elsewhere who do not have so much as a name? What of starving mothers with starving children in Somalia and the Sudan? I recently saw a news photo of a tiny black child with spindly limbs and bloated stomach, fallen forward with his forehead on the ground. A vulture sat about twenty feet away, patiently awaiting the moment when that child became mere carrion. *Kyrie eleison!* sing the choirs in Oxford's

King's College Chapel and the Brompton Oratory. Does the cry reach higher than the vaulted ceiling?

C. S. Lewis approached the riddle in a series of five sonnets. The speaker in the poems makes the point early on that people who think the universe is meaningless have the luxury of simply shaking their fists at the cosmos and blaming whomever is responsible for the whole drama. Like Baal, this god must be off on a hunt or in the bathroom (Elijah tossed that jibe at the dancing priests of Baal on Mount Carmel). But we Christians, who believe that the Omnipotence is also the Father, must forever (or at least until the hour of our death) labor with the impossible paradox that the One who ordains all things is not only not a cosmic sadist but in fact the One who loves us.

In my own case I think the great anchors of faith have been daily Mass, a daily rosary, the office of readings, and the Liturgy of the Hours—at least morning and evening prayer. There is an objectivity about Catholicism that is greatly lacking in the sectors of Christendom not in communion with the See of Peter.

Despite my "low" view of my migraines as qualifying for the label "suffering," I do believe that they, along with the smallest daily adversities (and joys), may be offered at the altar. At the very least I can pray for those similarly afflicted, and I can carry the pain (when it outstrips the medicine, which it can do at times, even now) *for* others, as Our Lord did.

Pain is a great leveler, like death. You find out that you are not in some privileged, immune elite that has the luxury of escaping the afflictions of our poor flesh. Readers who have read the Tolkien books (*The Hobbit*, etc.) will know the character Sam Gamgee. He is a most profoundly ordinary person (well—hobbit, actually). But he is immensely ennobled in our eyes by the end of the great saga, for even though he cannot be the Ring-bearer (and hence the obvious hero), he can *bear* the Ring-bearer Frodo when Frodo's strength is exhausted.

There does come, I am bound to testify, a shift—a transfiguration, even a "transubstantiation"—in the grim precincts of pain when one makes the decision to "offer it up." In so doing one is raised from the grim solitude of thinking, *What an unfortunate person I am, with this affliction forever at me*, to the fellowship of the whole Church, which is the body that participates in the great offering at Calvary.

"By the mystery of this water and wine, may we come to share in the divinity of Christ, who humbled Himself to share in our humanity," we hear the priest say at every Mass. Pain seems to be the agent that ushers us into certain depths of that fellowship not open to us by any other means.

Forgiving the Unforgivable

Mike Clarey

"Oh, no, it can't be time to get up already!" I said sleepily as I felt Kathie get out of bed. She is always the first one up. I looked at the clock—5:00 A.M.—and wondered to myself, *What day is this? . . . Thursday, May 9, Ascension Thursday! Oh, good . . . a light paper day . . . and then Mass at 7:30. I'll just grab a few more minutes of sleep.*

As I dozed off, I heard Kathie praying out loud.

"Good morning, Lord" Kathie said her morning offering softly. "What a beautiful day You created for us to celebrate Your Ascension into heaven. May all I do, think, and say today be for Your honor and glory and that of Your Blessed Mother." Kathie had the morning routine timed just right—making coffee, folding and bagging the newspapers for Susie and Katie—all before baby Josie would wake up, hungry and wet.

Kathie and I were married August 8, 1970. We soon began a family, deciding that Kathie would be a stay-at-home mom. We also wanted to live in the general area where Kathie grew up, so we eventually settled in Sioux Falls, South Dakota. We were very successful in the family-making business. Our first child was a boy, Brian, born June 16, 1971; next came Theresa on August 18, 1972; then Danny on June 5, 1974. Our fourth child, Susie, was born on September 8, 1976, and Katie on August 23, 1979.

Katie and Susie were the bridge between our oldest three children and our youngest three: Paul, who was born February 6, 1986; Maggie, born December 30, 1986 (that is right, two children in one year!); and baby Josie, born March 5, 1991. That makes eight children, all from the same mom and dad!

For many reasons, but mostly because Kathie was a stay-at-home mom and because we had a large family, our life was not exactly what you see in the movies. We struggled through many crises, but we knew we had a sacramental marriage and that God would give us the grace to withstand any trial. Although we did not have an easy life, we were very happy knowing we were trying to do God's will.

Still lying in bed and trying to get one more minute of rest, I heard Kathie calling our children from downstairs, "Susie, Katie, it's quarter to six. Time to get up!"

I knew the daily drill, even without being downstairs to see it. By 5:45 A.M. Kathie already had the newspapers folded and bagged and ready for the girls to make their deliveries. Josie was nursed, diapered, and dressed for the day—or at least for a while.

"Theresa, time to get up! You better shower first," Kathie called out. It was common knowledge that our eighteen-year-old Theresa took forever getting ready for work.

"Danny, you wait and shower while the girls are delivering their papers," Kathie added.

Katie and Susie usually left the house at 6:00 A.M. for their paper routes, which only took them about fifteen minutes.

That morning Kathie reminded Katie and Susie not to dilly-dally.

"We need to leave early for Mass," she said. "Did you forget this is Ascension Thursday?"

"Mom, I've got to tell you about my funny dream last night," Katie said, smiling.

"Katie, get your shoes tied," Kathie said. "You can tell me about your dream when you get back."

By 6:25 A.M. Susie was back.

"Good timing, Susie!" Kathie said. "Why don't you jump in the shower while I get Paul and Maggie ready for Mass."

As she waited for Katie to return, Kathie thought through when everyone would attend Mass that day: *Dad and I, Susie, Katie, Paul, Maggie, and Josie will go to 7:30 Mass at Holy Family Center; Danny will go to the school Mass; and Grandpa can go to 5:30 Mass with Theresa after she gets off work. I hope Brian remembers that this is a holy day.* Our oldest son, Brian, was in the Marines and stationed in California.

At 6:35 A.M. the phone rang, and Susie answered.

"Mom," she said, "somebody on Garfield Street didn't get his paper."

"Wait, slow down, Susie, and tell me again," Kathie said. "What address didn't get a paper? . . . That is on Katie's route."

Kathie knew that Katie should have been home by then.

Even at this point, Kathie told me later, she already knew inside that something was wrong. Too many details did not add up. Since Katie's route was closer to our home than Susie's, she had always been back to the house first. And since we had just trimmed the girls' newspaper routes down, their entire routes would only take ten minutes, or fifteen minutes at the most. Katie knew her route and had never missed a house before.

By now it was twenty-five minutes past the time that Katie should have returned. Something *had* to be wrong; there was no other explanation for her delay. Katie was not an "explorer." She would always come straight home.

Kathie rushed into our bedroom at 6:45.

"Mike," she said, "Katie's not back from her route. I am going to go look for her in the car."

I jumped out of bed and threw on some clothes. Kathie took Grandpa's car, driving around Katie's route, while I too drove around the neighborhood. Although the routes were smaller now and it took me only five or six minutes to drive Katie's route, it felt as if a lifetime were unfolding before me.

We had been temporarily taking care of a couple of neighboring routes until replacements could be found. It occurred to me that maybe Katie had forgotten and delivered the wrong route and was now trying to fix it. As I drove around the streets looking for Katie, I prayed, confident that there was nothing wrong and that she was safe. Yet the longer I looked, the more frightened I became. I drove the old and the new routes several times, including the alleys. But still no Katie.

I went home to see if she had come back, but she was not home yet. It was now 6:55.

"What are we going to do, Mike?" Kathie asked.

That is when I grabbed the phone and called 911. I knew the police would send a squad car over right away to help us look for her. I glanced at Kathie and the kids but was afraid to look at them for too long or too closely, knowing they might recognize the fear in my eyes. I did not want them to panic or become overly frightened.

So I prayed silently to Saint Michael, to Katie's guardian angel, and to our Blessed Mother: *Please protect Katie. Lord, I know you would not let anything happen to her.* In my mental anxiety I implored all the saints, praying specifically to every saint I could remember. I paced the floor for what seemed an hour but was in reality only a few short minutes.

I realized then that I could not just stand there and do nothing any more, so I said to our son, "Danny, go down Susie's route and check once more; I'll go over Katie's route again."

Kathie looked at me and then stared at the window.

"I'll just stand here and watch out the back door," she

said. "Maybe she'll just come skipping up the sidewalk any minute."

As I drove slowly through Katie's route this time, I saw out of the corner of my eye what looked like a carrier bag. I backed the car up and pulled into the driveway of a car wash. Oh, my God, it was a carrier bag! I began to tremble and instantly begged God to protect Katie. I got out of the car, ran over to the bag, and recognized that it was Katie's. *Oh, my God.* There was blood all over the bag. I picked it up and put it in the trunk. I did not want Kathie or the kids to see it.

On the way back to the house I was consumed with anxiety and fear. *What could have happened? Maybe she is hurt and some kind person is taking care of her. But why didn't she call home? Or maybe she was taken to the hospital. Or maybe . . .*

I stopped and prayed desperately, not really a request but more of a statement: "Lord, you wouldn't let anything happen to Katie. I mean, we do go to Mass nearly every day. Mary, do not forget we are faithful to the rosary. . . . And besides, I know you love Katie far more than we do. You would not allow any harm to come to Katie."

I tried to convince myself that I believed what I was stating out loud to God, but deep inside I knew something was dreadfully wrong. Yet I refused to allow myself to even consider the worst possibility. *The Lord will take care of everything*, I kept telling myself inside. *And did He not say, "Not a hair on your head would be harmed"?*

As I drove up to the house, I saw Kathie nervously looking out the window. I knew Katie still was not home. When I realized that the police had not arrived, I became furious.

I walked in the house, grabbed the phone, dialed 911, and screamed at the operator, "Where are the police? Our daughter Katie is still missing! You've got to start searching!" The 911 dispatcher assured me that the police were on their way.

I was angry, thinking that Katie could be wandering around hurt somewhere and no police had bothered to come.

We found out later why the police had not come right away. Shortly after our first 911 call, someone called to report that it looked as if someone was burying what looked like tools in a pile of sand. Because the site was eight or nine blocks from Katie's route, and because of our call about our missing daughter, we now believe the police already suspected that a little girl had been kidnapped and murdered. We had no idea what had happened, of course.

About 7:15 A.M., a few minutes after my second call, two squad cars showed up. I rushed out to meet them. I had to tell them about the bag that I had found, but I did not want Kathie and the kids to hear me.

Kathie told Danny and Theresa to call their rides and tell them they wouldn't be going to school. "You can't leave until we find Katie," she said simply. "And please call Father Phil at the Holy Family Center and ask everyone to pray at Mass that we find Katie safe."

One of the officers spoke with Kathie and got a description of Katie: "She is wearing jeans, a blue and white sweatshirt, her white jacket, and white tennis shoes. She is eleven years old but small for her age. She has greenish brown eyes and light brown hair, about shoulder length. She is short and thin . . . but full of energy and love."

I rode with the other officer to the exact place where I had found the bag. Other police officers were already there. The officer assured me that the police were doing everything they could to find Katie.

I remembered how tiny Katie was at birth—and how tiny she remained all her life. She was full of life, kind and generous, and she had an unusually deep love for the Lord. Katie had been due August 15, the Feast of the Assumption. But true to her considerate nature, she had waited till eight days after Kathie's mother died (also August 15). We even had time to collect all the sweet corn from our big garden and store it in the freezer before her arrival.

When the police dropped me back home, they told us someone from the department would keep us informed. Kathie asked me where I had gone with the officer, so I finally told her about the bag. We looked at each other in disbelief, trying desperately not to think about the worst and hoping to protect the children from the horror of our thoughts. Theresa, Danny, and Susie were old enough to understand that something very bad may have happened. Paul and Maggie were simply confused.

"We need to pray," Kathie said. Although we all had been praying already, our words now had an extreme sense of urgency. We prayed aloud, then we prayed silently, and we waited for Katie's return.

Kathie and I endlessly paced the floor in quiet prayer. She kept looking out the window, knowing that any minute Katie could come bouncing up the sidewalk, oblivious to the commotion she had caused.

"Mother Mary," Kathie said quietly to herself, "keep her safe. Tell her not to fight—just to live! No, wait! I am sorry, Lord. That's not what You would say, and that's not how we raised our kids. It's better to die than . . . Oh, Lord, help us!"

We heard some movement in the hallway.

"Oh, no!" Kathie whispered, "my dad is awake. All this has awakened him early. How do I tell him Katie's missing?"

Kathie's dad had been staying with us while recuperating from an illness. He loved the children dearly, and they loved him. He was a joyous addition to our family. Although in poor health, he never missed our family's evening rosary. Kathie went into the hallway to meet him, wondering how to tell him that Katie was missing.

"Dad, Katie left for her paper route and has not come back," Kathie began softly. "The police are looking for her."

The look in his kind eyes broke my heart. He did not say a word. He just turned around and shuffled back to his bedroom.

By now it was nearly 8:00 A.M., and we still had no word of Katie. Our dear friend Father Larry came to be with us.

"Oh, thank you, Father, for coming," Kathie said as he hugged her. We all gathered around him, and again we prayed and waited in anguish.

"Father Phil is still saying Mass, and everyone there was asked to pray for Katie's safe return," Father Larry assured us. "Ruth got on the prayer chain before Mass, so you have a lot of people praying that Katie is found unharmed."

Father Larry Rucker, Father Ray Vega, and Father Phil Elmer are from the religious order Priests of the Sacred Heart. They lived and worked at the Holy Family Center, our parish and the place where we spent most of our devotional time. The weekday morning Mass time was perfect for our family. After the newspapers were delivered and the kids were fed and dressed for school, we regularly attended Mass together. Then the girls would walk across the street to school, just in time for the first bell. After school Katie and Susie normally returned to the Holy Family Center about the same time as the priests, and they would all share with each other the events of the day.

Father Phil is our family's spiritual director. Whatever family celebration we have, Father Phil is an important part of it. Katie received her First Holy Communion from him. He baptized Josie. And he heard our confessions and brought all of us into a deeper love and trust in our Lord Jesus and His mother, Mary. Father Phil taught us the infinite value of daily Mass and the importance of a daily rosary and frequent confession. Perhaps the Lord was using Father Phil and these other two holy priests to prepare us for the suffering we were about to undergo.

A detective arrived shortly after 8:00 A.M. and asked to speak with Kathie and me, alone.

"Susie, please take Paul and Maggie downstairs. Danny, you'd better go too. And, Theresa, take Josie down with you, please. The police need to talk with Dad and me," Kathie said nervously. "Can Father Larry stay with us?" The officer nodded.

"Mr. and Mrs. Clarey," the detective began, "a short time ago we got a call from a man who saw someone burying what he thought were stolen tools just a few blocks from here. When we investigated, we found the body of a little girl. We have not made a positive I.D., but . . ."

"What does it mean? You think it's Katie? Oh, no! No . . . no . . . is she alive?" Kathie cried out. The officer remained silent, and we broke out in uncontrollable sobs. *It can't be, Lord. Please tell us it isn't so!* We were in shock. *It can't be true! Lord, please . . . this is just a terrible nightmare.*

It is very hard to describe the darkest day of your life. Kathie and I sat on the couch weeping, alone with our pain and grief —a deep grief that sapped all our hope and strength and all that was good in life. Words and hugs could not remove the suffering. There was no comfort, no peace.

My soul desperately tried to unite with Jesus, to have Him make everything all right. But He was not there. *My God, my God, why have You abandoned us?*

I wanted to die right there. But we had other children. Even in this moment of utter emptiness and hopelessness, we had to try to control ourselves as we thought of the children. *What do we say to them? How can I tell them Katie will no longer be with us? How do I explain the evil that has been done to Katie? But I must. I must somehow find the strength and words to tell them and to hold them and to try desperately to lessen the greatest heartache we have ever experienced.*

Then Kathie softly said what I was thinking, "We have to tell the children."

We called the children together. We could see by the fear and sadness in their eyes that Theresa, Danny, and Susie were already thinking the worst. Paul and Maggie could not possibly understand what I was about to tell them.

"Katie won't be coming home," I began. "She has been . . . she has . . ."

We began to weep. We were helpless. Paul and Maggie could not comprehend what I had just said, but they understood by our tears and anguish that Katie would no longer be watching over them. And they too broke down and cried. We held the little ones close to us, desperately trying to lessen the grief. Even Josie, only two months old, squirmed in discomfort.

Father Larry called us together for prayer. This time we would not beg the Lord to bring Katie home safely but rather pray for her soul and ask for the strength to draw another breath. Once again we turned to our Blessed Mother with the rosary. *Mary, Queen of heaven and earth and Queen of our family, please come to us in this our greatest hour of need!*

Thus began what had promised to be a beautiful spring celebration of our Lord's Ascension with our friends at the Holy Family Center. Although the sun was still shining brightly, the grass was green, and the tulips and lilacs were blooming, it was the darkest day of our lives. It seemed as if the world dimmed, from full color to gray. It felt as if the purpose of life simply left. And there was nothing but an emptiness and a feeling of being all alone. Even though we were together, I still felt alone.

At 9:30 A.M. the police called to inform us that they had arrested a man with a history of sexual crimes. He was identified as the man trying to bury the body of our precious Katie.

The phone began to ring shortly after that, and then it seemed to never stop ringing. Friends and even strangers immediately began to stop over, to drop off flowers and food and to express their sympathy. Our little house quickly filled with friends and family. The news media also started to call, and camera crews showed up at the house. Someone answered the door and informed me that reporters were there and wanted to interview us.

"Not now, please, not now," I pleaded.

We simply could not deal with everything that was happening. But somehow we had to. There was so much to do and so much confusion.

I realized there were many calls to make. *How do I tell my mom and dad someone murdered their granddaughter? What do I say to poor Brian, so far away and with no one to comfort him?* I am the oldest of ten children scattered all over the country, and I knew that each of them had to be called. I could barely speak without sobbing, and now I had to tell them Katie was murdered. *Oh, my God, help me! Mary, please give me the strength to tell them.* I asked the Holy Spirit to put the words in my mouth and began to make my calls.

"Hello, Dad, this is Mike . . ."

I could not reach Brian, as he was on leave, but his master sergeant promised he would find him and have him call as soon as possible. Our bishop, Paul Dudley, heard the news on the car radio on his way out of town, turned around, and came directly to our home to pray with us. We gathered around him and hugged and cried together. Bishop Dudley offered a beautiful prayer and words of comfort.

We were all trying desperately to make sense of everything. *Jesus, where are You? We need You so very, very much.* But He was there. He was with us in His priesthood, in His people, our friends, our family, our neighbors, and most of all in our suffering. We just could not understand that then.

The rest of that morning and afternoon remains a blur in my mind. There was an endless parade of people coming to our house: our pastor, Monsignor Donald Kettler; Father Charles Mangan; Father Jim Zimmer; our closest and dearest friend, Father Phil; neighbors; strangers; friends; and of course family members. They all came to comfort us and perhaps to find a little comfort themselves.

We greeted each one with hugs and whispered prayers. The look of pain and bewilderment in their eyes only renewed our own pain. But how could we offer comfort to them? What words could be said? There were no words, just anguish, groans, and weeping. Amid all the commotion, Kathie had the presence of mind to remember that it was a holy day, so in the early evening Father Larry offered Mass in our home.

The phone rang later that evening. The sergeant had been true to his word, and it was our son Brian on the phone.

"Dad, I got your message. What's wrong?"

"Brian," I began to cry again, "Katie has been killed . . ." I could not finish the sentence.

"Dad, I'll be home as soon as I can get a flight."

Sometime after midnight we tried to get everyone to bed. We were all exhausted, but sleep would not come. Kathie and I went to bed, kissed each other, and found ourselves alone with our thoughts. I felt Kathie's unease and heard her sighs.

I wanted so much to take the pain away, but I was helpless. We had not had time throughout the day to be alone with each other, but even if we had, what could I say or do to lessen my wife's pain? I could not take her grieving away, and she could not take mine away.

Ours was a very personal, intimate depth of feeling— almost despair, except that we did not completely give up. Our hope seemed to be taken from us, snatched from us. What was left was a sudden feeling of betrayal by everything that we believed and held sacred.

Kathie tossed and turned in bed, shattered and weary, her eyes swollen shut from all the tears. In the still of the night I could hear her whispered prayer.

"Oh, Lord, this pain is too much for me to bear. I do not know if I can go on or even if I want to. . . . Mother Mary, help me! You watched as your only Son was beaten, mocked, and then put to death. You know how I feel. You know my anguish. Help me to have the courage to go on. I know I must be strong for my husband, for my children, for my dad, and for Mike's parents. But how it hurts me to see the pain and puzzled looks in their eyes." Kathie then sobbed. "Jesus, please give me Your strength! Oh, Katie, my poor Katie. Jesus, Mary, please hold her for me."

I rolled over in bed, afraid of my own thoughts. *Lord, why did You not save her?* The thought of my defenseless, frightened little Katie being overpowered by her killer was too much for me. What fear she must have felt, with nowhere to run. I was swirling in a terrifying sense of despair.

Were you there with her, Lord? Did You go to her and comfort her? Why didn't You stop it? Lord, she was one of Your most faithful and innocent little ones. Why? Why couldn't it have been me instead? I could not protect her, but You could have. Why, Lord, why?

I was trying desperately to understand how this could happen. Could it be that all we believed to be true in our faith was just a terrible hoax? No! It could not be true! Our life, Katie's life, would have been meaningless. But why? Did we not pray enough?

Were we not worthy of Your protection, Lord? And you, Mary, we consecrated our family to you long ago. Couldn't you have spared Katie? Were all our prayers in vain? And where were her guardian angel and Saint Michael? We never failed to ask their protection every day!

I could not grasp it all. In my bitterness I cried out to the Lord, "You could have saved her, but You didn't! I trusted in You, and You abandoned us! But who can we turn to if not You? There is no one else."

Saint Augustine says that God only permits evil if there is a greater good that can come out of it. That may make sense, but when you are in the middle of the pain and the misery, it is just not good enough.

I rolled over, and in my mind I saw the Lord's face in agony on the cross. I could see blood and tears dripping from His pain-wracked face, and I could see His heart was breaking in His horrible agony.

Oh, yes, Lord! You were there with Katie. Yes, Lord. I do know You love her more than we can comprehend. Then I saw Mary weeping at the foot of the cross. She too was helpless, but I could see her love and deep trust and confidence in her Son. I understood then that not only was He with us now but He was also with Katie that morning, and He too was in agony over Katie's death. Little by little I began to surrender my despair to Jesus, trying to touch Him, trying to feel Him, knowing only He could make it all right. Only He could help us understand the mystery of this "valley of tears."

I felt Kathie get out of bed. It was 7:00 A.M. on Friday.

Kathie later shared with me her anguished thoughts as she awoke that second morning, which she wrote in her journal:

Another day to face without dear Katie. Lord, only You can help me through this day—You are my strength. We have lost grandparents, classmates and friends, my brother in a car accident, and my mother to cancer. But all these pale in comparison to losing my own child, my tiny baby whom I cared for and nurtured for so short a time. Lord, You are surely testing our faith this time. . . . Katie's death is more than I can bear unless I truly believe You love her and us more than I can fathom. Maybe in Your great mercy You called Katie home now, while she is so pure and innocent, to spare her from the temptations of the unholy trinity: the world, the devil, and the flesh. And, Lord, it is only in my faith in You and in the resurrection that I can believe and begin to hope to be reunited with Katie in heaven. Lord, I believe, please help my unbelief!

One by one we began to gather around the kitchen table. None of us had slept. Again we tried to pray, but it seemed so empty. Once again the phone began to ring. And once again our little house filled up with friends and family. So many people. So much to do. But I just did not know how to begin. There was not time to think. I walked into the living room to check on Grandpa, wishing we could be alone. I could see he was still crying.

"You are blessed to have so many friends," he cried, a little overwhelmed by all the attention. "So many good people."

Thankfully, Monsignor Kettler called and said that he would take care of all the funeral arrangements. He would stop over later in the day to discuss what needed to be done.

Someone turned on the TV, and there it was. The story of Katie's murder seemed to consume our city of a hundred thousand people. We quickly sent the little ones away, for we could not allow them to see or hear any of this. There were live shots of our home and the grizzly details of how she died and where they found her. The newsmen reported how quickly the police had arrested the man and the horrible details of his sex crimes of the past. They were saying that Katie was raped and then murdered.

The thought of Katie being confronted with such evil frightened us. How afraid and alone she must have been. *How I wish, Katie, that I could have been there to protect you. Oh, Jesus, she was so innocent, so pure. Please, tell us You were there to give her strength. Tell us You were with her to console and comfort her.*

A police officer called to clarify some minor details. After I answered a few questions, the officer said, "And do not believe all you hear in the news. The medical examiner only found some evidence of an attempted rape. She was not raped. The man told us that when he tried to grab little Katie, she fought him so violently it scared him. He was afraid that he would be seen, so he struck her with something. He thought that he had killed her, but she was only unconscious. But then to make sure, he took a knife and . . ."

Katie had been familiar with the story of twelve-year-old Saint Maria Goretti, who died defending her purity. I found great comfort in thinking that our little Katie had also died defending her virtue.

Monsignor Kettler stopped by. He had taken care of what he could. We would have private time with Katie, and there would be a time for visitation. A wake and the funeral would be on Monday morning, and she would be buried in Kathie's hometown, Alvord, Iowa. But we needed to make a few decisions. We had to pick out a casket and the clothes she was to wear. Did we want an open casket?

"And one more thing, Mike, they want to broadcast her funeral on TV."

I resisted. I did not want this to become a circus. I did not want it to become one more news story. The grief that we were feeling was very private, and I was not sure I could stand up publicly to the scrutiny that we were going to get.

But Monsignor Kettler gently said to me, "The whole city is mourning for Katie and for your family. They can't all be at the funeral, and we're all hurting. This would offer them a way to show their compassion and perhaps receive a little consolation. You won't even know the cameras are there."

When he explained that the cathedral could squeeze in about a thousand people but that there were a lot more people who wanted to come to the funeral on Monday, I was stunned. I was overwhelmed with the outpouring of love from the community. It was a difficult decision, but I relented.

Again and again reporters called wanting to talk to us. I thought about what Monsignor Kettler had said about how the city was also mourning, and I glanced over at a huge pile of cards. I began to realize what an impact Katie's death had on the whole community.

"Mr. Clarey, the city needs to hear from your family," one reporter said. "We all want to share our sympathy and to know more about little Katie." I consented to an interview, but with no cameras.

On Saturday we finally had a few minutes to be with Father Phil alone. He looked a little weary and very sad. Father Phil and Katie had been close friends. They had many discussions while Katie and Susie waited at the Holy Family Center after school for a ride home.

"Father," I asked, "ever since I can remember, we have prayed for a good death. But Katie was not even given the chance to receive the last rites."

"But she was provided for nevertheless, Mike," Father Phil said. "Just last week all of you attended First Friday Mass, and the next morning First Saturday Mass. I heard all of your confessions, but I particularly remember Katie's. I remember thinking what a beautiful confession it was, from so young a child. And do not forget, she wore the scapular. Yes, she was well provided for. Our Lord and our Blessed Mother had been preparing her all her life for that moment."

Father Phil talked to us about suffering and how we must try to offer it to Our Lord. We were cradle Catholics and were raised with "offer it up" for any and every complaint we had. How many times were we reminded to "make a morning offering" so our whole day would be like a prayer. Sometimes it was almost automatic, without much thought. Then as we became older and the trials and suffering increased, we began to wonder why. Why should we "offer it up"? What good did that do?

"But, Father," Kathie said softly, "we have spent many years making our morning offering. It seems we are just given even more suffering—and this one is just too much."

But dear Father Phil insisted and went even further.

"Kathie, we can not always understand why these things happen," he said. "The mystery of evil has confounded theologians from the beginning of time. Sometimes all we can do is surrender it to the Lord, who alone can produce some good from this tragedy. I believe, and so should you, that somehow God is going to do something wonderful with Katie's suffering and death and also with your suffering.

"There is something more I am going to ask of all of you. Maybe you can not do it today, but I want you to try. I want you to not only offer your sufferings to the Lord but also offer prayers of praise and thanksgiving to Jesus for the opportunity to suffer with Him. Unite your suffering with Him on the cross for the salvation of souls."

This was too much for me! *Doesn't he realize we want the Lord to take this misery away? How can we "thank Him" for this? Something more precious than my own life has been torn from me and left all of us with an emptiness that cannot be repaired! And I'm afraid that even the Lord can't fix it.*

All of us were trying to grasp what Father Phil was asking when little Paul blurted out, "Father, when is the resurrection?"

Now I understand why Our Lord said we must be like little children. Our five-year-old had no doubt about what our faith teaches us. He knew Katie was with Jesus and Mary in heaven, and someday we would all be together again. He did not question Jesus' promises. He just wanted to know when.

Father Phil hugged Paul and whispered, "Soon enough, Paul, soon enough." He then got up to leave, "I'll see all of you tomorrow."

Kathie went upstairs to Katie's room to find something for her to wear in the casket. She was hurting terribly and crying so much she could hardly see the clothes she was holding so tenderly. She shared with me later the battle taking place inside her mind—and her heart. *How can I come to thank the Lord for this pain?* she wondered. *But I have got to try.*

Then she began to praise God and to thank Him. The words were barely out of her mouth when a sense of peace came over her. The agony was still there, but there was also a glimmer of hope. It was the beginning of abandonment and a trust that, somehow, Jesus would turn all this suffering into something good—and that eventually He would take away the pain.

Later that afternoon the reporter came to interview our family.

"Hello, Mr. and Mrs. Clarey. I am John Smith[1] with Chan-

---

[1] Name has been changed.

nel 13 News. I know you do not want any cameras, so I'll just record our interview. We want you to know how sorry we are for you and for Katie. In all my years here in Sioux Falls, I do not recall any story that has touched this community as this one has."

He asked us about our faith and how important it was to us at that moment. He told us he had interviewed Father Phil and many others, and the one thing that stood out was the unusually mature faith Katie had for her age.

"I understand you would go to the abortion clinic to pray?" he asked.

"Yes," I replied. "Katie could not understand how a mother could destroy her own baby, especially after the difficulty we had in bringing Josie into the world."

He asked all the children questions about Katie: her favorite clothes, her favorite games, and her favorite song. Susie told him her favorite song was "I Saw My Lord This Morning" by Dana, a contemporary Catholic singer.

He turned to Kathie and asked, "Do you have anything you would like to say to the man who killed Katie?"

We were taken aback by the question. Not once had any of us said anything about her murderer. Our attention was focused only on Katie and her life and our faith.

Kathie very slowly but deliberately said, "Yes, we do. We would like to tell him we forgive him."

The reporter just stared in silence, then murmured something about how this could be possible, but Kathie immediately said, "It is what God asks of us. It might not be our way, but it is His way. We ask in the Our Father every day, 'Forgive us our trespasses as we forgive those who trespass against us.' We do not necessarily understand it, but we must trust in what Jesus tells us to do."

After Kathie's comments the reporter did not seem to have much else to say, and neither did the rest of us. He thanked us for our time and for sharing Katie with him, and then he left.

That evening we finally had a little time by ourselves, and we began discussing what Kathie had said about forgiveness. It was true. Not one of us said we hated the man who had killed Katie. We did not even think about him. We chose to remember the joy of Katie's short life, not how she died. It seemed as if at least part of the burden and pain was already being lifted. We were experiencing the grace of God. After our rosary and night prayers we all drifted off to bed alone with our thoughts. It was another restless and lonely night without Katie.

When we say we forgive the man who killed Katie, it is not a denial of what happened. It is not a denial of justice. Forgiveness is like love. It is an act of the will. Ultimately you surrender to Our Lord, and He applies the grace after that.

The next morning Kathie tried to get out of bed quietly, but I was already awake. It was early, but as usual she had to feed Josie. The early morning is important to Kathie. It is the only time of the day that she has for herself and for her time of prayer. As she had countless other mornings, Kathie made her morning offering to the Lord, this time asking the Lord for grace to face the day and requesting guidance for me. She also thanked the Lord for the unexpected grace of forgiveness.

The phone began to ring early that day. "I just wanted to thank you for sharing your faith with us," the first caller said. "You gave me the courage to forgive my daughter-in-law."

Apparently our interview had been on TV. We had no idea that we had said anything profound or important. But the phone rang all day, with people thanking us, explaining their own difficulty forgiving a loved one, saying they now had the courage to do so, as well as assuring us of their prayers. Over the next few days we received hundreds of cards and phone calls expressing these sentiments.

We heard from a priest from another diocese, "If you can forgive your daughter's killer, I can forgive a brother priest who hurt me long ago." A young woman lying in the hospital with a terminal illness thanked us for showing her how to forgive her husband. *Yes, Lord, you can turn this act of evil into some good!*

That evening we all got into the van and went to the airport to meet Brian, who had not yet met his baby sister, Josie. Because of Brian's enlistment, the sad reality is that there was never a time when all of our eight children were together.

This was a sad and tearful reunion. But now Brian finally had someone to console him. We drove home, and again we prayed. We stayed up late that night, talking, reminiscing about happier times—perhaps afraid that we would forget them and return to the reality of Katie's death.

On Sunday morning Kathie woke up startled.

"What time is it?" she said out loud. Kathie glanced at the clock. It was nearly 7:00 A.M. Then without warning the reality of Katie's death enveloped her, and I heard my loving wife cry out, "Oh, Lord, she is gone. . . . How can I get through another day without Katie?"

Then Kathie remembered it was Mother's Day.

"I should be celebrating motherhood today," she said, trying to breathe, "but instead I'm preparing to bury my eleven-year-old Katie. Mother Mary, please be my strength today."

What could I say to Kathie today, of all days, Mother's Day? Throughout her life Kathie has sacrificed everything for our children and for me. But how could I wish her a happy Mother's Day amid so much pain?

I had forgotten what day it was. Earlier in the week I had promised to take the little ones shopping on Saturday. They had been excited, poring over the sales ads as they looked for that special gift for Mom. Katie and Susie had been saving a little money from their paper routes, and Paul and Maggie were going to contribute their sizable fortune, a little over two dollars.

I am not sure how they did it, but somehow the kids found a way to buy a little gift on their own. One by one they got up and went to Kathie and hugged her and wished her a happy Mother's Day.

Because it was Sunday, it was decided that Father Phil would celebrate Mass in our home. My mom and dad, Kathie's dad, eight of my brothers and sisters, as well as Kathie's brothers and sister, their spouses and children, all gathered in our family room. Kathie's brother Dennis brought a rose for all the mothers and one for our Blessed Mother.

As Father Phil began the Mass, I looked around at all the family we had gathered there. Some were no longer practicing Catholics; others had left the Church. I thought of the petty personal differences that some of us had with each other. At that moment they all seemed to melt away. *Katie, I thought to myself, look at your family — all your aunts and uncles and cousins. See how by your horrible death and suffering you have brought us all together for the first time in years to worship Our Lord. Could it be, Lord, that Katie's death was not meaningless?*

I looked around at all the food and flowers and cards that people had sent and were still sending. *Katie, did you know you had so many friends?* Our family was astonished and humbled by the outpouring of sympathy and love.

A priest once told me that God uses "the ordinary means" to accomplish His will. And I began to understand that all of us are His "ordinary means." These compassionate and loving people, most of whom we did not even know, were being Christ for us. I prayed: *Yes, Lord, I can see You now. I see You in every tear-filled face, I hear You in every mumbled attempt to offer us sympathy, and I feel You with all the hugs from this, the body of Christ.*

The time came for us to go see our Katie. We were met at the door of the funeral home and escorted to a large chapel. The room was overflowing with flowers, and there, in the middle, was a small white casket holding our precious little girl. As we timidly approached, I began to fear what we would see. Would we see the wounds and signs of struggle? Would we see the terror in her face?

I prayed again: *Mary, you saw your Son's body taken down from the cross, and you prepared Him for burial. Be our strength as we also prepare our daughter for burial. Oh, my God! This is not a nightmare. Katie is really dead—what a horrible word!*

She was as beautiful in death as in life. She looked as if she were just sleeping. Kathie had chosen a white dress and scarves to cover her wounds. I saw the bruises on her little fingers, which clutched her First Communion rosary. I remember thinking how sweet and peaceful Katie looked. We began to cry uncontrollably. *Yes, Lord. You now have our daughter. Mary, take care of her. See how little she is!*

"If I could just pick her up and hold her again," Kathie said to me. I pulled my rosary out of my pocket, and we began to pray the Divine Mercy chaplet as we looked at her lifeless body. Katie looked the same and felt the same. *Why, Lord, can't she be alive?* We did not want to leave her, but we knew we had to let her go.

We had arrived early for Katie's wake in order to have a few private minutes with her, but the funeral home filled to overflowing very quickly. Father Phil led the service and gave the homily. He has suffered for years from a throat disorder that gives him permanent laryngitis. But that night he could be heard and understood loud and clear. He knew Katie very well, as he was her spiritual director and confessor. Father Phil compared Katie to Saint Maria Goretti. The similarities were obvious. Saint Maria, the patron saint of teenage girls and youth, was a twelve-year-old girl from Italy who refused to give in to Alexander Serenelli's seductions and was stabbed by him fourteen times. On her deathbed, Saint Maria forgave Alexander, and even after her death she appeared to him in a dream and gave him a bouquet of flowers. Alexander not only returned to his Catholic faith but was later pardoned according to the wishes of Saint Maria's mother. He was released from prison after twenty-six years and became a lay order Franciscan before he died.

Toward the end of his homily, Father Phil looked at each of us and quoted John 16:20: "Amen, amen, I say to you, you will weep and mourn . . . but your grief will become joy."

After the homily our family led our friends in saying the rosary. As we were praying, my thoughts went back to happier family times with Katie. Every night after supper all of us go to the living room to pray. We normally have each of the children take his or her turn leading a decade of the rosary. After I offer our petitions and opening prayers, I usually nod or wink at one of the kids, giving the signal to begin the next mystery. Most of them just give a little nod back, but Katie would always smile and wink back at me.

Katie's funeral was on Monday. Kathie shared with me this entry from her diary for that day, four days after the murder:

Monday, May 13, 1991, the anniversary of Our Lady's appearance at Fatima.

Dear Lady, please grant me the strength to face this day —Katie's funeral. It is with heavy hearts that we all get ready to be at the funeral home by 9:15. We want to pray one last family rosary with Katie before her body is put into the ground.

Kathie would later write:

I thank God for Mike's strength as he led us so calmly in the prayer we have prayed so many times as a family. Thank You, God, for my mother, who instilled a love of the rosary and a devotion to Mary in me so that we could now feel comfort in these prayers, knowing that Mary is with us every step of the way. Thank You, God, for bringing all our siblings to be with us from so far and near.

As much as I love the holy sacrifice of the Mass, I both dreaded and longed for this one. What a comfort it was to see the magnificent cathedral full of people whom Katie's life and death have touched. I see now what Saint Paul meant when he said, "When one member of the body of Christ suffers, we all suffer with him." Thank you, Lord, for the Foxhoven family, such dear friends who traveled to sing at the funeral. What a blessing to have fourteen priests and Bishop Dudley to give our little girl a final blessing and to plead to the angels to take her to paradise.

The dreaded time came to lay her body to rest next to Mom and brother Bill. Part of my life was put in the ground today and will remain there as long as I live. I believe a piece of my heart will remain broken until we are all together in heaven with Jesus. Dear Father Adams had such a beautiful quote, "The day Katie was born, she cried and her family smiled. Today her family is crying, and she is smiling because she has seen the Lord."

In the weeks and months that followed Katie's death, our family tried to return to our daily routine. But no matter how we tried, things could never be the same. Sure, we could return to school, work, and daily household chores. But each day brought reminders of our sorrow.

Through endless tears and prayers we began to treasure even more our faith, and the Church, the body of Christ. We found out that each time we surrendered our suffering to Jesus, we were healed just a little more. And all of us grew in togetherness and in love and trust in Jesus.

More than a decade has passed since Katie's murder. The grief is still there. But God has been faithful in His presence and in His healing. Part of the healing process was the hundreds of people who would ask, "How do you live with this?" We would receive healing as we attempted to help others heal from their own deep wounds.

There seems to be a kind of bond among people who have suffered the unexpected loss of a loved one. We tend to seek each other out. Each time someone comes to us to share his or her own tragedy and look for answers, we let the Holy Spirit speak through us. As we share each other's pain, we begin to weave another bond, a bond with the Lord. We have shared something very intimate and very personal with Him.

In the final analysis, every one of us is going to die, whether we die at eleven years or a hundred years of age. Ultimately, this is a short life. We're confident that Katie is in heaven. And that gives us hope. Our goal is to be united with Jesus forever in heaven. That vision changes everything. Things that used to be important to us are no longer important. Bickering, material things—they no longer matter. We now have a deeper sense of reality, a deeper sense of truth, a deeper sense of purpose than before.

But we still have to struggle to hang on to that, and we have to practice it. Prayer, the sacraments—those are the remedies the Church offers us and the sure way to remain faithful. If it was not for the Church, if it was not for our faith, if it was not for the sacraments, I do not know if we could have survived this.

We know suffering will come again in this "valley of tears." But God waits. He waits ever so patiently for us, saying: "Come to me, all you who are burdened, and I will give you rest" (Matthew 11:28).

Moments of Grace

Grace D. MacKinnon

The steady, rhythmic sounds of the train had finally lulled me to sleep. Then suddenly, I knew we were nearing our destination. I knew it because Mother's arm around me had grown tighter. How we had dreaded this moment. Terror gripped me. If only we could turn the train around and go back! I wanted to scream, *Why does this have to happen?* Wasn't it enough that I had been born crippled? But I was six and did not understand.

In the distance I could see the train station, and as we approached, I sensed that the secure world created by my mother's love was about to shatter. I loved and needed her so much. Why did I have to say good-bye to her?

This painful episode from my childhood is engraved in my memory. Thinking back, and knowing what I do today, I firmly believe that it was all part of God's plan. Yes, even this wrenching experience was necessary, yet only God knew why. It is a great mystery when a child is born with a permanent physical disability. In it there is a sign and a message, and it involves a mission. The strength for it comes from the "moments of grace."

For me many of these came through people. In the persons that He sent into my life, God showed me how much He loved me and how I would eventually understand what it was He wanted from me. And what He wanted was far more than I could ever have imagined. One day He would reveal to me the "secret" of suffering. But before that, I would have to undergo many trials and much pain.

To feel rejected, unwanted, and "different" is a suffering that takes deep root in the human heart. It affected my entire life and, for many years, my relationship with God. But through it all, He gave me strength, even when I did not feel His presence. In His infinite love God had chosen me to bear a painful cross from the moment of birth. What would make this cross unique is that it was to be a visible one.

The crippling illness, later identified as cerebral palsy, did not manifest itself immediately. Because of my inability to sit up, it became clear by the time I was six months old that something was very wrong. Unfortunately, in the 1950s, my doctor did not know how to diagnose my physical condition. He simply prescribed vitamins in hopes that they might provide the strength I needed. Little did he realize the seriousness of the case he had before him.

At home my family tried to provide the best possible care for me. Like so many others in the Rio Grande Valley of south Texas, we lived in extreme poverty but with hearts full of pride in our Hispanic culture and identity. After my father's departure due to unfaithfulness, Mother struggled alone to provide for her eight little girls.

We lived in a two-room house in an alley. A meal often consisted of two potatoes and one egg for all nine of us. Sometimes we were so hungry that we would sit anxiously on the curb waiting for our mother. When my sisters would see her coming, they would jump up and down in the alley yelling, "Look! She has food! She has food!"

Mother had been abandoned by her father, and now by her husband, the only man she had ever loved. Yet she was the most courageous, noble woman I have ever known. Her entire life was dedicated to raising her children. She was an example to us all of the love that God has for every human soul.

My first six years were lived as an invalid in a protected world where everything was done for me. Crawling on the floor was my only means of mobility. This earned me the nickname "patito," meaning "little duck," because of the way I waddled on my hands and knees from one place to another. Everyone seemed to tower over me, making me feel small and weak. Even though it was frustrating to move about, mine was a world filled with love and attention. But that was soon to change dramatically.

One day, when I was six years old, the physical therapist at the clinic that I was attending told my mother, "Your daughter cannot go on like this. Something has to be done. But there are no facilities here for the type of total rehabilitation that she needs." My survival, nonetheless, depended on it. I had to be sent away, and it would be for an extended period of time.

"I can't let her go!" Mother agonized. "She won't make it without me. Who will take care of her?" These thoughts tormented her as she pondered the prospect of taking me four hundred miles away to the Moody School for Crippled Children in Galveston, Texas, and leaving me there indefinitely. She had no money to do this. And even though she had been told that the state of Texas would pay the expenses, she knew there would be no means to come visit me.

But the decision was made, and this is how we found ourselves on the train to Galveston that terrible day. As we pulled into the station, I knew that nothing in my life would ever be the same again. I was about to be abandoned! Panic seized my heart. Clinging to Mother, I thought at that moment that I would rather die than be separated from her.

"Please take me home, Mama!" I pleaded. "Don't leave me here!"

"I have to do this!" Mother said.

She told me later that she had to convince herself. *Someday Gracie will understand.*

As I was being introduced to some of the children at the school, I turned around and she was gone. My mother was gone! I had been left with strangers!

"Come back, Mama, come back! I can't run!" I cried.

My body shook violently as the nurses tried to hold me down. With every fiber of my being I wanted to run from there, but escape was impossible. I could not even walk! How on earth could I flee? Was this all a terrible dream? Would I soon awaken to find myself safely back home? Would I ever see my mother again?

Where was God if He loved me so much? What had I done to deserve this? To be torn from the person you love most in the world is a terror that only those who have experienced it can ever understand. A loneliness I had never known before began to creep into my heart.

The school seemed enormous. A ward filled with row after row of crib-like beds became my home. The bars on my bed made me feel even more trapped. At night I often lay awake, listening to the crying of the other lonely and suffering children. I too cried but silently. How swiftly darkness and gloom had entered my life, breaking the spirit within me. Each day brought only more sadness. I felt abandoned, as if I had been thrown into a prison and forgotten there.

Into this world would come a bright light, bringing a ray of hope I so desperately needed. Her name was Carmen. She had soft eyes, a warm smile, and a wonderfully clean smell. Carmen was a nurse at the Moody School who, in many ways, became like a second mother to me. Every day I waited to see her happy face. I felt special in her eyes. She had a way of getting me to do things that no one else could. I was angry and resentful inside, except when I saw Carmen. With her encouragement I began to participate in activities and to learn the tasks necessary for my survival. God had sent this angel at the right moment, a great grace in a very difficult time.

Among the first tasks I had to learn were how to feed myself and how to eat properly. At home my sisters had taken turns feeding me each day. Mother had insisted on it. What a great effort it took now to bring food up to my mouth—such a laborious chore that seemed to take forever. My mother, I realized, had overprotected me. By allowing myself to be babied, I was acting contrary to the independent nature that was the real me.

Letters soon began to arrive from my mother and sisters, promising that I would, indeed, be going home—but I had to learn to walk first. I missed them so much. Yet it seemed impossible that I would ever walk. And if I could not do it, did that mean that I could not go home, ever? *Do they not want me if I can't walk?* I wondered. *Why did You make me this way, God, so that no one would want me?*

I had an overwhelming fear of falling. One day, outfitted with leg braces from waist to toes, I was led into a gym, pulled up out of my chair, and ordered to fall on a floor mat. The idea was to teach me how to fall down properly so that I would always know how to protect myself. Stubbornly, I refused to do it. After a solid five minutes of refusing, the therapist was forced to push me over. Down I went. I eventually learned how to fall and many other things, but at this point, I wondered if this nightmare would ever be over.

The weeks drifted into months, and the months became a year. I worked hard, promising God that I would be good if only He would let me see my mother again. Then one day, when I had just about given up hope, we were told we were going home. The children were all congregated in the dining room waiting for their parents. Could it really be true? Would my mother really come for me? Was it actually over? My heart pounded with excitement. I could not wait to surprise her.

Many of the children had already been picked up. Every passing minute I grew more worried. Then, as I was bent over a water fountain, the school administrator called my name. I turned around, and there she stood!

As long as I live, I will never forget that glorious look, the huge smile on my mother's face. Wearing the heavy braces and with the crutches that I had mastered, I walked to her for the first time. This was the moment I had dreamed about all those months—my mother holding me. She cried when she saw me walk to her. We were so happy! And then she took me home.

I had learned a great deal during that year in Galveston, but still the questions in my mind and heart remained. Why was I so different from everyone else? Why did people stare at me all the time?

I yearned to be like my seven sisters—to run and play outdoors. They tried to include me in their games by slowing down for me, but often I felt left out. The frustration of not being able to make my body do what I wanted was so intense at times that I longed to just disappear and never come back. *Maybe they would all be better off if I weren't around at all*, I thought. To cope with my loneliness, I developed an imaginary friend.

Our house on Levee Street in Brownsville had three large mesquite trees in front. At one of these trees I would meet my friend each day. No one, of course, could see her but me, and it was our own secret. She had a little sister who could not walk. I often refused to let the sister join us. "No, I don't want her to play with us!" I would say.

Later when I grew up and remembered these buried experiences, I realized that it was my own desperate way of dealing with the rejection I felt as a child. By making myself one of them in my imaginary world, I was able to become what I considered "normal." Often I thought, *If only they knew how it feels to be stared at with a look that says, "I don't want to come near you."*

Although I was being raised Catholic, God seemed distant somehow. I do have memories, however, of a tall Irish priest who would bring Holy Communion when I could not get to church. Sometimes he even celebrated Mass in our home. Father Casey had a kind face, and I was naturally drawn to him. Love and compassion flowed from his heart. God was reaching out to me in these moments of grace. But I was still too busy feeling rejected to know it.

Mother had made sure that catechists came to prepare us to receive the sacraments, but she did not attend Mass herself. Deep within her was a terrible pain. She had grown up with the knowledge that her father had given her away on the very night she was born. Since she had discovered this fact at the tender age of five, it was difficult for her, as it was for me, to see God as a loving Father. I myself felt that I was being punished for something that either I or someone else had done. Nothing else made any sense to me. The seeds of rejection had taken root in both of us in various ways.

After returning to Brownsville I was placed in the Gateway School for Crippled Children. The headmistress there was not prepared, however, for the battle that was to come. God had a plan. To achieve it He gave me a fighting spirit and a determination that would not quit. With the odds against me, fighting was the only way I knew to survive.

A hungering desire for knowledge was brewing within me. Besides, a message had come through loud and clear: "Surely Gracie will never marry. She may not have a normal life, but she is going to be smart!" And even though this hurt me deeply, I kept it to myself and accepted it as my fate.

As I increasingly complained of how bored and unchallenged I was there, Mother fought for my release from the Gateway School. Because of my physical disability, I was often treated as a retarded child. This was simply intolerable. I had a mind of my own. Why could they not see that? The puzzles they gave me to do were too easy—and I wanted more than that! With impatience and anger welling up inside of me, I repeatedly insisted, "I want to go to a normal school! Will somebody please listen to me?" And eventually someone did.

Every day after classes I spent an hour or so in physical therapy at the clinic next door to the school. It was that same therapist, Miss Putegnat, the one who had originally urged my mother to send me to Galveston for rehabilitation, who also took her aside one day and told her in a hushed voice, "You must do something to get Gracie out of this school. She doesn't belong here." But the school refused to release me.

Had it not been for Mrs. Virginia Garcia, the principal at our neighborhood elementary school, I might never have made it into public school. Taking a chance, even risking her own job, Mrs. Garcia allowed me to enroll at Skinner Elementary School when no one else would, thus making it possible for Mother to remove me from Gateway School.

I entered at age ten and was placed in the third grade, as I was too old for the first or second. God had brought into our lives the right people exactly when we needed them. These were indeed moments of grace, and there would be many more.

Our family had no car. How would I get to school? It was only four blocks away, but that was a tremendous distance for me. No matter what it took, however, I was determined to get there! One of my sisters was assigned to walk on each side of me. Along the path was a railroad track. The loose gravel terrified me because of the way it could easily cause the tips of my crutches to slip away.

"Hurry up, Gracie!" my sisters would shout. "We're going to be late for school! You're taking too long!"

Why did they have to make me feel so slow? I was trying as hard as I could. Why could they not understand how afraid I was? I wanted to go as fast as they did, but the heavy braces and crutches were holding me back. Becoming impatient, they would take hold of my arms and say, "Come on, we'll help you." Frightened and shaking, I would trudge along. Anything to get to school.

By fifth grade the girls at school had discovered boys. This would present a whole new alienation for me. I would listen as they talked and daydreamed of having a boyfriend. I dreamed too but only in my thoughts. I did not dare tell anyone. One day, however, as they were teasing me about being shy, I blurted out that I liked a certain boy in my class.

"Gracie! You like a boy? But you can't even walk!" one said. The pain of that statement shot straight to my heart. I longed to ask, *Don't I have a right to be happy too?* Why was there always pity in their eyes when they looked at me? From that day until after I graduated from college, I never again told anyone of my interest in any young man. The words that had rung in my mind were, *No one will ever want you.*

Making friends in junior high and high school was a struggle. I fervently yearned to be accepted by my peers. But how could that happen when my body simply could not keep up with them? Walking on crutches meant that I was much too slow at doing everything.

There was also the problem of how I looked when I walked, swaying from left to right. (It is not easy to walk a perfectly straight line when using crutches.) Appearance means everything to young people, and no one wants to be stared at for the wrong reasons. Thus, many of my classmates did not want to be seen with me.

How well I remember one particular occasion, when I was in seventh grade, that brought this to light. Since I was never invited to parties, I decided that I would have one of my own. As my birthday neared, I begged my mother to allow me to have a real party with invitations and all. Normally Mother did not like this sort of thing, but seeing how much it meant to me, she agreed. As a special gift, she ordered an elaborate tray of party food that cost $50, a significant financial sacrifice for her! Mother only earned about $200 a month at that time, so this was a sign of how much she wanted the evening to be everything I hoped for.

Excitement filled the air in the days prior to the big event. I gave out forty invitations to my friends at school. Since some of the most popular students were in my classes, I daydreamed about how this party would finally make me feel a part of them. Everything would be different. They would see that I was just like them.

But it was not to be. Except for my family, only three people showed up that night. We did our best to have a good time, eating, talking, and listening to music.

"Gracie, what happened?" Mother kept asking me.

"I guess they were all busy," I answered.

After everyone had gone home, I went to bed and cried alone. My heart was broken. What was so wrong with me that caused them not to want to be around me? I thought I was attractive enough, fairly smart, and quite friendly. I did not have a contagious disease!

During those years my life revolved mostly around family and studies. It was such a simple, sheltered life in many ways. Household chores always fell on my sisters, as Mother would never hear of my doing any of them. Meanwhile, their lives were going on around me. I loved so much to sit and listen to their adventures and experiences.

Where could I turn when there was no one to talk to? God was about to answer my prayer. When I was about fifteen years old, a religious sister at our parish asked my sister Diana and me if we would like to join the Legion of Mary. I did not know what that was. In fact, I did not know much about Mary at all. But a little prayer booklet with pictures of the divine mysteries and the rosary opened my heart to the healing power of God. Gradually I drew closer and closer to my spiritual mother, Mary. I would pour out my heart to her. She understood all the things I could never say to anyone else. And I sensed that she had something to tell me.

Although I loved my earthly mother immensely, she sheltered me so much in her attempt to protect me from being hurt that it was difficult to imagine living a "normal" life. It was not easy to talk to her about these things. What I wanted more than anything was to be like everyone else, to not stand out. Mary knew that. Sitting quietly in the chapel of Saint Joseph's Church, I would converse with her and beg her to help me understand the reason for my affliction. In my heart I could hear her say, *Jesus loves you just as you are, my child. One day, you will know how much.*

It was Mary who was leading me to her Son, and fittingly so. Her heart was so full of mercy. The profound sense of peace and love that I experienced in that chapel was to remain with me for the rest of my life. I knew that I belonged to God and that He loved me. I did not understand it, but I knew it. The beauty of this truth resounded sweetly in my soul.

I wanted to love Him the way that I should, but there were still many unanswered questions in my heart. Why had He made me this way? And what did He want from me?

We were now at a house on MacDavitt Street, the last

home we lived in together as a family. I had a small bed by a window. In the evenings I would often go to bed before everyone else because I delighted in lying down and looking up at the night sky. There I could slip away from the real world into one of make-believe.

I would imagine that I was a beautiful young girl who loved to dance and that a handsome man with kind eyes was in love with me. They were such beautiful dreams. Were there really men like that in the world? How I wanted to believe that one day God would send one to rescue me.

At the age of nineteen and with high school graduation approaching, I faced another major decision. When I was a young child, Mother had told me she hoped that I would die before her because she feared no one would take care of me the way that she did. But now I was growing up. What would become of me in the future?

"I want to go to college!" I announced one day. It was so important to demonstrate to myself and to others that I could make it on my own.

What a challenge this would prove to be. At the age of twenty-one, after spending two years at a smaller college, I left the security of my home and embarked on a journey that had been appointed for me by God. I had an adventurous spirit for someone so physically limited, and it was all His doing. I found myself on the forty-acre campus of the University of Texas at Austin, where architectural barriers were everywhere.

Before leaving home, people had asked how I was going to make it on campus all by myself. "I don't know," I had replied, "but when I get there, I'll find out!" It was to be a time of enormous physical, emotional, and spiritual struggle, culminating in a deep and lasting spiritual experience.

The state provided funds for a student to push me in my

wheelchair to classes. Ads were posted on campus, and several young men called to inquire.

"May I come by your dorm to discuss it with you?" one of them asked on the phone. I agreed, arranging a time for later that evening. After we sat and talked for a few minutes in the lobby, he suggested taking me for a stroll through campus so we could see if the way he pushed my wheelchair would be acceptable. It was a nice evening, and there were many students walking on campus, so it seemed safe enough.

As we were passing one of the beautiful water fountains, he leaned down and said, "Would you like to stop and sit on a bench for a bit and talk?"

"Sure, that sounds fine," I answered.

He sat on the bench while I sat in my wheelchair, and the time passed quickly as we talked about many things. I soon found myself becoming more and more comfortable with him, yet never in my wildest dreams would I ever have predicted what happened next.

Looking straight into my eyes he said, "You know what? You are a very nice girl." And then he kissed me!

It was so unexpected. I had never been kissed before. What did this mean? Did it mean that he really liked me?

Sleep was impossible that night. Dancing in my mind were all sorts of romantic thoughts. Never before had I experienced such elation. Wondering what was to come, I spent the entire next day thinking of the things I wanted to say to him when he called me. After all, wasn't that the next step? When a boy liked you, he would call and ask you out.

But he did not call, and I never saw or heard from him again. For days I drifted in and out of anger, hurt, and emotional pain. What a fool I had been! I yelled out to God, "Why? Why did you let that happen to me?" No answer came. I felt torn up inside. Why was I considered such a nice girl but not good enough to take out on a date? The campus was swarming with thousands of students, but I felt invisible. *Can anybody see me? Me! Not my wheelchair! I'm here! Please let me be like you!*

Life at college would have been devastatingly lonely had it not been for the Newman Club, a Catholic student organization on campus. A girl in my dorm, not wanting to go to the first meeting alone, had begged me to accompany her.

"Go with me just this one time and I won't ask you to go again," she promised. Reluctantly I agreed. But as it turned out, I was the one who joined and she never went back! God can be very sneaky. He was up to something.

This group of young people brought me out of the interior world where I had locked myself. It was as if they knew what a sheltered life I had led. They insisted I do everything they did—from horseback riding to "tubing" down the Guadalupe River! They loved watching me have fun.

Suddenly life was full of social activity. The shyness was melting away. Since everything was done as a group, most of the time it did not even matter to me that I did not date. At last I had friends who truly wanted to spend time with me. An undiscovered side of my personality began to emerge. I loved to joke and laugh and express my opinions. Like a wilting flower that only needed to be watered to come back to life, I had been starving for love and attention.

Everyone is like this to some extent, I believe. But the physically disabled feel it in a particular way because much of the attention they receive is pity. We all want to be loved and acknowledged for who we are. I needed to know that people could look beyond the wheelchair and see my heart, my mind, my soul. I had interests, needs, and desires just like everyone else. Not having grown up with a father or brothers, I was especially in need of a male friend. It was then that God sent Monte into my life.

Monte joined the Newman Club about the same time that I did. I did not understand why, but he took an instant liking to me. When he realized that I needed a ride to some of the meetings, or a push in my wheelchair from the dorm, he immediately volunteered. We became inseparable friends. We did such crazy things together. I will never forget our wheelchair "rides" down 21st Street, one of the steepest hills on campus. I would sit in the wheelchair and lean forward to balance the weight, while Monte would position his feet on two bars below the chair. We would roll downhill at full speed!

"Gracie," he would say, "I may be vain, but I love it when people stare at us wherever we go!"

To me he was the most magnificent person in the world, and I daydreamed of what it would be like if he were interested in me beyond friendship. But I knew that he loved my best friend, Cathy. I thought she was the luckiest girl on earth. When we graduated from the University of Texas in 1973, Monte and Cathy were married, and I was a bridesmaid at their wedding. Our friend Mike, a very handsome young man, was my escort. I felt so sorry for him as we walked down the aisle together that day.

Poor Mike, I thought, *having to walk down the aisle with me on these crutches.* How funny we looked! I was more nervous than the bride. But I was so happy for Monte and grateful that he had come into my life, for he had been the first man to ever make me feel human and normal. He had loved me for who I was as a person. He did not care about the wheelchair. He cared about me.

Another wonderful part of God's plan in having me join the Newman Club was that now I was able to attend Mass on Sunday. Through my teenage years our family attended Mass irregularly. Mother had always been consumed with the responsibilities of work, home, and the heavy burden of raising eight girls. And since she did not go to Mass herself, we did not go either. But in college Mass was right down the street.

The liturgy held a mysterious attraction, offering me a profound awareness of belonging. Yet a distance between God and me still existed. I knew He loved me, and I wanted to believe that I loved Him, but I had not yet forgiven Him for creating me in this physical condition or for allowing me to suffer. The truth is that God had been at work in my life all along, but I did not know it, or why. A total surrender would be necessary. He had to bring me to that moment.

While I was with my friends at college, I felt accepted and happy. But I noticed that as soon as they had dropped me off and gone home, an incredible loneliness would take hold of me. I had no one to go home to, no one person to whom I was special. How I dreaded the end of an evening. It was on one of those nights, as I sat in my darkened dormitory room, feeling lost and alone, that I gave up my grapple with God. Out loud, I spoke to Him.

"You have been after me for a long time, haven't You?" I asked. "And I have been running away from You. Well, there's a reason for that! I am not good enough for You! Look at me, how crippled I am! I'm not good enough!"

The tears began to flow, and it was then that God's mercy and love permeated my whole being. I was enveloped in a peace I had never known. After a while I spoke again, this time with calmness.

"If You think You can come into this life of mine and make it better, then go right ahead and do it. I am inviting You to come in. Forgive me, my God, for being angry with You. Help me to be everything You want me to be."

It was my turning point.

In abandoning myself to God and to His love, a new realization flooded my mind. He had not created me this way.

THE MOYLAN FAMILY

Janet, Ann Marie, and Tim on Ann Marie's first birthday (January 1996)

Our last Christmas with all seven of us was in 1995. From left: Tim, Janet, baby Ann Marie, Michaela, Amy, Jenni, and Daniel (kneeling)

Jenni on her tenth (and last) birthday holding Ann Marie, the baby sister she had wished for. (August 11, 1995)

A great picture of Jenni and Tim as it captures the peace that both had in life. This was the photo we sent with our thank you notes after the funeral. (May 1994)

Jenni's last photo. Tim took this photo on the beach shortly before they died.

The family photo we took for the church directory in the fall of 1996. This was the first family photo after the loss of Tim and Jenni. It was very difficult for us, but I knew we needed to do it. Clockwise from top left: Amy, Michaela, Daniel, Ann Marie, Janet

A picture in the summer of 2002 at our home.
From left: Michaela, Amy, Ann Marie, Daniel, Janet

To see more pictures of the Moylan family,
visit the Amazing Grace Family Album at www.AmazingGraceOnline.net/album

THE CLEVELAND FAMILY

We had it all! Christmas of 1994, almost three years to the day before I (Carl) went to prison. Top row: Kitty, Patricia; 2nd row: Joey, Carl, Caitlin; Bottom row: Caroline, Connie, Beth and family pet Ellie

This picture was taken the night before I reported to prison. I am sitting with friends Barbara and Dan Wauks. (December 28, 1997)

I had the opportunity to accompany New Orleans Archbishop Philip Hannan on a pilgrimage to Rome and the surrounding areas. Although we knew that an investigation into my law practice was underway, the archbishop (on the left) insisted I serve as his deacon on this trip. Here we are in the catacombs. (Spring 1996)

With my pastor, Father Albert Ernst, on the day of my ordination to the permanent diaconate (December 1989)

Thanksgiving 2000. We had great reason to give thanks this year– my release from prison! Clockwise from the top: Connie, Beth, Caroline, Caitlyn, Patricia, and Kitty

Kitty's wedding in October 1994: Left to right: Patricia, Connie, Kitty, Caroline, Beth and Caitlin. Joey and I are so proud of our girls.

Two blessings we have experienced since my release from prison were the births of our first two grandchildren. Abigail (left), was born in January 2001. Adeline (right), enjoying her first birthday party.

Carl and Caitlin challenging the Nantahal River in North Carolina. (Summer 2000)

Patricia's engagement party. I was not released for her wedding. Top row: Connie, Caroline, Beth and Kitty; Bottom row: Caitlin and Patricia. I was in prison for both Patricia's and Beth's weddings.

Alleluia! My homecoming party in April of 2000. (The Jubilee Year!)
Top row: Caroline, Carl and Connie; Bottom row: Kitty, Beth, Caitlin and Patricia

To see more pictures of the Cleveland family,
visit the Amazing Grace Family Album at www.AmazingGraceOnline.net/album

PEGGY STOKS

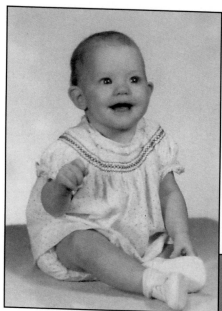

Me at age six months.

A second grade school picture. I was seven.

A seventh grade school picture. I was twelve. The expression on my face captures how I was feeling at the time.

The day I graduated from
nursing school in June 1981.

Mother's Day, 1994. I was in the
midst of post-partum depression.

A recent photo

To see more pictures from the life of Peggy Stoks,
visit the Amazing Grace Family Album at www.AmazingGraceOnline.net/album

TOM HOWARD

U.S. Army, 1959

A picture just after my engagement to Lovelace, 1964.

My other sweetheart – a TC-MG.
(That's J.S. Bach on my sweatshirt)

Dr. Thomas Howard, associate professor of English, Gordon College, Wenham, Massachusetts (1975)

My daughter, Gallaudet, and I at her Harvard graduation. (As a proud papa I have to say that she graduated summa cum laude and Phi Beta Kappa.)

With the Pope in January 2000

My wife, Lovelace, and me.
Mount Lafayette in
Franconia, New Hampshire,
is in background.

To see more pictures from the life of Tom Howard,
visit the Amazing Grace Family Album at www.AmazingGraceOnline.net/album

THE CLAREY FAMILY

Katie, age seven, holding her new baby sister, Maggie. (January 1987)

This was Josie's baptism at the Holy Family Center Chapel. All the children are here except Brian. Also pictured are Grandma Clarey, Grandpa Kramer, and Father Phil, who baptized Josie (March 18, 1991)

Katie at two years old. She was very tired and didn't want her picture taken, thus the sad face. (1981)

Katie at four years old. This was taken before she started kindergarten in 1983. Of all the pictures of Katie, this one best captures her personality: happy and full of energy (and a touch mischievious).

This is Katie's eleventh birthday, which we held shortly after we moved to Sioux Falls, South Dakota. (August 23, 1990)

We were never all together for a picture because Brian was in the Marines when Josie was born. We had Katie's last school picture added so she could be with us in this picture. (December 1993)

GRACE MacKinnon

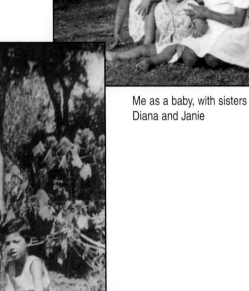

Me as a baby, with sisters
Diana and Janie

Me (on the ground) with my
mother and sister Sandy.
This photo was taken just prior to
my journey to Galvestion for my
year of rehabilitation. It shows my
my invalid condition.

In this photo, I look on as my sisters Perla and
Sandy play with the family dog. My mother, always
protective, watches from the door.

Original house where my sisters and I grew up as young children in the 1950s in Brownsville, Texas.

Route showing the railroad tracks I had to cross when I walked to school on crutches.

Me at age thirteen.

Me in my high school "cap and gown." (1969)

Me with my mother, in 1994, three years before she died.

My mother and sisters at a family reunion in summer of 1994.

Teaching courses in Catholic doctrine in the Diocese of Brownsville.

Me with my daughter, Crystal. (1998)

On the set of my TV show "The Joy of Our Faith," which aired on KMBH-TV in south Texas and northern Mexico in 1998.

A recent photo - "I know there are no wheelchairs in heaven."

To see more pictures of Grace MacKinnon,
visit the Amazing Grace Family Album at www.AmazingGraceOnline.net/album

THE HARDEY FAMILY

Our backyard. Brad's fort was located in the back, between the two trees pictured in the center. I was standing on the patio to the left when I had the "vision" about the sins in my life.

Brad was nine and in the fourth grade when he died. This is his class picture and the last picture that was taken of him. (1990)

Brad with a largemouth bass. The two of us went fishing often. (1988)

This is the original picture drawn by our friend Rhoda Boone two weeks after Brad's death.

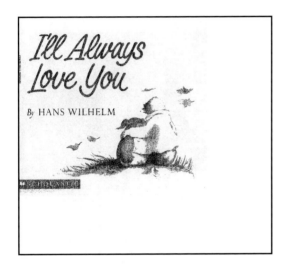

I'll Always Love You

By HANS WILHELM

SCHOLASTIC

This is the cover of the book Jennifer brought home three weeks after Brad's death. She had actually ordered the book a month before his death. To this day, we're amazed at the similarities between these two drawings, and believe it was a grace that God gave to comfort us after the loss of Brad.

Brad's gravemarker featuring the drawn image.

BRADFORD THOMAS HARDEY
"THIS WORLD WAS NEVER MEANT
FOR ONE AS BEAUTIFUL AS YOU"

OCT 2, 1980   MAY 3, 1990

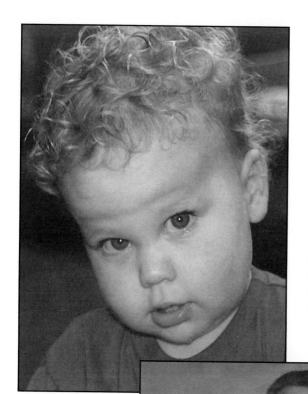

We experienced new life in more ways than one after Brad's death. One of those ways was with the birth of Stephen, shown here at eighteen months. (1993)

The Hardey Family. Clockwise from left: Jennifer, Kim, Stephen, and Bonnie (2000)

To see more pictures of the Hardey family,
visit the Amazing Grace Family Album at www.AmazingGraceOnline.net/album

THE HARDING FAMILY

My modeling headshot (1987)

Cheering on the team and spending a happy moment with a child from the Special Olympics. (1981)

Clowning around in the leaves on a beautiful day: Gabriel, Mikaela, and Noah (September 2000)

David with his little princess Mikaela during the building of our home. (March 1996)

Noah, age five, Gabriel, age two, and Mikaela, age eight (2000)

David greets a native from the village during his pilgrimage (2000)

Noah at age two-and-a-half kneeling on The Children's Prayer Station. (1997)

A memorable moment with Mother Angelica
outside of EWTN. (October 1999)

Me and Mikaela with my mom and dad. (Thanksgiving 1994)

To see more pictures of the Harding family,
visit the Amazing Grace Family Album at www.AmazingGraceOnline.net/album

DEB HEADWORTH

My wedding day. From left: sisters Tami and
Denise; mom Rosemary; Deb; dad Butch; and
brother Todd

Russ and I were married on
June 4, 1994. Neither of us
could predict the challenges
we would face over the next
eight years.

In 1997 I made this portrait as a
gift for Russ, who often contem-
plates in the same position as our
Holy Father sits here.

This photo was taken in 2000, just before I began chelation treatments to rid my cells of toxic mercury poisoning.

In 1999 I began sculpting this crucifix. Truly, God was carving me more than I was carving the wood. An understanding of sacrificial suffering was being chiseled into my very being.

Madonna (close up): My meditations while creating this image were, "Mary, how did you bear the weight of the cross? How did you find the strength to watch God being killed? How did you stay your hand?"

Christ (close up): My prayer during the creation of this image was, "Christ, help us offer our sufferings through You, with You and in You, in unity with the Holy Spirit, so that all glory and honor is Yours, for ever and ever, Amen."

To see more pictures from the life of Deb Headworth, visit the Amazing Grace Family Album at www.AmazingGraceOnline.net/album

JOAN ULICNY

This picture was taken at a wedding about five months before my accident in December 1986. I was working at IBM at the time this photo was taken.

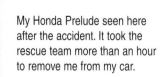

My Honda Prelude seen here after the accident. It took the rescue team more than an hour to remove me from my car.

Here I am with a character actor at a party. After years of tears, God alone would restore my laughter.

Here I am with my mother, Rita Ulicny, in Breckinridge, Colorado. One ski facility there has an excellent program for teaching the disabled how to ski. (Winter 1998).

I joined the YMCA right after I was dismissed from Harmarville Rehabilitation Center in 1988. The YMCA staff selected me to be in this advertising campaign, presumably because of the strides that were made in my rehabilitation. Although the ad copy says, "The Y made me realize all the things I can do," I came to see that it was in Christ that I could do all things.

To see more pictures from the life of Joan Ulicny,
visit the Amazing Grace Family Album at www.AmazingGraceOnline.net/album

To learn more about the contributors
to this book visit:

www.AmazingGraceOnline.net

The almighty, incomprehensible God surely loved me! And He could heal me whenever He wished, but instead He was "allowing" me to suffer. I had not been rejected at all!

I had been chosen. And it had to be for a reason. I did not know what the reason was, but I was being called to trust Him. Why had it taken me so long to see it? Suddenly my life took on a new meaning. There was a purpose for the disability. I had a mission, and it was to be a substantial one, although at that moment I had no clue what it was.

If only I could write that my life was totally wonderful after that re-conversion experience, but of course it was not. In fact, it was just the beginning of many more difficulties. And I made numerous mistakes. Satan never likes it when one says yes to God. The difference, however, was that now there was an acceptance. The "why" questions were gone.

This does not mean, though, that the pain I had felt from so much perceived rejection was completely gone. On the contrary, it manifested itself many times through the years, and still does occasionally to this very day. But the Lord has always been with me, pouring out His healing grace on my wounded heart during some of my most difficult moments.

After college graduation in 1973, my determination to be independent and prove that I could make it on my own took me to Houston, Texas. Everyone thought I was crazy to move to one of the largest cities in the country to live alone, but as it turned out, my sister Sandy decided to go with me. It was frightening for both of us, as we had been so sheltered all our lives. We struggled financially and in various other ways, but at least we had each other.

A few years later, however, Sandy left to pursue a life in California. It was a lonely period, but I refused to go home defeated. Not driving at the time, I found rides to work and continued on, but I would always wonder, *Will I be alone forever?*

Desperately longing for love and a normal life, I was married in the spring of 1979. My family was very much against it, insisting that James and I had not known each other long enough, but I convinced myself that it would work. We met when I was working as a personnel specialist in a local government office. He swept me off my feet with all the attention he gave me. He asked me to marry him after a very brief courtship. It was the first time a man had ever proposed to me. Never before had someone focused on me as he did.

I was "in love with love" and naïve about marriage. I did not then understand the Church's teaching regarding this most beautiful sacrament. What I thought of instead was that at last someone wanted me. All my life I had been looking for a good man, the one who would want me and love me forever, just the way I was.

Four years later we were blessed with our first and only child—a beautiful daughter, whom we named Crystal Ann. I wanted so much to believe that our family would be together forever. Sometimes, however, there exists in a union between two persons an impediment from the beginning of a relationship, something that blocks or prevents a true marriage from coming into existence. Sadly, ours ended in divorce after fourteen years, and the details are too private to discuss. Two years later the Church declared the marriage to be null. The divorce was the most difficult and painful experience of my life. My heart was broken.

Over and over there were instances when I was tempted to give up the idea that I could ever be truly happy or feel fulfilled, but it was especially at those times that the Lord—in His moments of grace—would remind me that He had a plan for my life and also that one day, if I would wait patiently, He would bring along the man who would look deeply into my soul and love me. Gradually, through prayer and the help of friends, I acquired a peace about it all that I had thought impossible. As the door to one part of my life was closing, another was quietly opening—one that would propel me toward God's plan with such a powerful force that there would be no turning back.

It was while I lived in Humble, Texas, in the early 1990s that I first heard and responded to the Lord's call to help build His kingdom. In the beginning I dismissed it, thinking how crazy the notion seemed. Me? The Church would not want me!

The first pastor I encountered there certainly did not want me. I volunteered once to be a lector, and his response was, "Thank you, Grace, but I do not think it would be feasible with your wheelchair." I felt discouraged. As nice as he tried to be, I always felt a barrier between the two of us.

All that changed, however, the day that Fathers Paul Procella and Philip Wilhite came to Saint Mary Magdalene Church. Jesus wears many faces. In these two priests He revealed once more how much He loved me and that I had a very important role in His Church. They wanted and needed me! And I was yearning to serve.

Now the mission began to unfold. I soon found myself invited and welcomed to serve on the parish council and also to be a lector for Sunday Mass. No one had allowed me these opportunities before. I knew then that I was caught. The doors to the Catholic Church had opened to me. I gradually began to feel not only that I belonged but also that I was very much needed. The disabled were needed in God's Church like everyone else!

Never would I have dreamed that my journey would eventually lead to a university master's degree in theology. Nor did I envision I would work one day for a bishop, assisting him in teaching the beautiful truths of our Catholic faith. And I also never would have guessed that I would today be writing a weekly newspaper column called "Dear Grace," answering readers' questions on the Catholic faith. How amazing it seems when I look back now and see how God worked it all out.

My hunger for God and for knowledge of Him were almost unquenchable. Many circumstances had kept me from Him for so long. "I want to learn about You. Help me!" I prayed. I also turned to Our Lady, "If this is God's holy will, help me, Mary. I will do whatever it takes. I will struggle, I will sacrifice, I will work hard." She heard my prayer.

In the fall of 1992, after having been out of school for nineteen years, I decided to attend the University of Saint Thomas Graduate School of Theology. It was a fifty-mile commute every day for the first two years, although later I moved and lived across the street. I had never driven into Houston alone. The prospect of driving those eight-to-ten-lane freeways terrified me.

I can't do this! I thought.

But a soft voice persistently said, *Yes, you can.*

On my first day of class I quickly picked a spot over in a corner. After a few minutes twenty-five young men walked in, all seminarians studying for the priesthood. I was the only woman in the class! When the professor began to teach using words I had never heard before, I was certain I would never make it.

I was thinking, *Grace, when this class is over, you are going home and never coming back here again!*

That sounded like a great idea. But Mary would not leave me alone. *Just go back one more time*, she would say.

Okay, just one more time, I would answer. But soon I was absolutely hooked. Nothing would have torn me away from that seminary. I knew that I belonged there just as I knew the sun would rise the next morning. I was falling more and more in love with God, and I had to know about Him.

One of my biggest challenges was one professor, a priest.

"Father, I write very slowly because of my disability," I explained, hoping that he would understand. "When we have exams, I will need more time." I knew the work but could not write fast enough.

"What you want is special privileges, and I will not give them to you," he said coldly. "If you cannot do what everyone else can, then perhaps you should get out."

I went home and cried, "What will I do? Should I let this man stand between me and what God wants of me?" I could not. What he was doing was wrong. I went to see the dean. Within two days a letter went out to the faculty, informing them of the school's commitment to provide accessibility to all disabled students.

Still the professor's attitude did not change. One day, in a meeting with him before class, I could see the repulsing look in his eyes as he spoke to me. I felt a strong desire to say something. The students had not yet come in, so we were alone.

"Father, I want to study with you," I began with sincerity, "but I feel that you just don't like me for some reason."

"You're a big girl," he responded. "Cope with it."

I was stunned. But he went further, "You are average, nothing more, and you are not going to make it here."

With all the courage I could muster, I looked up at him from my wheelchair and confidently declared, "Oh, yes, I will!"

Later that day a seminarian took me aside and told me that he had been in the hall and heard the conversation. "Grace, I stood out in that hall and felt such anger at hearing him speak to you that way. I would never allow anyone to speak to me that way. Why should you have to? But I hope you understand that I am powerless to do anything about it." I did understand.

And what would I have done without Father James

Anderson, one of my teachers? In him I witnessed such love for God and the Church. His lectures were like sermons because his faith was so strong. He spoke with conviction and helped me to see that the truth is symphonic—like beautifully played music. There was no doubt that he was a godsend to me, a true moment of grace. Having him for a teacher was like finding an oasis in the desert.

I would often say to him, "Father, I am just not smart enough! I wish I were brilliant. Why didn't God make me smarter?"

And he would shake his head and respond, "Grace, Grace! You don't need to be brilliant. Some people may be brilliant, but they can't teach a thing! Besides, you have something many do not have. You love God so sincerely, and you love the Church so passionately. As far as the smarts go, you have enough."

On campus there was a very steep ramp up to the main classroom building. Often I would remember Father Anderson's words as I started up. Then I would pray Hail Marys and push as hard as I could. Sometimes, just as I got to the top, my strength gave out and I would roll all the way back down, with the books falling from my lap to the sidewalk. Frustrated but determined, I would pick them up and start all over again. Overcoming physical barriers has been a part of my whole life, but I have never given up fighting for access. The world was meant for all of us, not just for some.

So much has happened since that lonely night in my dormitory room at the University of Texas. Living in a wheelchair has never been easy. If people only knew what it takes physically just to get ready every morning to face the day. The disabled have to go through a lot just to keep up with what is average for the rest of the world. It is worth it, though.

Some of the suffering has been painful and personal. But

from all of it I have emerged stronger. The world is wrong to teach us to run away from suffering. Jesus never did. Look at the cross. He accomplished the greatest "good"—our salvation—by way of the greatest evil.

Suffering is indeed a great mystery, but the Lord has revealed to me its secret. It is all about love. If we look beyond the suffering of the cross, beyond the nails in His hands and feet, we will see love. That is why today we wear the crucifix —to remember the love that Jesus' sacrifice took. We must never forget. If we attend Mass, for example, and witness His suffering for us in the sacrifice, yet walk away from it not transformed in Him, not ready to go out and love, then we have missed the whole purpose of the Mass.

This is why I believe suffering is unique when it takes place in a visible way. It becomes a transforming sign of love. If I suffer in a manner that can be seen through my life, I can show the world that when we live in Christ, although we may look weak, in Him we are strong!

And this leads people to love. It takes divine power from God to suffer with joy, and people see that! Suffering visibly with a disability is no accident. Jesus suffered in a visible way, and some today are called to do the same. Jesus glorified the Father in His suffering body, and so can we.

Through much study, prayer, and reflection I have come to realize that if He is allowing me to suffer visibly, it is because He is using it as a sign of love for others. God has allowed it, and I am privileged to have been chosen.

Does this mean it does not hurt any more to be stared at, to be left out of activities, to feel unwanted just because I am different or too much trouble? I can honestly tell you that it hurts a great deal sometimes.

The wheelchair, for example, can be such a barrier for some people. They seem afraid to come close to the person in it. They do not need to be. In true love there must be a willingness and sincere desire to "suffer with"—that is authentic compassion.

Suffering is never to be enjoyed, but it is to be embraced. When it does hurt, I remind myself of Who it is I am living for, Who it is that I love above all else. When I feel sorry for myself, I run to the cross. It always helps me regain my perspective.

The disabled have an opportunity to inspire people just by their very presence in our world. Who else gets a chance to do that? We can be sharers in God's mission in a very special way. When I focus on that, I do not mind if people stare at me. Jesus was different. Therefore I do not mind being different.

There are times when I want to stand up and walk across the room, or run in an open field, or dance and feel free. In heaven I know I will. I have been honored, however, through my suffering, to be a part in the changing of lives. God chose me not only to be a sign of His love but also to teach others about Him and His ways through the writing and lectures that I am able to give in my work for His Church.

My heart's desire is to teach others about Him for the rest of my life. This was God's plan all along, His mission for me. If my physical disability inspires a single soul to come closer to Him, then I do it willingly and with joy.

And He has a mission for each one of us. God loves us so much. All we must do to realize it is open our eyes and see Him in our everyday moments of grace.

From Death to New Life

Dr. Kim Hardey

It was supposed to be a typical Thursday at work. In my job as an obstetrician-gynecologist, May 3, 1990, was a "call day," which meant that my primary responsibility would be to deliver babies and handle emergencies. I had anticipated for some time the 6:00 A.M. office meeting, where my three partners and I would each receive about $20,000 in bonus money. For doctors practicing in the small town of Dothan, Alabama, this was more than pocket change.

Money had become very important to me in the months prior to this bonus. I had come to see how I could lose everything I had worked for in a single lawsuit—even if I were innocent. I had recently won a major malpractice suit against me that had made national news, but I won only because the jury looked at the facts, which were clearly on my side. What if another jury ignored the facts? I would lose everything, and my family could be in debt for the rest of our lives. This haunting experience showed me how vulnerable a doctor can be in this litigious age.

So I began to hunker down, work very hard, and save money. I was not motivated by greed but by a fear of losing everything in a fractured legal system. I had plans to retire in ten years and live off my investments on a tropical island, where there would be no lawyers. My plan required that I invest $10,000 in bonds every month. Not only was I on schedule, but this bonus would be enough to make my next two payments.

There was a second very important part to this master plan: no more children! My wife, Bonnie, and I had been married for ten years. I did not want anything to interfere with my early retirement at the age of forty-six. So we used the diaphragm as our mode of contraception. We could definitely afford the two children we already had—Brad, nine, and Jennifer, seven—but no more!

It was Brad who would surprise me that early morning in May. As I walked toward the front door, ready to leave at 5:30 A.M., he asked me if I could sit down with him as he ate a bowl of cereal. My initial thought was to say no, thinking that nothing could delay my office meeting. Since doctors had to start surgery at 7:00 A.M., all meetings had to begin promptly at 6:00. My partners would not appreciate it if I were late. But for some reason I felt compelled to stay. So Brad and I talked for about ten minutes as he ate his bowl of Frosted Flakes.

The office meeting went well. I was pleased with the amount of the bonus, which was about what I had expected.

By the time I arrived at labor and delivery at seven that morning, it was clear that it would be a busy day. There were five women in labor. The patient in room four was one of my nicest. She was scheduled to deliver twins that day. No one was near delivery, but it would take at least a few hours to evaluate each patient and fill out the related paperwork. I was caught up by noon, and so I stopped to take a break.

Suddenly my beeper went off. There was a strange message on the pager: my office phone number, followed by the ominous numbers 911. Since I was already at labor and delivery, I knew the emergency was not there. Labor and delivery was normally the source of most of my action, and the nurses who might need me were already sitting next to me.

As I dialed the phone, I wondered if one of my patients might be miscarrying. Stan, the manager of our office, answered my call. I asked this of Stan. "No," he said. With a trembling voice, he said that a car had hit Brad. He had no details, but his voice made me fear the worst.

A myriad of questions immediately raced through my mind as I considered what to do next. Why was Brad not in school? How did he get off the playground? Why wasn't someone watching him?

I went to the emergency room to contact the ambulance assigned to Brad's case. The news I received went like a knife into my heart. They were having trouble stabilizing him.

My training as a physician had included emergency room work. I had been on the other end of too many radio conversations like this one. The worst possible thoughts raced through my mind: death, brain death, severe handicaps—the most serious of injuries.

I raced back to labor and delivery. How could I get everyone delivered as quickly as possible? When stabilized, Brad would be transported to the closest hospital, which was five miles away from the hospital where I worked. I was aware that I could not go to check on Brad until everyone had delivered.

After a few very long minutes, two of my partners came to relieve me without being asked. They had been told about the accident and hurried in to take over for me. I was relieved to see them. However, the dire look on their faces confirmed that they knew this was not a minor accident.

I used every bit of my Subaru's turbo engine to navigate the familiar five-mile trek to Flowers Hospital. Images of Brad filled my mind, as well as flashbacks of a friend's child, a three-year-old boy who had been hit by a car just two years earlier. Bonnie and I had kept a late-night prayer vigil with the parents of that child at the same emergency room. Their child died from a common fatal injury when cars hit children: the separation of the brain stem from the brain.

As I continued across town, all I could think of was that small boy on a ventilator. My heart sank with the thought that this nightmare could be repeated with my own son. *Please, God, keep him alive*, I prayed.

The ambulance that carried Brad beat me to the hospital. It was about 2:00 when I burst through the emergency room doors. I glanced at the waiting room and recognized a crowd of perhaps fifty familiar faces. In a small town news spreads fast. We had many friends, and it seemed as if all of them were there. Tom, one of my teammates at basketball, was there. So was the mayor's wife, a friend of Bonnie.

I did not stop to talk, walking instead toward the door reserved for doctors. Nurses in white uniforms seemed to be expecting me, and they escorted me to the small private waiting room where Bonnie and a few close friends kept vigil. Although I was a doctor, hospital policy did not allow me in to see Brad. I was anxious for some answers.

I found out that Brad had gone on a field trip that morning to practice songs that he and the third-grade class were going to perform at the school's end-of-the-year program. On the way back to school, the class had stopped at a park to eat lunch.

Details after that were sketchy, but the other third-graders claimed that while role-playing the "Ninja Turtles," Brad had crossed the street by crawling through a culvert. Realizing that he was not supposed to be across the street, the others urged him to come back. As Brad stepped into the street, a car going forty-five miles an hour in a twenty-mile-an-hour zone hit him. The young man driving the car had reportedly been late for work.

Bonnie was one of the chaperones for the field trip. In a

strange way, I was relieved to know that she had been there. While I realized this was an accident, the fact of Bonnie's presence kept me from the added pain of laying blame on the schoolteachers.

Bonnie heard the screech of the brakes and the thud from the impact. When she looked at the street and saw the bright colors of the outfit, she knew right away that it was Brad. A lady passing by had tried to do CPR on him. I knew the ambulance team had done their best. All we could do now was pray and wait.

We would not see Brad until 3:30. We would have gone crazy during that hour-and-a-half wait had it not been for the many friends who were there with us, consoling us and praying with us. One of our parish priests came by and was allowed to administer the anointing of the sick to Brad. The orthopedic surgeon came in to say that several bones were broken but that he did not know any more about Brad's condition. The general surgeon, whom I also knew, explained that the liver and a kidney were bleeding, but the C.A.T. scan (computerized pictures of the body using data from multiple x-ray images) was still in progress. This was of utmost importance.

Bruce Woodham was our local brain surgeon and a good friend. Bruce had been at the hospital the night our friends' three-year-old died. When he entered the room that day, a chill went down my spine. He began by explaining that Brad's injuries were identical to the three-year-old's. This meant, essentially, that there was no hope. Our only son was going to die.

Brad's pediatrician, Bill Barron, was also a good friend and a fellow parishioner at the Catholic church in town. I found out that Bill had been at Brad's side for the two hours that Brad had been at the hospital. I knew that he was an excellent doctor. He and I had worked together many nights on difficult neonatal cases. I trusted his opinion when he said that, barring a miracle, our situation was hopeless.

Our first prayer was for a miracle for our son. Our friends suggested that we storm heaven with petitions until we received a miracle. We prayed for this but somehow found the courage to add, "Not my will, Lord, but Yours be done."

I will never forget Bonnie's difficult but true insight that she expressed within these first few hours: "As Catholic parents we are given children to assist them on their journey to heaven. It would be selfish of us to want Brad here when he is so close to attaining his eternal goal." My heart rejected this statement at first because I wanted my child with me, but I knew she was right.

Finally we were taken to see Brad. He was such a handsome little fellow, always full of life. Seeing him connected to cold, sterile tubes and covered with swelling and abrasions shook us to the core. He was bruised, motionless, and helpless. Only a parent can fully understand the utter helplessness and heartache we felt as we saw our son lying unconscious on the hospital bed.

A spirited and happy child, Brad loved to be tickled. Yet my tickles this day yielded no laughter, nor even a response. Standing there next to him, Bonnie and I wondered how this could have happened. We prayed for Brad, and for ourselves, because we knew unimaginable pain still awaited us.

Brad died at five that afternoon. We were with him for the final ninety minutes of his life. We caressed him and talked to him as he lay unconscious. We watched his heart monitor trickle down to a stop. Our world had ended.

Bonnie and I drove the short trip from the hospital to our home in silence. There are no words to describe the numbness that each of us felt inside. We were in shock. Because this all had happened so quickly, much had not sunk in yet. To this day I cannot remember many details about those first few days and weeks after Brad's death. I have often wondered whether God allowed this "fog" so we would be protected from experiencing the full force of the loss.

When we arrived home around 5:30, some friends were there. They had prepared a meal for us. Realizing we probably needed some time, they left us to ourselves. We went to our bedroom. It was there that we first talked.

"Bonnie, I think we have been selfish by refusing to have more than two kids," I started the conversation, surprising even myself with this statement. The thought had simply popped into my mind and out of my mouth.

As I shared my thoughts, the hole in my heart from the loss of Brad seemed to grow. I can't say exactly what made me think about this either, but I was struck hard by the reality that we now had just one child—because we had not been willing to have more. "We have denied God children for selfish reasons," I added.

The loss of a child is crushing no matter what the size of the family is—small or large. But somehow my pain was magnified as I thought of living in my large home with just my wife and daughter. The house seemed so empty.

If the truth be told, it was not that "we" had been selfish but that I had been. Several times over the years Bonnie had tried to convince me not to use contraceptives. She would have had more children if I had been open to the idea. But in my blind selfishness I simply would not consider it. Now that my most treasured possession had been taken from me, I saw clearly. That very night we threw the diaphragm away. We promised God that we would be open to any and all children He would send us.

Jennifer was brought home around 6:00 P.M. We then told her what had happened. She did not understand what the words really meant or how Brad's death would change our family forever. She mostly seemed hurt and saddened about not being able to tell him good-bye. As God would protect Bonnie and me in these first few days and weeks from the full force of the pain, He would protect our young daughter even more by limiting her understanding of this type of suffering. Her youth was her ally here, not giving her the range of life experience to feel the spirit-altering pain.

One of the few consolations I had during these first twelve hours was the gratitude I felt in having had those ten minutes with Brad early in the morning as he ate his cereal. I do remember saying good-bye. Those ten minutes will forever be etched into my mind. How I would have regretted it had I not made time for him that morning.

Friends started to arrive at our house around 7:00 P.M., bringing us meals for the next few days and offering all sorts of help. Many remained with us until past 10:00 that evening. Administrators from the Methodist school Brad had attended came by to see us. I immediately sensed their fear of a lawsuit and told them there would not be one. After experiencing such suffering from my own lawsuit, I did not wish to inflict the same pain and fear in them. And frankly, I also reasoned that perhaps if I showed mercy to the school administrators, God might extend His mercy to me, making the expected appeal on my malpractice case disappear.

Bonnie and I fell asleep late that night, exhausted from the emotionally draining events of this horrible day.

I woke up early the next day, Friday, wondering if everything had been a bad dream. But then the reality set in. During those first few hours alone, Bonnie filled me in on more of the details of her experiences the day before.

Brad had been looking forward to the field trip and had woken up excited that day. During the third-graders' rehearsal, Bonnie had talked with a woman whose husband had recently died. Bonnie sought advice from her on how to offer support to her own sister-in-law, who had recently experienced the death of her husband (Bonnie's brother, Jerry). Amazingly, Bonnie had said to the woman that she did not think that she could ever endure the loss of a child. And equally amazing, the last song Brad sang on that field trip, "As the Saints Go Marching In," would also be the last of his life. A scriptwriter could not create a more surreal set of events. Bonnie and I have taken comfort in these two coincidences, believing God gave us these signs to show us that He was, in fact, watching over us.

Bonnie also fondly remembered how impressed the other mothers had been when Brad was not embarrassed to give her a kiss in public. What a joyful thought this was for her mother's heart.

Friday began what I now consider three days of extraordinary grace. People from all aspects of our lives came to share in our grief. Men with whom I played cards, co-workers from the office and hospital, patients, and fellow parishioners all came to offer their condolences. The pattern with each was the same: We would cry, we would remember some special moment or funny episode with Brad, then we would cry again as we realized that we would never share these moments again with Brad.

Our first major task on Friday was meeting with the funeral director. We spent at least two hours going over all the details of the funeral and wake. We were blessed to be accompanied by the friends who two years before had buried their three-year-old. They were such a tremendous support. The funeral director was a friend from the parish and a patient's husband; this too made the process a little easier.

Bonnie and I decided to have the wake that night and the

burial on Saturday. We did not want a long process. Bonnie chose a child-size casket with angels on both ends, symbols of the angels protecting and guiding our son.

Later that day Bonnie had the heart-wrenching task of preparing Brad's burial outfit. While ironing the clothes, Bonnie became very angry with God. She told me later how she asked God out loud *why* He allowed our son to die. She heard a distinct inner voice say, "Now you know how I felt when I lost my Son."

Her response was, "But You knew that Your Son was coming home and that You would have Him back."

The voice replied, "And one day you too will be with your son." Suddenly, and without any further need for explanation, her anger disappeared.

The wake that night began with the rosary. Most of our family members who could come had already made the seven-hour trip from our native Louisiana. The long receiving line passed quickly. Bonnie and I were still being sustained by the grace God provided through the love and prayers of our friends and family. We were able to keep our focus on our belief that Brad was now in heaven, which diminished greatly our own pain. Thinking about this gave us some peace and even some moments of joy.

Many who had come to console us were surprised to find that we seemed to be consoling them. As I look back now, I can see that we were starting to experience some sort of transformation—a conversion to a greater depth of faith.

The wake went on for many hours. A reception at our home followed. Bonnie and I went to bed very late, exhausted again.

Saturday began in much the same way as Friday, as new visitors completed their pilgrimage to Dothan to console us. We were kept busy, and this seemed to help us in our grief. The immense love expressed by so many people made the burden of our loss seem lighter, as if all of us carried it together.

The funeral was set for early afternoon. The church was packed. Grace, once again, sustained us, temporarily keeping away the sadness that wanted to stalk us. We buried Brad in a grave next to that of our friends' three-year-old. Hundreds of balloons were released into the air, symbols of the hope and prayers we offered that day.

Jennifer's First Communion was originally scheduled for the next day. Our parish priest offered to perform a private service at a later date if we did not feel up to attending the class-wide First Communion. But Jennifer seemed to be doing well, and we knew that this event was one of the most important she would experience in life. We decided to keep to the original plan. In addition to being important for Jennifer, we thought that this moment of joy for our family would give our sorrow some additional reprieve. Grace was abundant for a third day, and we were able to participate without any outward sign of the deep sorrow that lay beneath. We celebrated Jennifer's special day with our closest friends.

On Monday the new and ugly reality finally set in. The faithful friends who had comforted us had to get back to their own work and families. The genuine empathy they offered was intense and real, but their grief would heal quickly. Although they loved us, their lives had not been shattered by Brad's death in the way that ours was. We had given life to the child, taught him to walk and speak, marveled at his first discoveries, celebrated his joys, and comforted his pains.

When a parent loses a child, it is impossible to think of anything else but that loss for a very long time. Grief becomes the predominant part of you and your life. Ordinary things become tainted. I remember walking into a Wal-Mart that Monday and realizing that no one there could possibly know the grief I carried within me. This awareness was a sharp contrast to the love, sympathy, and attention that our family had experienced the first seventy-two hours. The sadness and grief welled over me like a relentless assault of ocean waves.

For Bonnie it all seemed like a bad dream—a terrible nightmare—that should end. She kept thinking she would look up and see Brad coming around the corner, smiling. He would not. It would be several days before the sad and overwhelming reality would set in with her: Brad was not coming back. Then the pain was so intense, it would become physical, absorbing all her energy and effort. The sense of loss would consume entire days, enveloping her mind, heart, and spirit.

That Monday I also did some yard work to pass the time. We had specifically picked for our home site a two-acre lot in a cul-de-sac of a brand new development. Our landscaper had created a masterpiece of a yard, which was surrounded by tall trees and a large expanse of adjacent woods. It was the perfect sanctuary for our kids and our family.

As I looked out from our deck, I began to cry as I saw a glaring reminder of our loss: Brad's tree house fort. The fort was a custom-designed wooden work of art, perfect for young boys' play with toy guns and for little girls' tea parties. It was nestled between two large oak trees.

My mind played tricks with me that day as I imagined Brad sliding down the slide and running after make-believe enemy soldiers in retreat. The scene continued in my mind, and frankly, to this day, I am not sure whether what I saw next really happened or was just the result of a grieving heart and mind run amok: I saw a very bright shining light, like that beaming forth from a projector in a movie theatre. I could not control nor stop the stream of images playing in front of me. The images were of my sins of the past. This "vision" seemed to last about thirty seconds.

As soon as the scenes ended, I was filled with an overwhelming and powerful sense of forgiveness. Although I had confessed these sins in the past, I now truly felt forgiven for them. At that moment I knew God loved me. I cannot overemphasize the consolation and peace I received in this brief but extraordinary experience.

I returned to my office practice on Tuesday. I knew I had to begin my new life without my son. I had to fight the strong temptation to feel sorry for myself.

My first appointment that morning was with a new patient who had two sons who were hemophiliacs. One had died a month prior from HIV, which he had acquired from the multiple transfusions needed to keep him alive. Her other son was also HIV-positive and was not expected to live long. That morning we shared our common grief and consoled each other. I felt as if God had sent this woman to console me, and I was very grateful.

Prior to Brad's death Bonnie and I began to desire a deeper commitment to God and our faith. As a result of this vision, I came to believe that God had allowed us to experience the loss of Brad for some deep reason. If I could be patient and trust God through this time of suffering, the reason would be revealed.

The loss of a child affects people in different ways. My loss led me to an intense desire to identify and eliminate sin from my life. I am not sure whether this primarily came from the vision. It might have come from some other instance of illumination, like the one I had the night of Brad's death, when I admitted to Bonnie my selfishness in not being open to other children. Either way, I was now on a mission.

Serious sin can jeopardize one's very salvation and union with God. I desired more than anything for our family to be together in heaven. So examining my conscience became a thrice-daily activity.

I would realize soon enough, though, that this mission faced at least one "small" problem. Although Bonnie and I had already resolved to no longer use contraception, I still believed I had to prescribe the contraceptive pill to make my living as an Ob-Gyn. Although I had yet to understand why the Catholic Church strongly condemned the use of artificial contraception, I had come to believe in the authority of the Church. I believed that in matters of faith and morals, the Church spoke with the authority of Jesus. So a week after Brad's death, I decided to seek the counsel of my parish priest.

Father Smith[1] and I were good friends, and even now I believe that he meant well. Brad's death had greatly troubled him (he told me that in his thirty years of priesthood, Brad's burial had been his most difficult) and he wished to spare me more anguish. But his advice, I would eventually find out, was incorrect. He reassured me that we live in a "tough world" and that we "had to do our best" within that reality. Therefore, continuing to prescribe birth control pills would not be a problem. At the time I was relieved by his recommendation, and I did not consider the matter further.

Bonnie shared my overriding concern to see Brad again. There really was a "divine paradox" resting in both of our hearts. The loss of our son was deep and irreparable (at least here on earth). Yet that loss was the catalyst to our new life —a life of more intense and devout faith. In time this faith would grow and become our greatest joy. We would even come to believe that the conversion that came about because

---

[1] Name has been changed.

of Brad's death may very well have been *necessary* for our salvation.

Prior to Brad's death, neither Bonnie nor I would have been considered a bad person. Bonnie always had a strong desire for God and even did daily spiritual reading. She participated in prayer groups, taught religious education, and was an extraordinary minister of the Eucharist at the parish. I was president of the parish council, a lector, and an extraordinary minister of the Eucharist too. We had been tithing regularly for two years and, in recent years, were attending Mass at least twice a week. I had also been reading the Bible and a devotional called *My Daily Bread*. But in many ways we were living our faith on our own terms, some of which were contrary to God's will. So at this critical moment in our lives (and even because of this critical moment), we felt called to go deeper, to walk daily with God, trusting that joy would return and that His plan would be revealed.

After Brad's death, *My Daily Bread* became my daily source of wisdom, insight, and consolation. A particular chapter in one issue, "The Value of Adversity," became my favorite. I would read it dozens of times in the coming months and years. The author notes that we Christians can deceive ourselves into thinking we are "walking the walk" when things are going well. But it is only when we suffer that we can truly see and know ourselves as we really are. Each day I trusted that my suffering would lead me to become a better person tomorrow.

During the first few weeks following Brad's death there were many things to do. We constructed a fence in Brad's memory around the park where the accident had occurred, using the $8,000 we received in lieu of flowers at the funeral. A bronze plaque was posted to remind passersby of Brad's death. Trips to the park were very difficult, especially for Bonnie, but the idea that others would be protected from a future tragedy brought us comfort.

Even before this, we faced the difficult dilemma of what to write on the grave marker. What do you put on the grave of a child so young? Brad had a basset hound named Buffy, whom he really loved. So Bonnie asked an artist friend, Rhoda, to draw a picture of Brad with his arm around Buffy. After Rhoda completed the picture, we conceived the inscription: "This world was never meant for one as beautiful as you." One day when Jennifer came home from school, a small paperback book fell out of her backpack. Bonnie was shocked to see the cover. The book was called *I'll Always Love You*. Brad would say words very similar to these each night as we tucked him into bed. But even more amazing was the picture on the book's cover. There was a plump basset hound sitting next to a thin boy, as both looked off into the sunset. The picture was nearly identical to the one Rhoda had drawn!

Bonnie called Rhoda, thinking she surely had copied the picture from this book. Rhoda said she knew nothing about the book, a story about a boy who loved his dog and who experienced the dog's death. Jennifer had ordered it several weeks before Brad's death, not knowing what it was about. To Bonnie and me, the book was a wonderful gift from a loving God, who knew of the tragedy we faced and sent us this sign as a source of hope.

In time life would begin again, in more ways than one. Six months after Brad's death Bonnie found out she was pregnant. We were both so excited at this glorious news. I felt that a new baby would restore some of the joy that had been lost. At a sixteen-week ultrasound we found out that Bonnie was carrying a boy. It seemed that God was giving us another chance to raise a son.

But two weeks later Bonnie began to bleed. As an obstetrician, I knew that this was common and that only rarely did it mean something bad was happening. I had Bonnie come to the office. In the exam room, however, a sick feeling came over me. There was a problem with the developmental size of Bonnie's uterus. An attempt to listen to the baby's heartbeat was met with an ominous silence. The ultrasound confirmed our fears. Our new baby was dead.

Bonnie handled the news much better than I did, perhaps because growing up she had watched her mother suffer through five miscarriages. We set up a D and C with one of my partners for the next day, February 14, 1991. It would be a Valentine's Day that I would never forget.

Bonnie came through the surgery fine. I, on the other hand, was not doing so well. Before Brad's death I had an unusual experience after a weekday Mass. A new parishioner came up to introduce herself to me. I had already heard that she was believed to have unique spiritual gifts.

"I have a prophecy for you," she said to me when I first met her.

This was an unusual greeting from someone I had just met, but I was intrigued by what she might say. Maybe she would predict some good news, perhaps that the retrial of my malpractice case would be dismissed. But, no, her prophecy was dire. Very dire.

"Your life will be filled with great suffering," she said.

This was not what I wanted to hear. As each new suffering occurred in my life, I thought about the prophecy and wondered what further suffering my family and I would face. *Will anything ever go right again?* I asked myself. *Will I just drift from disaster to disaster from now on?*

The night of the surgery friends came to the house to try to console us. "The baby probably had some kind of abnormality," they reasoned. To which I responded with a snap, "Why didn't God just fix it?"

This was my rock bottom. I did not understand why God had allowed this to happen. I no longer cared about much. I actually wished for death. I thought death would end my pain and enable me to see Brad again. What I did not see then is that I was far from ready to give God an account of my life. And mercifully, He did not allow me to die.

Bonnie healed quickly from the miscarriage, and the very next month she was pregnant again. This time things would go differently. Our new son, Stephen Paul Hardey, came into the world on January 10, 1992. Joy and hope re-entered my life that day. I began to believe that maybe good things could happen to us after all. And that year did embody the best that life could offer. Stephen was a joy to all of us. He became an instant celebrity to those who knew of our suffering.

Stephen's birth also brought about a new resolve. After experiencing the intense and profound joy that comes from new life, Bonnie and I decided to continue to be open to the possibility of new life. Even Natural Family Planning (NFP) was not an option. Bonnie and I knew we did not have a serious reason to avoid pregnancy, which is the condition the Church requires to be present in order to morally use NFP.

I had always considered myself pro-life. Since my first days in Dothan I had offered free ultrasounds to women who were contemplating abortion. But the combination of the death of our son and our newfound awareness of the amazing gift of life produced in me a firmer resolve about the pro-life issue. Because most of the other OBs in town described themselves as "pro-choice," I was left alone to counsel young women to choose life. I began to volunteer frequently at the local crisis pregnancy center.

Because of this work my OB practice had attracted a large group of pro-life women, and my business was booming. We had good friends, a new baby, material wealth, and a good parish. In short, life was now very good. But on a crisp

December afternoon in 1992, this would all begin to change. My faith would be challenged yet again.

As I pulled into our cul-de-sac in my zippy red Miata, I remember thinking how nice our house looked. I parked the car and walked over to Bonnie, who was sitting in a rocker on the front porch. She quietly handed me a letter from a Catholic lay-run organization. The letter included a copy of a pastoral letter written a year earlier by Bishop Glennon P. Flavin of Lincoln, Nebraska. The letter was entitled *A Pastoral Letter to Catholic Couples and Physicians on the Issue of Artificial Contraception.*

My instincts told me this would not be good news. Although I thought that I had already settled this issue with my local priest, I decided to read the letter.

It said: "Catholic physicians and others who prescribe contraceptives or recommend their use are cooperators with those who use them. Such cooperation is gravely sinful."

Reading these words set in print had a dramatic effect on me. I instantly became angry. "How does an Ob-Gyn doctor survive without prescribing the pill?" I asked rhetorically.

The document continued: "It should be obvious that Catholics who practice artificial birth control and those who cooperate with them in their immoral actions may not receive Holy Communion without committing sacrilege."

The message was clear. If I continued to practice medicine as I had been trained, I would be cut off from the grace that comes through the Church. And I would be unable to receive the Eucharist, which I treasured.

In a final admonition the letter quoted the Pope, whom I loved and respected. I truly valued what he had to say, due to the authority given to him as the head of the Church. His statement said: "It has been noted that there is a tendency on the part of some Catholics to be selective in their adherence to the Church's moral teachings. It is sometimes claimed that dissent from the Magisterium is totally compatible with being 'a good Catholic' and poses no obstacles to the reception of the sacraments. This is a grave error."

Wow, I thought, *"grave error" are serious words from the leader of the Church.* I knew my catechism. To me, "grave error" meant that the action was mortally sinful, which cuts one off from God's grace and results in the loss of one's salvation. Following this logic, my deepest desire to see Brad again was now being threatened.

I looked at Bonnie and said, "Do you realize what this means?" I then waved my hand, gesturing toward the house, the beautiful yard, the cul-de-sac, and added, "It's over. All of this will be gone. Is that what you really want?"

Bonnie had long suspected that my work practices in this area were in opposition to the Church's teachings. She even had mentioned it to me on occasion. But I had always shrugged off the idea, not really wanting to deal with a change of this magnitude. Yet now I had no choice but to seriously consider it.

Bonnie said nothing. She would later tell me that that night she gave my fate to God. She knew she had done her part to challenge me with the truth. Now God would have to change my heart.

For several days after that I was deeply upset and could think of little else. The first option that I considered was to join the Episcopal Church. Episcopalians were nice people and seemed happy. Surely one could be saved as an Episcopalian. The problem was that I knew too much.

A few years prior my older brother had sent me a Catholic audiocassette by a convert to Catholicism named Scott Hahn. Like many converts, Hahn had wrestled intensely with the teachings of the Catholic Church. And like many others, he had come to see the clarity of Catholic teaching on issues such as salvation and authority. He had explained these teachings in a way that persuaded me of their absolute truth. So I truly believed that Jesus Christ had established the Church and that, despite some human failings, the Church possessed Jesus' full authority and the fullness of truth revealed by God. Running from the truth was not an option.

What was I to do? Should I enter a different aspect of medicine where these moral dilemmas did not exist? No, there were too many problems in doing another residency. And as a family practice doctor, I would still have to deal with this issue. All other medical training programs would require leaving Dothan for three to four years. Besides, what was the point? I liked obstetrics and was good at it. Yet I could not fathom the idea that you could practice gynecology without prescribing the pill.

Two weeks later I saw an ad in a medical journal for an employment opportunity at a crisis pregnancy center in Cincinnati, Ohio. Perhaps this would be a way out, I thought. I spoke with the woman in charge, and she assured me that I would not have to prescribe the pill as a part of my work. Could this be what God intended?

The problem was that I wanted to stay in Dothan. It was a great place. I had built a good life there. The fifty thousand people who lived there were basically God-fearing, hardworking, and kind. The town's economy was booming and diversified. Recreational opportunities were unlimited. There was adventure just eighty miles away on the most beautiful beaches in Florida.

But Dothan was not Catholic. There was one Catholic church in town to serve just eight hundred families. There was no Catholic bookstore. We could not get the Catholic television network EWTN. The critical question lingered, "How can an OB practice survive without dispensing birth control in an area of the country where there are few committed, practicing Catholics?"

In all honesty, I had no idea why the Church thought that contraception was wrong. My only reasoning at the time was that the Church wanted people to have bigger families. Although I would eventually discover the deep and profound reasons for the Church's position, I was not there yet. All I knew was that being able to prescribe the pill stood between me and Brad and God—and this was unacceptable. What I decided to do next would be out of obedience yet without understanding.

I walked into a business meeting the first week of January 1993 and announced to my partners that I would no longer prescribe the pill. The reason I gave was that the pill could act as an abortifacient. In other words, sometimes the pill works by preventing a *fertilized* egg from implanting in the womb after conception, and the mother would not even know it. This had been brought to my attention by patients over the years, and it had troubled me, but never enough to act on it.

My partners' collective response was that I could give it a try. I am sure they thought I had lost my mind. Maybe if they let me try my new policy for a while and it failed, I would come to my senses.

My new decision resulted in daily challenges. I would explain my decision to each patient and show her a photocopy from the PDR (Physicians Desk Reference), which explained the pill's action. Patients were generally nice, but many were skeptical. Some decided to switch doctors, while others began to use barrier methods.

I was handicapped because I could not teach NFP, which, contrary to popular opinion, is highly effective (and more importantly, considered morally acceptable for spacing children under certain conditions). Nor could I refer patients to some other local NFP teachers; there were none. My goal was not to convert everyone to NFP. I was simply trying to eliminate the occasion of my own sin.

Looking back at what I did and how I did it, it is easy to see why it could not work. My partners resented the fact that their patients began to ask them if the pill was really an abortifacient. I believe most doctors do not enjoy a moral confrontation. Psychologically I was a mess. One day things would seem great and I would be excited. The next day my patients would seem reluctant to stop the pill, and I would arrive home deeply discouraged.

I sought outside advice. I called a national pro-life organization to see if they knew of any Ob-Gyns anywhere in the country who ran an NFP-only practice. The president knew of none but directed me to Dr. Thomas Hilgers, a medical researcher who taught NFP in Omaha. I called Tom, and he was very helpful and encouraging. He suggested that Bonnie and I come to Omaha that summer for the *Humanae Vitae* Conference.

"What kind of conference?" I asked. I had never heard the words *Humanae Vitae* before.

He explained that *Humanae Vitae* (which means "Of Human Life") was Pope Paul VI's document, released in 1968, reiterating the Church's long-held position that the use of artificial contraception is always immoral. I decided that Bonnie and I should go to the conference.

We arrived a day early and walked around the vendor area. Representatives from the Couple to Couple League, an organization dedicated to teaching NFP, were on hand, and they gave us a copy of the short but profound encyclical. We took it back to our motel, and I wept when I read it. Never had I encountered such a beautiful vision of marital love. The truth was liberating but painful, particularly paragraph 17, which spoke of how contraception feeds into our human weakness and causes us to lose respect for the marital act and even our spouse, turning them into actions and instruments of selfish enjoyment.

My observations of the world had for a long time led me to believe that something was terribly wrong. Now I had the answer. Women were suffering from the effects of the sexual revolution. Countless women patients had expressed the loss of joy in their marriages. Many of them were depressed and had poor self images from past abortions. Many suffered physically and emotionally because of sexually transmitted diseases. I had personally tried to console the brokenness of scores of women who had been betrayed and abandoned by men. I could see Pope Paul VI's predictions in *Humanae Vitae* were correct. Contraception was, in fact, at the root of many societal ills.

The Pope wrote: "Each and every marriage act must remain open to the transmission of life. . . . By safeguarding both these essential aspects, the unitive and the procreative, the conjugal act preserves in its fullness the sense of true mutual love and its ordination toward man's most high calling to parenthood." In contracepting, men would lose respect for women, the document warned, forgetting "the reverence due to a woman, and, disregarding her physical and emotional equilibrium, reduce her to being a mere instrument for the satisfaction of his own desires, no longer considering her as his partner whom he should surround with care and affection."

I learned that the "unitive" and "procreative" aspects of marital love mentioned in the document are fundamental to the act's very meaning. When either one is intentionally removed, the act itself changes from one of total self-donation to one in which each individual is trying to get what he or she can. The two are no longer one flesh. They who are invited by God to become "co-creators" with Him actually remove the Creator from the equation.

Also, as a doctor I had dedicated my life to leading people to health. Yet, ironically, the pill and other forms of artificial birth control were treating fertility, which is the normal, healthy state, as a sickness that needed to be remedied. Pharmacological solutions should be used when we are sick, not when we are healthy. I could see that things thrive when they are done in accord with nature. When we contradict nature (and God, for that matter), problems arise. Again, no wonder there were so many societal ills that seemed to be related to the injection of contraception into the culture.

For the previous six months I had struggled daily to comply with the Church's prohibition of contraception. Never did it occur to me that the Church was actually right. I now saw that, not only did the Church have the truth, it also had the most beautiful concept of marital love. But the whole world was disregarding it and paying a terrible price. Suddenly I felt energized.

I went back to the booth area with one question: "If a doctor wanted to practice in an area of the country where Catholics followed this Church teaching, where could he go?" Two places were mentioned: Arlington, Virginia, and Lafayette, Louisiana.

Lafayette was well known to me. I had lived there twice as part of college and residency training. My mom and sister lived there. Ironically, an Ob doctor whom I knew from my residency had called just a few weeks earlier to invite me back to Lafayette to work with him. We still did not want to leave Dothan, but if we were going to move, it would at least be a move home, not to a faraway part of the country. We headed back to Dothan, praying for the will of God to be revealed.

Once we were back, I called a hospital in Lafayette that I had been told was recruiting. The hospital was familiar to me from my undergraduate days. I asked the physician in charge of recruiting whether it would present a problem if I did not prescribe contraception or do sterilizations.

"No problem," he said. "We are a Catholic hospital." I planned a look-and-see visit for mid-August.

For the trip to the conference in Omaha, I had asked one of my partners to switch weekends with me. He later asked why I wanted to switch.

"You don't want to know," I replied, as he was the partner most bothered by my new practice habits.

He insisted, "No, really. Where did you go?"

"I went to a meeting to celebrate the twenty-five years that the Church has taught that contraception is immoral," I replied. I did not know at that time that the Church had actually taught that for two thousand years.

"You were right, I didn't want to know," he replied.

A few days later he came to my call room to talk. I could see the anger in his eyes. He said that the Pope had no right to tell us what to do and that very few Catholics followed those teachings anyway. I sensed a change in the wind.

Things did not look good for my future in the group. I soon received a proposal, which seemed more like an ultimatum, from my partners. I could stay in the group if I would at least do tubal ligations for patients who delivered when I was on call. Friends who knew of my situation thought this was reasonable enough. I would have to do about fifty sterilizations a year. Surely, they reasoned, this would be okay with the Pope since I would be doing them against my wishes. And I was certainly acting better than all the other Catholic doctors, they added, who did all kinds of things that the Church said we should not do.

I knew better. My mind and heart had already been firmly

convinced by the truth of the contraception issue. Bonnie and I decided to go to Lafayette in early August 1993 to check things out.

Even then, we still fought the idea of leaving Dothan. I had hoped that I could stay in Dothan and, if needed, perform a rare tubal ligation, only when a woman had repeat cesarean deliveries. In my ill-formed theology this seemed acceptable to me. We considered the trip to Lafayette a "just-in-case" visit in the event that things did not work out in Dothan.

At the Omaha conference a few weeks earlier, Bonnie had purchased a set of cassette tapes by Scott Hahn on the book of Romans. We brought the tapes with us. As I pulled onto the interstate to begin the seven-hour drive, I popped the first tape in.

One of the first points Hahn made was that obedience to Christ was, in fact, necessary for salvation. Prior to this trip, my Protestant friends were attempting to persuade me that because Christians were now "under grace, not law," I could morally perform some tubal ligations and not be concerned with whether this "sin" would separate me from God. Hahn explained that the Church clearly taught otherwise. Obedience to Christ was necessary if one wanted to avoid rupturing one's relationship with God.[2]

---

[2] Man owes obedience to God through observance of the natural moral law, which God has written on the hearts of all men and therefore can be known by man's "natural" or God-given ability to reason (cf. Romans 2:14–16; Catechism, nos. 1954–57, 1776–77). However, as the Church teaches, "the precepts of natural law are not perceived by everyone clearly and immediately" (Catechism, no. 1960). For example, whereas the sin of adultery is self-evident to almost everyone, the sinfulness of performing tubal ligations is more easily known by a well-formed Catholic. Nevertheless, performing tubal ligations can be a mortal sin for both a Catholic and a non-Catholic, depending on three factors: (1) if the wrongdoing is grave matter, which in this case it is; and if an individual commits this grave wrongdoing with

By the time the tapes were done, I was convinced that, when it came to matters of faith and morals, Christ wanted me to submit my will to the authority of the Church. This would be a major turning point in my life. I knew I had to take seriously this possible move to Lafayette.

We met with the physician recruiter and a financial representative at a restaurant in Lafayette. They expressed their need for a doctor with my specialty and their hope that I would start soon. They said we could look at some office space and see the labor and delivery facility the next morning. Bonnie then mentioned that I did not plan to prescribe the pill. The financial representative seemed shocked but said nothing. In the morning I received a phone call.

"Did you really say that you won't give out the pill? Don't you know that most Catholics take the pill?" he asked. "I am afraid we aren't sure we want you."

Later he called to say I could have the job at a significant reduction in pay from the original offer. So we went back to Dothan to pray and consider our fate.

In the meantime things were coming to a head with my

---

(2) "full knowledge" and (3) "complete consent" (cf. Catechism, nos. 1858–59; cf. nos. 1854–64). One should never act on a doubtful conscience (cf. Catechism, nos. 1783–94), nor should one presume that he will be saved regardless of his grave sins (cf. Catechism, no. 2092).

For more information regarding the salvation issue, see the aforementioned Catechism citations and consult the following resources: *FaithFact: Persevering to the End: The Biblical Reality of Mortal Sin* (Available by calling 1-800-MY-FAITH (693-2484); Dr. Scott Hahn's cassette tapes *Romanism in Romans* (available from Saint Joseph's Communications, 800-526-2151, (www.saintjoe.com); *Catholic for a Reason, Vol. I: Scripture and the Mystery of the Family of God*, which includes Richard White's article "Justification as Divine Sonship: Is 'Faith Alone' Justifiable," (available from Emmaus Road Publishing, 800-398-5470; emmausroad.org); and James Akin's book *The Salvation Controversy* (available from Catholic Answers, 888-291-8000, www.catholic.com).

partners in Dothan. If I could not stay in the group, I considered the possibility that they would let me start my own practice and provide call coverage for me so that I could have an occasional weekend off. In return, I would cover for them and even take some of their more difficult shifts. We set a meeting for September 17. This would be a providential date.

A few months earlier someone had given me a desk calendar with Scripture meditations for each day. One day the calendar had fallen open to a particular quote: "When you find yourself in times of trouble, wait on the Lord and He will answer in His time." Because I liked this Bible verse, I had left the desk calendar open to it and the corresponding date, September 17! My answer was in this verse. I would wait for God's answer.

I went to that meeting with an overwhelming sense of peace. My partners informed me that they would not cover for me. I would be in practice totally on my own.

Bonnie and I decided that it would be best for our family to move to Lafayette.

I still did not believe that an NFP-only practice would survive. God knew otherwise. I predicted that after a year of failure (the length of my contract with the hospital), I would retire and fish for a living. Today, eight years later, my business is not only surviving but stable and even very strong at times, although there were very challenging moments.

At the time of my conversion to the NFP-only belief, there were only a handful of Catholic gynecologists in the country who were faithful to the teachings of the Church. Today there are nearly four hundred who are part of a national NFP-only doctors directory. There is also a website (www.omsoul.com) to support these doctors with free and low-cost pamphlets and other resources for their patients. I have had the opportunity in recent years to share my experiences with these doctors and to hear of their own struggles and blessings.

There is a new excitement moving across the country about NFP. Catholic and Protestant couples alike are discovering that, even though the practice of NFP requires some sacrifice, the benefits are manifold.

When I look at my professional life, I see that the adoption of these strong Catholic beliefs has brought a unique form of suffering. It has made me an anomaly in my field and caused daily rejection by patients. Especially disheartening is to be rejected by fellow Catholics, who have been given access to these profound truths through the teaching of the Church. This is a great source of frustration for Catholic Ob-Gyns who know the physical and spiritual dangers that artificial birth control can bring.

And as a Catholic doctor who believes and promotes the Church's teaching, I must fight the sins of pride and self-righteousness that come with knowing that I am making serious sacrifices for the truth. I assure you, though, I still have far to go in this area.

Although I have witnessed some conversions to this important teaching on human life, I have come to see that the fruit of most of my efforts will not be seen in this life. I must learn to be content in knowing that my life is based on the truth and that God will somehow bring good from the effort I bring to my practice.

God has used suffering as an instrument in my conversion, primarily in Brad's death but also in the death of my self-centered beliefs. I am pretty sure that I would not have come to understand God's glorious teaching on marital love without the catalyst of my son's death. I would not have my renewed faith. I would not have my other son, Stephen (nor the little baby whom we miscarried and who, we believe, will be in heaven with us too). I would probably be retired by now, living on an island without attorneys, and I almost certainly would not be truly happy. I see Brad, in one sense, as the sacrificial lamb for our family, just as Jesus was the sacrificial Lamb for the family of God. And just as Jesus rose to eternal glory, so too will my son rise to eternal glory.

It has been more than twelve years since his death. Bonnie and I still miss him dearly but take enormous comfort in our belief that we will see him again. We often think of the unimaginable joy we believe he is experiencing now in heaven and the joy he must have in seeing his parents' renewed faith. And although we have not been blessed with more children, the past ten years with Stephen and Jennifer have been incredibly fruitful. We have received countless blessings.

We have Brad to thank for this. In his death he found new life. And in his death we found new life. Thank you, son.

Ask and You Shall Receive

Debbie Harding

It was late at night, and the anger within me was reaching a boiling point. I felt abandoned and betrayed in my greatest hour of suffering, and no matter how I tried to rein it in, my anger would not subside. My hands shook. My stomach burned.

Finally I exploded.

"Why weren't you there for me when I needed you the most?" I wailed. "Why weren't you there for me?"

The response was a deafening silence.

Oh, my God, what have I done?

I heard the stairs creak as my husband, his body broken and thin, slowly crept to the basement. I heard the door of the gun cabinet open.

Dear God, what do I do?

I held my breath and tiptoed down the darkened hallway, afraid that if he heard the slightest move, it would set off a catastrophic response. I then heard him cock the gun, and I grabbed the stair railing to support my weight. Slowly I descended, my heart pounding.

"No, David, please, no," I pleaded. "We love you."

Silence again.

And then, with a gut-wrenching cry, David burst out, "I'm sorry I couldn't be there for you. I'm so sorry, Hon. I am so, so sorry."

And in my heart I tearfully rejoiced, *Thank you, God, thank you, God.*

With deep sorrow David and I held each other and wept.

Four months before this fateful night, at the age of thirty-eight, I was diagnosed with breast cancer. Our family of five, including three small children, was on the verge of bankruptcy. My husband, David, in the throes of his drug addiction, was battling for his life. Though our situation seemed quite hopeless, I knew that God, in His infinite wisdom and bountiful love, was good. I knew that a love of the cross conquered all!

I grew up in Fitchburg, Massachusetts, one of five children. With each child vying for attention, my parents were challenged, especially since we were all different in so many ways. As an adolescent I faced the usual temptations, uneasiness with self, and questions about life. My parents' unconditional love sustained me through these challenges, as did their constancy in teaching the truth.

My father was a well-respected dentist who worked long hours to provide a good home and a Catholic education for his kids. Mom had the difficult job of staying home to raise her children. She managed all the tasks that entailed with relentless love. My parents never tolerated any behavior that was offensive to God. He was revered. Sin was not watered down. And the commandment "Thou shalt honor thy mother and father" was enforced.

Still, I had to make my personal faith journey as most of us do—the hard way. Along the way I asked God for many things. The proposition "Ask and you shall receive" grounded my desires, and receive I certainly did. Yet it was never in the way that I expected. I realized, through much self-discovery and heartache, that my parents' deep faith had been instilled in me. What they had given me had firm and lasting roots.

I studied ballet and modern dance for fourteen years, before putting this love for the performing arts aside near the end of high school. But during my sophomore year in college, I realized that I missed performing. I felt unsettled and sought something more than academics. It became apparent that my solid academic schedule was a bit ill-conceived. I was about to transfer to a New York fine arts school when I heard that the New England Patriots were holding auditions for "The Spirits," the cheerleaders for their 1981 pro-football season. I knew this was for me.

I made the team, and the next two years were like a dream come true. Aside from the demanding practice and game schedule, my new life involved countless promotional and charity fundraising appearances for groups like the Special Olympics and the Muscular Dystrophy Association. There were also sports promotion events, speaking engagements, autograph signings, and many parties. In addition to being selected to be a part of the Spirits' poster my rookie year, I was also chosen for the Spirits Revue, a select group of talented dancers within the team who performed at nightclubs throughout New England.

I remember many wonderful moments of camaraderie when I tailgated with my cheerleading family after each home game. My fondest memory is of looking up at the rowdy bleachers and seeing my dad's proud smile and two thumbs up, with his eyes fixed on me—instead of watching star quarterback Steve Grogan pass the winning touchdown. Those were awesome years, and my experience with the Spirits promised to open many doors in my future.

I asked God for fame, that I might have the praise of my peers.

I was given doubt and misfortune, that I might seek only the
will of my heavenly Father.

After graduating from Providence College in the summer of
1983 with a bachelor of arts degree, I packed my belongings
and drove to California to pursue a performing career. Audition after lonely audition diminished my hopes of dancing
professionally. There was always someone prettier, someone
with the right look, someone with the right connection. How
I longed for my family.

Within the year I returned home and opened up what
would become a lucrative health and beauty business. This
occupied my next five years. Yet this financial success was not
enough for me, so I pursued modeling, obtaining some com-
mercial work in print and television. I was completely taken
with the world and its shimmering lights and promises, but
I was never really satisfied. Looking back, I see that I was
always reaching higher, always wanting more.

I married David Harding in October 1989. Seven months
later, through the grace of our heavenly Mother, I accompanied my parents to a remote little village in Bosnia-
Herzegovina named Medjugorje. My parents had told me
that, since 1981, the Blessed Virgin Mary allegedly had been
appearing there daily and giving messages to the world
through six young visionaries.[1] Mary's messages were of

---

[1] The alleged apparitions of Medjugorje are claims to private revelation.
Private revelations are not offered or held by the Church as an article of
faith—there is no obligation to believe them, even if the events should some
day be judged by the Church to be of supernatural origin. The references to
these alleged apparitions in this book are not to be viewed as an affirmation
of their validity on the part of the contributors or the publisher. As with all
matters of faith and morals, we should give our assent to the Magisterium
of the Church, which Christ established to teach and govern in His name.

peace and love, reminding the world that God exists. She asked everyone to convert and to re-center his or her life on loving and serving God.

I do not know why I went on this journey, except that I felt called by the Holy Spirit to do so. Once I heard about it from my mom and dad, I felt a deep need to be on that plane with them.

I asked God to help me live a life free of worry. Instead He let me feel the weight of my sins, that I might confess and be free.

My journey to this special place became a personal pilgrimage. Although my life was full, it was void of real meaning. I felt an incredible emptiness; something was missing. My heart and soul were ready for a deeper level of spirituality than I had ever known.

I witnessed many miracles there, but the most extraordinary one was the conversion that took place within me. I experienced one of the greatest confessions of my life on this trip. Many hurts and sins melted away. I started to find much-needed answers to the questions troubling me. I was starting to take off the mask that hid my pain and confusion.

This cleansing and inner healing allowed me to open up to God's love, which I had previously felt unworthy to receive. I understood that despite my failings, I was unconditionally loved by the only One who truly mattered, God! I finally felt forgiven by God's transcendent mercy, His amazing grace.

Before the pilgrimage ended, and as a gesture of thanksgiving, I decided to climb "Apparition Hill," believed to be the place where our Blessed Mother first appeared in this small European village. Teary eyed, I stood barefoot before the rocky mountain. I then began my ascent as an offering of penance for all my past transgressions, feeling each jagged edge of the stony terrain on my bare feet. With each jab against my skin, I winced, while repeatedly whispering, "Jesus, I do this out of love for You."

A feeling of peace and courage came over me, and I realized that offering anything out of love for Jesus is the answer for enduring the impossible. Accepting my daily cross with love and trust in Our Lord would be essential on my journey of faith. I was sad to leave this holy place but also ready to go home. I had gained a new outlook on life.

Soon after we returned, my father and mother found personal church apostolates in which to work. I had a feeling inside that I would be asked to do something in the future for Our Lady, but for now I was called to be patient. Miraculous things were happening to transform me. My life slowed down, and my priorities began to change. Life in general was taking on a whole new meaning for me.

My pilgrimage helped me understand that to "die to self" was the first step on the journey to true happiness and everlasting peace. I had to detach myself from the world and all the material wants that went with it. I also had to begin chipping away at my ego, which weighted me to the world. I had to become less so that Jesus would become more.

I recognized the importance of receiving the sacraments frequently and the need for a deep and active prayer life. Only through the graces of the sacraments would the changes in my life be possible. I finally turned in my pom-poms, blue suede boots, and worldly dreams for a scapular and rosary.

As I look back, I see how Mary was preparing my heart for the difficult trials ahead. She knew that had I not surrendered my will and my life to God, I would never have had the strength to endure the trials to come.

When I had married David, I had promised to be faithful "in sickness and in health, for better or for worse." My life over the next twelve years would include a lot of "sickness" and "worse," because I had married a drug addict. Each day would be a lesson in compassion and acceptance for me. I learned, through tremendous pain, what a true and redemptive gift suffering is meant to be. Yet along with the dark shadows that David and I faced through the addiction, Jesus also gave us some incredible graces.

In 1991 we suffered the heartache of two miscarriages. These losses hit me especially hard. I learned, however, not to question God's merciful plan, only to accept it and to find the courage to move on.

And as quickly as life was taken, life was renewed. Our first angel was born a year and a half later. Although she arrived six weeks early, Mikaela was perfect in every way. I was elated beyond words. I vowed to Almighty God that I would do my best to keep her heart pure and raise her with the constant love of Jesus in our home. I knew that if I wanted her to love and grow in a relationship with Jesus and Mary, then we had to plant the seeds of faith when she was young.

So to nurture our daughter's faith, David and I assembled a makeshift altar in her room when she was two years old. This became the place where we prayed nightly as a family. On a small table we placed a crucifix, a candle, a statue of Mary, and a rosary. A pillow for her little knees was on the floor. This became Mikaela's special place.

By the next year, however, Mikaela had outgrown this makeshift prayer station. We needed to create a more permanent and meaningful place of prayer to celebrate her budding relationship with Jesus and Mary.

In the early spring of 1995 I was blessed with a profound dream in which I was shown a kneeler. The impression of that vision proved indelible, evolving two years later into a

family-owned and operated apostolate of building children's
kneelers. We called it "The Children's Prayer Station."

Several months after my dream Noah was born—and
motherhood in all its glory was being fulfilled. I was a busy
housewife and mother, efficient at diaper changes and runny
noses but not at wood construction. Yet, believing in my heart
that this kneeler apostolate was a direct request from heaven,
I made it my mission to see it to completion. After numerous
prototypes, and with invaluable help from my father, a final
product was created—a solid cherry wood kneeler designed
to "grow" along with the child to adulthood.

Our marketing consisted of local advertising and a beautiful brochure that we mailed upon request. But just as we
were making some headway with the project, I experienced
a third miscarriage, which put everything on hold. Then, in
July of 1998, God blessed us once again with new life. We
named him Gabriel.

Family life was full, yet I knew that for the prayer station
project to progress, it needed to be placed in expert hands.
After a series of events, I contacted Catholic author and TV
host Jeff Cavins. We corresponded for several months about
the project, which eventually led to an invitation to be a guest
on his show, *Life on the Rock*. My live appearance was to air
Thursday, October 21, 1999. The topic for this hour-long live
broadcast would be how to start an apostolate. But Providence had something else in mind.

On September 29, the day after my mother's birthday, I was
having a very difficult night. It had been one of those exceptionally long afternoons, and all I wanted was for the day to
end. David was at an Alcoholics Anonymous meeting. I was
feeling sorry for myself at being home alone, again. I was
tired.

It was bedtime, and the children seemed extra rambunctious. I looked forward to our nightly prayers, hoping I'd get a moment of peace and quiet. This peace and quiet never came. Instead, all three children wanted a piece of me—and I felt too worn out to give to them. So for the first time in their little lives, I sent them to bed on their own, without a story or a kiss from Mommy.

"You mean you're not going to tuck us into bed?" they all whimpered.

I jumped into a hot shower and enjoyed the simple sound of silence. But as soon as my nerves settled down, the "mother guilt" seeped in. How could I have sent them to bed without a last, reassuring hug of the day? I decided to go upstairs and kiss my children good night.

Now feeling calm, I took a deep breath and started up the steps. I had my left hand on the railing. Then suddenly my right hand crossed over to my left breast and rested on a very hard lump. I immediately thought to myself, *Why did I just do that?* It was as if God had directed that very awkward movement.

Then it hit me: *No, no, it can't be. It must be one of my medals!*

But it was not.

Panic ripped through me. I tearfully entered the rooms of my children. Mikaela was already sound asleep. I sat beside her and gently stroked her little head. I remembered the many times that our daughter would sweetly say, "Mommy, the reason why I was born six weeks early was because I couldn't wait any longer for you to hold me and to tell you that I love you."

I kissed her good night and then crept into the boys' room. Noah was asleep. I leaned down and placed my face close to his, taking great pleasure in just listening to him breathe. That moment was interrupted by the sound of Gabriel snoring just five feet away. I noted that his right hand was extended out of the crib rail. I reached over and gently placed my hand in his, delighting in his soft, plump skin and radiant innocence.

When David came home that night, he found me in bed, crying, clutching my rosary. After telling him what was wrong, he examined me. Because David's professional experience was in the medical field, working in the O.R., I paid close attention as he told me that the lump was suspicious. We decided that I should call the doctor first thing in the morning.

Within five hours of my call to the doctor's office the next morning, I saw my primary care physician. He did not like what he saw. Without saying too much, he booked me for an emergency mammogram. A half an hour after that screening, I was staring into the face of a general surgeon. He was holding my mammography film, and he was not smiling. He told me that he wanted the mass removed immediately, without even suggesting the option of a biopsy.

Was I hearing all of this right? I left the surgeon's office and stood in the parking lot, in shock at all that had happened over the past nineteen hours. I shook my head in disbelief, recalling my mother's reassuring words, "Don't worry, my honey, it is probably nothing but a cyst, which is very common in women your age."

But somehow I knew this was different. I looked up at the overcast sky, trying to feel the cool air against my face. I was numb with fear. Then all of a sudden I received an enormous gift of grace. Without question, I knew what I had to do.

I drove down the hill to my parish's perpetual adoration chapel, just a quarter of a mile away. As I opened the chapel doors, there before me was Jesus in the Blessed Sacrament, just waiting for me. I knelt before Him, trying not to disturb the others who were in prayer. I struggled to contain the emotions that flooded through me, then I burst into tears.

As I surrendered it all to Him, I knew the worst was yet to come. Finding the lump was only the beginning of a new cross that Jesus had in store for me—because He knew I loved Him that much. I knew that because I had received so many blessings in life, much was going to be expected from me. I felt that Jesus was asking me to accept this new suffering with confidence and a childlike trust.

Staring at the monstrance, the beautiful receptacle in which the consecrated host is exposed to view, I kept thinking, *There is no way that I am somehow immune to cancer.* Yet I remember not feeling any anger. There was simply none to be felt. I never asked, "Why me, Lord?" Instead I found myself saying, "Why *not* me, Lord?"

With complete acceptance I bowed my head and tearfully thanked Him for the new journey on which I was about to embark. Had I not had any faith, I wouldn't have had the ability to say, "Thank you, Jesus," in that questionable hour. But I did. I thanked Him from the bottom of my heart, because I knew He was allowing this particular cross out of His love for me, to accomplish something that I may never see or understand.

As crazy as this may sound, I felt special and chosen by God on this day. Whether God wanted to change me or to use me to accomplish something greater, it really did not matter. All I knew was that this cancer was allowed for a reason. God must have seen a certain courage in me that I never knew existed. All I asked for was the grace to bear the sufferings. In gratitude I remember telling God that I would do wondrous things with this cross and that I would offer it up in any way I could.

I never felt closer to Jesus or more loved by Him than I did in those few minutes spent with Him in adoration.

My acceptance of whatever God had in store did not spare me the human emotion in the following days. On October 6, five days after finding the lump, I had a lumpectomy. Then began the very difficult wait for the results.

As much as I tried to put the cancer test results out of my mind and get on with living, I was totally consumed with them. The fear of the unknown was agonizing. The biggest question of all remained, How much was Jesus calling me to suffer?

After a week and a half I began to feel I could not take the wait any more. I needed to know the truth. Each time the phone rang, I thought my heart would stop. I was exhausted to the point of paralysis. It was agonizing to know that my future lay in some cold pathology lab.

It was Columbus Day weekend and also our tenth wedding anniversary. It had been more than seven years since we had enjoyed a weekend by ourselves, free from parental responsibilities. We had originally planned to drive the back roads of Lake Winnipesaukee with the top down in David's antique MGB. But the preceding days had left us drained. How could I leave the children now? Instead David and I sat by the fireplace, relishing the warmth and quiet. Confident that our three children were asleep, I tucked my head securely underneath David's arm and let myself cry. Despite David's gentle touch and reassuring words, I was despondent. This time his outpouring of love could not soothe the pain I felt inside.

Why isn't my doctor calling? I thought. *Maybe he knows that this weekend is especially important to us and does not want to ruin it for us. Maybe he is enjoying a well-deserved weekend of brilliant fall foliage with his family, free of patients' concerns.*

By Monday afternoon, nauseated by anxiety, I decided to call the doctor's office, despite its being closed because of the three-day holiday weekend. I reached the answering service, and a woman confirmed that the doctor was on call. She asked if this was an emergency.

"Yes, it is to me," I said. "He has some information that I need." Within five minutes the phone rang.

My hands trembled. The most difficult conversation of my life was just seconds away.

Please, God, not now. David isn't home yet! I could not catch my breath. I was barely able to get out the word "Hello."

It was the doctor, who began by asking what I did over the weekend. I can not explain how, but I knew the truth without hearing a single utterance. Every fiber of my being began to collapse.

Then the doctor's voice shifted, and finally I heard the words I had anticipated.

"I am sorry, Debbie," he said, "but your pathology report was positive. You have cancer."

With the innocence and desperation of a child, clinging to some last bit of hope that perhaps the answer might be different, I pleaded, "Is it benign or malignant?" (As if cancer was anything other than malignant!)

He calmly repeated, "It's malignant, Debbie. You have cancer."

Somehow I ended the conversation and hung up the phone. As the weight of the horrific reality slammed my soul, I sank deeper into the chair beneath me. With my hands cupped over my face, I vigorously rocked back and forth, the tears flowing uncontrollably. And in that instant, as I gasped for air, I felt a breath from heaven.

Once again, in my deepest agony, I experienced the greatest infusion of God's love. In the midst of this unbearable grief, the deep roots of my faith were strengthened. The only words that I could speak were, "Jesus, I love you . . . Jesus, I love you . . . Jesus, I . . . love . . . You!" I must have repeated these four words a thousand times—until I was calm and every tear had dried from my now swollen face.

Mikaela was in school. The two boys were home with me but playing together in another room, unaware of what was happening. As I walked into the kitchen moments later, four-year-old Noah approached me.

Looking confused and concerned, he said, "Mommy, your eyes are all puffy. You look like you've been crying. Who was that on the phone?"

"Noah, you know how Mommy and Daddy have been waiting to hear some news from the doctor?" I said. "Well . . . that was him. He just told your mommy some bad news, but I'm gonna be okay!"

Looking into Noah's angelic face and his huge blue eyes, I was pierced by his sweet innocence and I could not stop the tears. I held him close to my chest, feeling the softness of his skin. I began to rock as I had done moments before. All I could think of were questions about the future. Would I see Noah grow up? Would I see any of my children grow up? I looked at fifteen-month-old Gabriel, enveloped in his secure little world and oblivious to the dark cloud that had befallen his family.

I called David at work, but I was choking so hard from crying that he had to guess what was wrong by asking me questions. Within twenty minutes he was home. David acted so brave, so unaffected, so clinical. Twenty years of working in the O.R. gave him the medical tenacity and know-how not to jump to conclusions. But I found myself thinking that he should be different somehow, because I was his wife.

David's objective was to calm me down; my objective was to make him feel. I had an urge to beat his chest with my hands and say, "Don't you understand that your wife has cancer?!" Why was he putting up such a front? Why didn't he cry instead of holding it all in?

Dear God, I thought, *how is he going to handle his sobriety now?*

In a soft and tender voice David reminded me of the count-less crosses we had already faced together and how through prayer God had always carried us. As he tried to lift me up, reassuring me that cancer did not necessarily mean a death sentence, my thoughts shifted to my poor mother and father. *They are going to be devastated,* I thought. *How am I ever going to tell them that their little girl was just diagnosed with cancer?*

I knew that Mom and Dad had been on pins and needles waiting for some information since the lumpectomy. Mom went to daily adoration, fasted, prayed the stations of the cross, and offered up every penance for me.

When David returned from picking up Mikaela from school, we all got into the car and headed up the road to Mom and Dad's house. As our car approached my parents' driveway, all I could feel, all I could hear, was the thumping of my heart. When the car was parked, I got out and just stared at their door. *How I love them,* I thought to myself. *This is going to crush them.*

I was so engrossed with my own thoughts about how I was going to break the news, I did not notice that my two older children had barreled out in front of me.

Before I could shout, "No, Mikaela, wait," it was too late.

The door swung open, and all I could hear was my daugh-ter's little voice screeching those dreadful words, "Mommy has cancer. Mommy has cancer . . . *cancer!*"

My mother met me at the door. The pain on her face was unlike anything I had ever seen before. At that moment her eyes seemed to be staring right at death. For the first time in my life I had a small understanding of what it must have been like for our Blessed Mother to watch her Son being nailed to the cross. This was the pain I saw in my mother.

A piece of each of us was crucified that day outside my parents' home. How I wished I could take away the sorrow that pierced Mom's and Dad's souls. Yet I knew I could trust that their faith would see them through this.

After a few days the initial shock and pain of the word *cancer* was slowly subsiding, and everyone seemed to be moving forward. The children were too young to be aware of the seriousness of our situation, so their playful lives continued as usual. Mom and Dad put my name on every prayer chain imaginable. David drowned himself in work.

The biggest changes were going on inside of me. I was a roller coaster of emotions, up one moment and completely down the next. But with each new corner I turned, God put something or someone in my path to make me stronger— usually at moments when I was at my worst. As the word got out, I started to receive well wishes from some kind people.

But I also had my share of disturbing ones.

I asked God to give me clear vision that I might know His will. I was led in a fog filled with obstacles and difficult people that I may pray harder to find my way home.

I'll never forget the afternoon when, just days after I was diagnosed with cancer, my brother Dan and his wife, Kathy, came to visit. It was a beautiful afternoon filled with light conversation and cheer. And then the phone rang. It was someone asking to speak to me, but David did not recognize the voice.

He handed me the phone, and I heard a woman introduce herself as a friend of a friend of so-and-so. I was polite and patient as she boldly imposed on me with a long dissertation explaining her tragic ordeal with breast cancer. I was not ungrateful for the call, nor insensitive. I know she meant to help. I just was not ready for it.

The woman spoke rapidly—and everything she said sounded foreign: chemotherapy, double mastectomy, partial mastectomy, centinal node biopsy, axillary node dissection, metastasis, reconstructive surgery, bone scan. On and on she went. And then, out of nowhere, she proclaimed that after she found out that she had cancer, she had waited more than a year before she decided to have any surgery. She said she needed that much time to figure out whether she wanted to live or die.

"Live or die?" What kind of a statement was that? I was horrified.

Then the woman ended her speech with, "So take your time, dear."

TAKE MY TIME, DEAR? I shouted to myself. *TAKE MY TIME TO DO WHAT? TO DIE?*

In a fury I started to pace, holding the phone away from my ear in a silent rage. *How dare this stranger call and force herself on me like this? What does she mean, she did not know whether she wanted to live or die?* My guts were being ripped to shreds. Streams of tears rolled down my face. I abruptly ended the conversation and went to my bedroom.

With dry heaves and my stomach churning, I threw myself on the bed, feeling totally shattered. From deep within my whole self was pleading, *I WANT TO LIVE, I WANT TO LIVE, I WANT TO LIVE.* I wailed, "You may not have a life, lady. You may not have three children, but I do, and I have a husband who is an addict on top of it. And if I die, who is going to take care of them? WHO IS GOING TO TAKE CARE OF THEM!?"

I asked God for strength, that I might have the courage to endure, and I was made weak, that I might learn to trust while crying on my knees.

That phone call was too much for me to handle. The woman's voice haunted me for days. I was new to the world of cancer. I could not process half of what she had said, not to mention the feelings going on inside me. The medical words she used were big and their meanings completely unclear. It was too much information too soon. I needed prayers, not negative statements. I prayed that nobody else would call to offer me help. My faith was rattled to its core.

Yet as disturbing as that phone call was, later I realized how much it had actually helped me. The fact was that the more I faced my greatest weakness, the more I felt God's penetrating love strengthening me. This cross was unlike any I had ever faced. Daddy could no longer wipe his little girl's tears and make them all go away, and Mom could not bandage the wound. My husband was too ill himself to comprehend my pain. I felt totally alone.

That call was, perhaps, my turning point in letting go and letting God take control over what was going to happen to me. I knew I had no control. The outcome was totally up to God. And that is exactly the way I wanted it! I did not want to try to control this situation by wishing it away.

After that day there were no more tears. I decided that cancer was not going to beat me. It might take my life, if that is what God wanted, but it was not going to pounce upon my soul. As time went by, a tremendous power was unleashed inside of me. In my agony I became spiritually strong.

"Come on, Deb," I would catch myself cheering. "You can do it. Just focus on the cross, focus on the cross, focus on the cross."

It was the beginning of a new and exciting journey for me. What perhaps sustained me the most was a prayer called "Your Cross" that I stumbled upon. There, printed in black and white, was what I had always believed about suffering:

Your Cross

The everlasting God has, in His wisdom, foreseen from eternity the cross that He now presents to you as a gift from His inmost heart.

This cross He now sends you He has considered with His all-knowing eyes, understood with His divine mind, tested with His wise justice, warmed with His loving arms, and weighed with His own hands, to see that it be not one inch too large and not one ounce too heavy for you.

He has blessed it with His holy name, anointed it with His grace, perfumed it with His consolation, taken one last glance at you and your courage, and then sent it to you from heaven, a special greeting from God to you, an alms of the all-merciful love of God.

—Saint Francis de Sales

I asked God for health, that I might be capable of doing the things I love. I received infirmity, that I might accomplish the things that mattered.

It was mid-October. In less than one week I was scheduled to travel to Birmingham, Alabama, to be a guest on EWTN's *Life on the Rock*. But I had to tell Jeff Cavins that my life had completely changed since he and I talked about a show on building an apostolate. I needed to reach him quickly so that he could get someone else for the taping.

Frantically I went to the computer and started to write an e-mail, "Dear Jeff . . ."

As I finished and clicked "send," something strange happened. The message would not go through. So I decided to shut down the computer, restart it, and try to send my e-mail again. The instant I turned off the computer, my phone rang.

"Debbie, hi, this is Jeff," was the cheerful greeting. "You were on my heart, and I wanted to call to talk about the upcoming show. So how are you?"

After we chuckled about my e-mail attempt for a minute, the tone of our conversation turned serious.

"Jeff," I said, "you'll never believe it, but I was just diagnosed with cancer." I explained that I was scheduled for surgery on November 2.

Although Jeff could easily have found a replacement guest, he suggested that what I was experiencing might be of help to people facing similar crosses. I told him I would do whatever God wanted. The show topic was changed from "How to Build an Apostolate" to "A Christian's Response to Suffering."

I was ready!

Only God could have orchestrated all of this. When I boarded the plane to Alabama a week later, with my cancer right beside me, I never had felt stronger. I prayed every second of my day to the Holy Spirit. I begged God to purge me completely so that I could be an empty vessel for Him to speak through, to give courage to others in their time of suffering.

It was the experience of a lifetime. There were no sad faces. I was met with love, hope, and much prayer. I was with a television crew and a group of people who obviously shared a deep love for God. It was a blessing beyond all blessings to proclaim my love and trust in God to the whole world. No New England Patriots-Dallas Cowboys football game could ever have compared to this experience! I felt completely at home and at peace during the show.

I still had to face all my real-life uncertainties and unanswered questions. The original pathology report had revealed that the mass of tissue the surgeon had removed had positive margins. This meant that not all the cancer was taken out. More surgery was required to see if the cancer had spread into my lymphatic system. Surgery was scheduled for less than two weeks later. I first had an appointment for an intake assessment by the team of specialists who would work on the cancer.

As I sat in the cold examining room, my rosary in hand, I felt completely content. I met several nurses, the surgeon who would be performing my surgery, two oncologists, a plastic surgeon, and several others. They were all kind and compassionate. Everyone remarked that I was very young to have breast cancer. Several of them asked about the perpetual smile on my face.

I was so at peace. We talked about the possibility of mastectomy versus the breast conservation surgery—and about radiation and chemotherapy. Nothing phased me. *Your will be done, Lord. Not mine, but Yours be done.* I'll never forget when the young psychiatrist entered my room.

"So how are you dealing with the fact that you have cancer, Mrs. Harding?" she asked meekly.

"Great!" I said.

She looked astonished. Perhaps she was analyzing my obvious denial.

"If not now, you may feel the need very soon to talk to someone," she continued as she gave me her card.

As I handed her card back to her, she persisted, "Mrs. Harding, really . . . how are you coping?"

"Faith," I said with conviction. "I have an incredible amount of faith and trust in Jesus."

She sheepishly left.

After the surgery I saw David's face as I drifted in and out of consciousness. He tried to keep me awake, but I was just too weak and out of it. Then, with one final, gentle effort, David shook me and said, "Honey, it's me." I saw him smile.

"They removed more tissue around the original mass," he said, "and took out a total of twenty-one lymph nodes. So far all the frozen sections appear negative for infiltration. Do you know what this means, Honey?" He continued to gently move me, with a gleam in his eye, as I drifted off to sleep.

Radiation treatments started December 7. For the next thirty-three days I traveled one hour each way to the University of Massachusetts Memorial University Hospital in Worcester, to receive what seemed like ten seconds of radiation treatment. I met some incredibly brave people during that time. We laughed a lot as we waited for our treatments, wearing our "johnnies" and sharing stories of pain and hope. And we cried. We also welcomed with open arms the newcomers, each of whom arrived filled with trepidation.

When I completed my allotted radiation treatment, I was given a diploma and a follow-up appointment with my oncologist. At that appointment my doctor would schedule the start of chemotherapy, or so I thought.

The night before my appointment I stared at myself in the mirror and thanked Almighty God for bringing me that far and for the knowledge that He would get me through the next phase, bald or not. I looked at my long, thick brown hair. Not wanting to experience its slow falling out, I laughed as I imagined a "shave-your-head party" with me, of course, as the guest of honor. At thirty-eight, I thought about my youth, a time when looks meant everything to my self-esteem. I smiled, realizing how little it all mattered now.

When I was young, I asked God for all things, that I might enjoy life. Long past my youth, I was given life instead, that I might enjoy all things.

Then came the day when I would find out the extent of my cancer and how much it had spread, as well as when chemotherapy would start. As the door to the examining room opened, I swallowed hard.

"Debbie," my oncologist greeted me, "it's better than we expected, and you do not have to have chemotherapy. All your lymph nodes—all twenty-one of them—show negative for cancer."

PRAISED BE GOD!!!

When David and I came home from the oncologist's visit, we met Mom and Dad in the cellar, where they were entertaining our little troops. The moment I saw them I shouted, "No chemotherapy, no chemotherapy!"

Mom and Dad burst into tears and grabbed me, knowing that no chemotherapy also meant that the treatment for my breast cancer was complete. There was nothing more to be done other than the normal follow-up protocol. It was over.

Then I heard the bellowing cheer from the children, "Yeah! Mommy's okay. . . . She's really okay!"

Little did they know that I was always okay, no matter what, because I was carrying my cross with Jesus.

I asked God to send me a knight in shining armor, that I might feel secure in this life. I was given an addict, that I might depend solely on God, so that I might have life in the next.

In the months that followed I became keenly aware of just how fragile David really was and how much my cancer had compounded his own internal suffering. Despite his severe challenges, he has always been a hard worker and a good provider for our family. He is bright and extremely gifted, and our children adore him. But he is an addict.

Relapse is a very real thing when you are dealing with a disease of the body; it is even more real when you're dealing with a disease of the spirit. At times I would forget that it was in God's time that David would be healed, not in mine. Then, on that terrifying night when he contemplated another way out of his suffering, I realized that David had indeed been there for me when I needed him the most. Perhaps not in the way I had hoped—by maintaining sobriety—but he had been present in the only way he was capable of at the time.

David had been physically there for me during my cancer. This spoke volumes about his love for me. He held my hand. He changed my drainage bag and bloody dressings. He was always there to comfort me and to wipe away my tears. He was lovingly present for our three children, for my parents, and for anyone who was in need of comfort, reassurance, or answers.

Being the wife of a drug addict is nearly impossible to describe. This evil disease is incredibly cunning and manipulative. It is relentless. It destroys everything in its path—one's love, one's life, one's soul. And no one suffers more than the addict, who wants relief and freedom from the obsession that rules his mind. When life gets tough, David's haunting addiction offers him the only way to cope that he knows, an escape through chemicals.

David's drug addiction has been the greatest cross in my life, more than even the cancer nightmare. There have been job losses, countless relapses, treatment centers, and constant tests to our marriage, where love, security, and honesty are so vital. There have been many times when I just wanted to lay down this cross, concede defeat, and walk away. And then a miracle would happen. God would show His face once again to my hopeless heart.

More often than not, He would make known His warmth and love by speaking through my mother. Mom would show up unexpectedly and say some unassuming words, never suspecting the tears of despair I had shed the night before. Her words often reminded me of all the reasons why I love David and of how he had been suffering tremendously too. I would then smile, offer it up, and pick up my cross once again. I pray that nobody has to carry this cross.

I have had many people tell me to leave David. "Let him go. Get on with your life." In this disposable society in which we live, we too often try to dissolve our marriages, jobs, and relationships in an effort to solve our problems. We curse our bad health. We run from the cross.

I have learned to look at the crosses as gifts. If God has given me David, with his troubles, as a gift, why would I want to let go of him? Struggling through the suffering could very well be the means God will use for my husband's salvation or my own.

Jesus never said the road to salvation would be wide and easy. What merit would there be in that? The road is narrow. The crosses are heavy. And, yes, they hurt. Jesus never told us to go around the cross and that He'd be waiting for us on the other side. He said, "Pick up the cross and follow Me."

Our acceptance of this daily cross of addiction has brought David and me closer to each other in our marriage and closer to our God. David's battle has given him a tremendous amount of compassion for the meek and the sick. His deep love for his children has made him an exceptional father.

My dear husband just celebrated his first anniversary of being a reader at our church, and our daughter is Saint

Denis' newest altar server. It brings tears to my eyes when I see them together on the altar. What miracles God has worked in all of our lives!

I teach a fifth-grade religious education class, and recently I took my class into the church. When I told them that we were going to learn to pray the rosary, I requested one simple thing. I asked that while they were praying, they would kneel before the crucifix out of love for Jesus. I said that if it was too much for them, I would understand if they sat. Fifty-five minutes later, we were all still kneeling. When we got back to the classroom, I asked the children what they had experienced. And the love of the cross was explained very simply by ten-year-old Ryan.

"Mrs. Harding," he waved his hand anxiously, "about halfway through praying the rosary, my knees were really hurting. Just when I was about to sit down, I looked up at the cross. I stared at the nails in Jesus' hands and feet. Then I said to myself, *If He can do it, so can I.* As I said this, the pain in my knees seemed to go away, so I continued to kneel and pray."

What wisdom we can learn from the young.

Our family has come a long way. I know there will be challenges ahead, but I know that God will send us only what we can handle. I know that in the cross we find the spiritual riches that will sustain us in good times and in bad.

I asked God for the world, and He gave it to me. Not the gold from this world but the gold that comes from carrying the cross with love. I got nothing that I asked for but everything I hoped for, everything I needed to reach my final home. I am blessed beyond compare.

I Obey

Deb Headworth

I hesitated before lifting the pill bottle. My hands trembled. Sores covered half my mouth. Infection gnawed at my head and my neck and slurred my speech. Dizzily I looked at Inky and Chessie lying beside me and petted them both. I did not want to swallow the pill, Chemet. Who would? The side effects were terrible. I procrastinated on this frigid December night in 2001 by grooming the cats some more. As fear threatened, I reminded myself that this was just another set of treatments. Vomiting, headaches, and nausea wouldn't kill me: It was just pain.

I tried to thank God for another opportunity to prove that I trusted Him. I knew I was dawdling, but it seemed to help. *God has carried me through my entire life. He won't abandon me now*, I thought. Memories of God's presence flickered and replayed in my mind. These took me back to my eighth-grade confirmation Mass.

~

The ceremony flowed beautifully, until the bishop paused, fumbled with his paper, then stopped altogether. In the awkward silence I felt the congregation's eyes bore into my back.

The bishop whispered to the attendant, "Does that read 'Maximilian Kolbe' next to Deborah L. Schoenborn?"

"Yes, it does," I said.

He gave me an inquisitive look. Blushing, I smiled and nodded with exaggeration. I heard him name me "Maximilian Kolbe" as I felt the oily cross on my forehead.

Really, I lectured myself, *if Saint Maximilian could stand in front of a Nazi soldier in an Auschwitz death camp and ask to take the place of a husband and father who was condemned to die of starvation, I can handle being a female with a male confirmation name!* In my mind I heard members of the congregation whisper, *Why would a twelve-year-old girl choose an old priest-martyr as her saint?* If they had asked, I would have answered that I was just obeying God's prompting—and I had submitted to it with blinders on.

It took me nearly eighteen years to understand why God asked me to choose Maximilian. But I had to practice obeying Him long before the scales would fall from my eyes.

～

My road to Calvary began with small tests in God's "School of Obedience and Repentance." The difficulty of the tests increased gradually, so that whenever God asked me to obey, I never really knew if I had the strength to follow through the next step.

That is true of the challenge I faced after my eleventh-grade retreat with Saint Anthony's Parish, in Grand Rapids, Michigan, in 1988. It was grace that fertilized my resolve to obey. I remember the music floating over the camp's room-divider. Candle light played hide-and-seek with the dark air.

"Take as long as you need; I am here all night," Father Fred gently encouraged from his seat in the confessional. He was so patient. Despite sitting on a hard plastic chair, he did not shift around. I barely noticed that thirty minutes had slipped by, so I kept confessing more. I confessed all. My test came the following day.

"What do you mean, you have to break up with me?" Tom[1] demanded, confused. "What did I do wrong?"

My announcement had hurt him.

"No, no, it is not you," I said. "It's me! I admitted last night every sin I could remember from my entire life. All of them! I am forgiven! I still can't believe how loving God is!"

"What does that have to do with our breaking up?" Tom's question jarred me. He sounded angry.

"I need time to develop my relationship with God," I stammered.

"But, Deb," he reasoned, "you can do that and still date me!"

"No, I spend too much time daydreaming about you, so I don't finish my schoolwork and other things. Plus, it's wrong to mess around; you're not my husband." My voice cracked. I could see the confusion cloud his brown eyes.

"Don't do this," he pleaded. His sad voice tempted me to rescind my words. I tried to soothe him.

"I'm? sorry I'm hurting you. Please understand."

He did not understand, and he mocked me for the next year and a half. The freedom that obedience and repentance produced had come with a considerable price.

Still, God supplied the grace I needed to endure the mocking. He covered me with grace during other trials too, such as the headaches that began in my senior year of high school.

～

As the airplane's motor squealed, my ears popped and the grenades in my head exploded.

"We'll land in Dallas in thirty minutes, Deb!" my friend Sue giggled. "We're almost there!"

---

[1] Name has been changed.

"There" was the National Cheerleading Competition. Winning first place at cheer camp and the years of dance and gymnastics had finally paid off.

"Do you think we're ready?" I wondered out loud, trying to ignore my headache and my churning stomach. I had been performing or competing since I was three years old, and I knew this particular headache was not due to nerves; it felt more like the flu. *How will I ever pull off back handsprings with a smile on my face?* I thought to myself.

The squad let me lead the prayer before we hit the floor. I do not think anyone else could have talked; their nerves seemed to have dried out their vocal cords. In the end God chose to supply the energy we needed to rank in the top quarter out of nearly five hundred squads.

On our way home Sue leaned forward and smiled. "We did our best."

"Yeah, we did," I grinned, eyebrows rising high.

"I can't believe it is over. Was it worth it?" she reflected.

"I don't know," I murmured, distracted. My head still hurt. *This is some flu*, I thought. What I did not realize was the pain would soon blend into me as a grain of sand settles into its desert. Nevertheless, God always granted reprieve when I needed it. I remember a great moment of joy that came from following His prompting.

~

It was a Sunday, and I bounded down the road in my big red Chevy. I yanked off my McDonald's visor and pins. I had changed from my uniform before leaving work but hadn't had time to finish.

"Heavenly Father, please send me a friend to pray with during Mass," I said out loud.

Although a high school senior, I had never gone to Mass alone before, especially at another parish. Because work had scheduled me for both the Saturday night and Sunday morning shifts, and since my parish did not offer a Sunday evening Mass, I had to go to a neighboring parish. Nervously I climbed the large stone steps and pulled open the heavy, hand-carved wooden door. Stained glass funneled the brilliant evening sun across the entrance. My eyes glided to the beam's end. There, veiled in dancing flecks of colored light, a young man stood smiling at me. I recognized him immediately. At a retreat held the weekend before with Saint Mary's parish in Marne, he had greeted my friend Katie and me and offered to carry our bags. Later he impressed us with an inspiring talk about "combating fear."

"Russ, what are you doing here?" I asked. "I thought you belonged to a parish across town."

"I do, but I come here quite a bit," he said. Then pausing slightly, "Do you want to sit and pray together?"

"Yes, I do." I grew wings and floated to the pew.

~

Over and over I have learned to trust God with my obedience, even though the purpose of His commands usually remains a mystery to me until after I obey. Slowly God has built my trust through small, everyday occurrences.

"Holy God, what college should I attend?" I asked in prayer one day. In my interior I heard God answer, *Go to Aquinas.*

I then thought, *My Aquinas scholarship covers only half of the cost; the others are offering more scholarship money!*

God responded patiently, *Stop worrying. Go to Aquinas College. I will provide.*

Okay, I'll wait and see, I thought, still feeling unsure.

I did not want to leave my family: Mom and Dad, three siblings, and Mini, our dog. *At least Aquinas is in Grand Rapids,*

I reasoned, thinking more about God's earlier instructions. Grand Rapids is only twenty minutes from my small western Michigan hometown, Marne. Both of my parents had come from large Catholic families and I had many relatives in both the city and countryside near my home.

Just before college applications were due, I slumped over our dining room table with a pen in hand. My tears blurred the forms.

"Deb, get that paperwork done today," Mom said. "It is due tomorrow!"

"But, Mom, I can't sign for Grand Valley University," I choked on the words. "God said to attend Aquinas!"

My pen dropped as confusion hounded me. *Why do I let money become such a roadblock?* I wondered. The ringing phone jolted me. My mom answered, listened, then winked and motioned to me with her finger to wait.

She hung up and said, "Deb, I was just offered a full-time position at Aquinas. You can attend for free as part of my benefit plan!"

And so God came through once again.

$\sim$

In the fall of 1989, just as God had instructed me, I began studying religion, art, English, and secondary education at Aquinas. My health began to worsen.

$\sim$

"Mr. Blovits, will you squeeze my head?" I opened my jaw and shut my eyes. The relentless aching throbbed in my head as the rest of the class continued its sculpting. They were used to this odd sequence of events. I had been asking our art instructor, who was like a father to all the students, to "squeeze the pain out" for several months now.

"Okay, break time," he announced. The class disbanded. Dizzily, I tottered to the restroom. The hallway spun around me. Bending over did not help. Suddenly everything went black, and my head smashed on the hard tile floor.

The nurse's chatter sounded rehearsed. "You must limit your sugar intake. You have hypoglycemia. Does diabetes run in your family?"

I could not answer because I was too busy digesting the news. I was a seventeen-year-old college student with a messed up pancreas who wished she could stop dreaming about hot waffle cones covered with chocolate malt ball ice cream and caramel drizzle. *Oh, Lord*, I thought, *why couldn't I limit my vegetable intake instead?*

~

In my third year of college God helped me discern my vocation.

"Will I marry You or someone else?" I whispered to Jesus in the silence of my dorm room. I was contemplating a vocation, but I knew I also loved Russ.

With my eyes clenched in prayer, I saw streaks of swirling satin, pure silver, and glistening white gold collect into a spiraling form. The whirlwind of metallic sparks transformed into a dress, a wedding dress. I did not see the face of my beloved, but he swung me backward as we danced and turned. I was filled with laughter and joy.

Once again God showed me that He listens, giving me just enough information to trust Him yet also asking me to practice trusting Him more. Two years later, in 1994, I would be sacramentally united to Russ Headworth, the retreat leader whom God had sent to me that day in church six years earlier.

~

In May of 1994, the month before my wedding, I graduated *magna cum laude* with a bachelor of fine arts degree: a painting major, a sculptural ceramics major, a drawing minor, a religious studies minor, an English minor, and a secondary education degree. Learning to mask my increasing headaches and nausea was much more difficult than obtaining my five-year degree from Aquinas.

~

In the first half of 1995 I delighted in substitute teaching and creating artwork on commission. But by late summer God revealed other plans.

Deb, get up. Go find your teaching position. I heard God in a clear but inaudible interior voice. The words jolted me from a good night's sleep. It was 9:00 A.M. I was not a morning person, and so I moved slowly.

Lord, today? It is raining and cold outside. My resume isn't printed yet. I made excuses.

Get up! God demanded.

I obeyed.

With the confidence that results from obedience, I visited three schools that day, explaining the humanities-art program I had designed. Over an eight-year period students would learn elements and principles of design while creating projects that reinforced an understanding of history and culture. By 5:30 that evening I had accepted two part-time positions.

~

About two and a half years into our marriage I was pregnant with our second child, having miscarried the first. I was having lunch with my friend Polly, enjoying a salad as she chattered.

Why am I sweating? I thought. The restaurant started to whirl around me. The volume of Polly's voice faded and then returned, funneled away and then crashed back—now louder than ever, like waves crashing against large rocks on a shore. *What is she saying?* I thought. Gingerly I excused myself from the table and headed toward the restroom.

Polly followed me. "Are you okay?" she asked.

"No. I'm bleeding. Can you drive me home?" My vision was blurred, and everything surrounding me began to plunge at me. I felt faint.

"What about your car?" Polly asked.

I squinted, trying to stop the movement. I held up a hand in front of me to guard against my hitting the ground or the wall. As Polly helped me to the parking lot, I mumbled, "I'll pick up the car tomorrow."

Polly dropped me off at home. I still felt sick. Later that afternoon I would lose my two-and-a-half-month-old baby. After calling the doctor, I lay down on my bed and thought about the pain I was in, about miscarrying a second child, and about how I was going to tell Russ. I did not want to call him at work. I would wait to tell him when he got home.

Russ and I were open to life throughout our marriage. I wouldn't say we were "gung-ho" about having a child, but we did not take any serious steps, like birth control, to avoid pregnancy. We casually used Natural Family Planning (NFP) to delay pregnancy for, perhaps, the first year into our marriage.

Despite being a deeply committed Catholic, I was affected by the culture, wanting to delay pregnancy because of the subconscious fear of being "strapped" with a child immediately after finishing college. I felt that I had to at least get my own career under way in light of my spending five years to get a degree. The few feminist professors had done an effective job in delivering the message that women had to be prepared to be on our own, considering the high divorce rates. I certainly trusted Russ and presumed we would always be married, but the culture's message of insecurity still subtly permeated my Catholic mind. It even created a coldness toward my first two miscarriages. I was sad about the loss of the children but was clearly more concerned about my own health and the fact that we might not be able to have children at all.

One good thing that did result from this second miscarriage was that my trust in and love for Russ deepened. I saw that he was with me in "sickness and health." The subconscious distrust of men that seemed to reside in at least a small part of my psyche was disappearing. The false security of material comfort that I had been taught in college was dissipating. I also began to trust in God more.

But little did I know that this sword would pierce my heart seven more times over the next four years.

~

Whipping in with the starkness of the winter of 1997, my health worsened.

A sharp, chilled rush swept through me. "Shut the door. You're letting all the heat out!" I whined to Russ, though I was barely audible over my shower.

"Get moving, Deb. It's already 6:15. I have to get in the shower, or I'll be late for work!" Russ said. Conditioner stung my tired eyes as I fumbled to wipe it away.

"Another rough night?" he asked.

"Yeah, you could call it that," I moaned.

"Did you get any sleep?"

I tried, unsuccessfully, to hide the self-pity in my voice. "Maybe two hours." Staring through swollen lids, I revealed a despondent half-smile in the steamy mirror. "Thanks for helping prepare my history lecture last night. After you fell asleep, I did some reading. Around 3:00 A.M. I corrected religion quizzes and wrote introductory subordinate clauses."

"How can we help you get more sleep?" he asked. "Two to three hours a night isn't enough!"

What I did not realize then is that from that point until the present I would average zero to four hours of sleep every twenty-four hours. I would visit the doctor at least once every other month during those four years. In early 2002 I would visit at least once a month. I returned to the doctor shortly after this conversation with Russ for an explanation.

∼

The whitewashed doctor's office looked as bleak as I felt.

"What do you mean, your blood is racing and your mind can't quiet down?" the doctor probed.

"Every time I lie down to sleep, my neck tightens, my back hurts, my head throbs, my blood races, and I see little white flashes," I responded.

Hesitantly he asked, "And your allergies, hypoglycemia, canker sores, bad breath, nausea, diarrhea, and fatigue haven't cleared up at all?"

"No," I grimaced. "My menstrual cramps are worse, and my waking temperature is dropping."

"Yes, yes, and your chart indicates you have weak thyroid levels too."

I nodded. "You're right; I forgot. By the way, I have been forgetting a lot lately. Do you think it is connected somehow?"

The doctor shrugged. Russ and I decided to get another opinion.

∼

"I have known Deb nine years. I really do not think anxiety is causing all her symptoms!" Russ sounded assuring. I gave him a smiling nod. This new doctor appeared unconvinced. He leaned back, repositioned my file, and crossed his legs. I cleared my throat, "But doctor, how can stress cause my hair to stop growing?"

Calmly he replied, "Stress does terrible things to the body."

"How can stress give me stomach aches when I eat meat?" my voice squeaked as I held back the tears.

"Everybody handles anxiety differently. Some people have a lower threshold than others. Others need help producing brain chemicals."

"But I have never heard of stress lowering someone's temperature," I stammered, "or causing severe menstrual pain!" The dam broke. I could not control my crying. *Geez, here I am bawling and proving his point*, I thought.

The doctor handed me a tissue. "Just try the anti-anxiety medicine for six months and see how you do."

I was humiliated. And as I figured, the medicine did not solve the problems.

～

At the end of my third teaching year I resigned from my part-time positions because of my deteriorating health. It would take all of summer 1998 to prepare my home-based studio. Clean white paint covered layers and layers of dirty, green-brown, cement-block basement walls. Slate blue oil paint unified the floor. Heavy curtains separated my portrait studio from my wood shop.

My spirit coaxed my body into slow motion to help my uterus cradle my third child.

Unlike with the first two babies, a deep reverence for the life within me had settled in my heart. I had come to realize how difficult it was to bring new life into this world. I definitely suspected that my medical conditions had caused the first two miscarriages, and so I was even more cautious with my body this time. The pregnancy was a primary reason why I stepped down from my teaching positions.

One morning I walked upstairs to stare out of the open dining room window. Flowers bloomed in a hanging basket just three feet away. I watched a mourning dove swoop to feed her babies nestling in the basket amid the foliage. A bright red cardinal gazed at me from the lilac bush. I realized this was the same bird I had seen a month ago when I discovered that an eternal soul was once again growing inside me. This bird witnessed my prayers for my third child.

Alone in my house a few days later, the hemorrhaging began. Even though I was on bed rest, my third baby could not pull through. I mourned the child this time, and not my medical problem nor the fact that we as a couple were not yet able to have a child.

~

Grief overcame me in relentless waves as I steadied the two-month-old twins in the center of one cupped palm. My fourth and fifth children were dead. All my miscarriages happened in the first three months, but this one was the most difficult because there were two babies.

"Lord, where were You a moment ago?" I cried. "Where were You while I pushed and cried and MY CHILDREN DID NOT CRY? They did not move as babies should."

Hot tears collected on my lap. Then I watched in prayer as Christ revealed to me His presence during this earthly hell. I felt His presence as never before in my life. He knelt down beside my sunken frame. His arms lifted my hands to heaven, the hands that shrouded my twins. His strength held me and my babies in the air. His Spirit spoke the words of offering through me.

I could not speak. I heard Christ proclaim to my soul, *Here are your children, the children of pain you offer Me. My Father has them. They live.*

I knew with my whole heart and soul that Russ and I would not be alone in our suffering. I knew—more than ever—that I had to rely on Christ. This was the moment of my deepest conversion to date. I think losing the twins was the catalyst. To witness the loss of two lives in one stinging moment was more than my heart and soul could stand.

It was also at this very moment that I began to understand the meaning of "sacrificial suffering." I began to see that all of us are going to suffer in this life, in either big or small ways. We will try to ignore this suffering because we live in a fallen world, but the maturing Christian will learn how to respond to this suffering in a spiritually healthy way. I began to learn to give my suffering to God with open arms. I would beg Him for all the grace He could give to help me endure and use this suffering for some good.

After this horrific loss I began to study. I wanted to know what the Bible, the Church, and the great saints taught about suffering, sacrifice, pain, and offering one's very self to God. I read the New Testament over and over again. I used concordances to study these words. I read the writings of Saint Teresa of Avila, Saint John of the Cross, and Blessed (now Saint) Faustina.

Over the ensuing days, weeks, and months, my reverence for life—my love for my twins—reached a level that I had never imagined previously. And I thought over and over about the vision I had of Christ holding up my twins and me. I meditated almost daily on what Christ was trying to teach me in this vision.

～

The winter snow of 1999 brought me another diagnosis: "E-n-d-o-m-e-t-r-i-o-s-i-s," I spelled into the online search engine. Site after site popped up in the results. "How can there be so many entries for something I had not heard of before this morning?" I said aloud to myself.

The obstetrician-gynecologist said it was a common disease, with diagnosis numbers on the rise all around the industrialized world. Infertility, sexual discomfort, ever-increasing pain, and divorce are the underlying themes. For pain control, doctors offer four common options: morphine, Eastern medicine and massage therapy, laparoscopy, and birth control pills.

I decided against morphine to avoid addiction. I used massage, but it did not cure or even ease the problem; it only lessened the pain. I had a laparoscopy, but the endometriosis regrouped with intense vehemence. The fourth option, birth control pills, was a viable one, as it eliminates or lessens the menstrual cycle, theoretically reducing the pain involved.

"Lord, why does your Church prohibit this pill, which promises me less suffering?" I wailed to heaven.

After research I discovered that through hormonal manipulation, the birth control pill actually worked in two ways. First it prevented the woman's follicles from forming into healthy eggs. (Although a woman has a specific number of eggs when she is born, these eggs are not fully formed.) Without eggs, pregnancy can not occur.

Yet sometimes, even if the pill is being used, a woman's body drops a fully formed egg into the fallopian tube. If a couple engages in intercourse, it is possible for the woman to become pregnant, even with the pill in her system. The pill will lower the woman's progesterone levels, which results in an insufficient uterine lining. Usually the baby can't implant in this type of lining. So the woman, often without knowing she is pregnant, will actually abort her own baby. She'll have a late "period" with exceptionally painful and heavy bleeding. In her ignorance she will kill her offspring.

Lord, do I stop my pain and risk killing a child, or do I endure the suffering of endometriosis? I prayed. Sharp, hot jabs poked at my ovaries. I bent over, rocking slowly. "I choose the pain. If that is what it takes, I choose the pain." The fact that it would involve even the possibility of an abortion was simply too much for me. Like my confirmation saint, Maximilian Kolbe, who laid down his life for another man who had children, I firmly believed that my Lord was asking me to have faith and offer myself for my children.

~

A few months later, when Russ and I were helping with our parish youth program, Brendan, another core team leader for the group, asked, "Deb, did you sprain your ankle?"

"No," I replied briefly.

Bemused, he cocked his head. "Then why are you limping?"

"Oh, it's just my burning ovaries," I answered with a dismissing flick of my hand. What else could I say? It would take too long to explain that for two weeks of every month the renegade uterine cells attack my ovaries, intestines, hips, lower back, and lower rib cage. The endometriosis cells, like all uterine cells, bleed. But in their case there is no place to which the blood can escape. So the blood forms scar tissue around each endometriosis cell. Every month the scar tissue cracks open into a fresh layer, giving the blood more and more tissue to break through. The pain is immense.

So I simply said to Brendan, "I'll feel better in a couple of weeks." I gave him a wink and wobbled away.

~

In early summer of 1999 Russ and I were about to enter church for Mass when a Boy Scout pointed to the pink impatiens he was selling.

"Russ, should you buy me a Mother's Day plant?"

Russ grinned as his hand gently guided my back. "How about after Mass so we won't have to carry it into church?"

"Good idea," I said as we walked inside.

We followed the readings in our *Magnificat* magazine. Peace closed my eyes as I became aware of the presence of the communion of saints.

Sweat beads slowly formed along my hairline. My hands began to tremble. Sharp stabbing pain seared my left ovary, jabbing my back into tight contractions. I straightened, jarring the pew. Pale and clammy, I looked at Russ. Alarmed, he leaned toward me.

"Russ, I am miscarrying this baby," I forced the whisper.

"How can I help?" Russ gasped.

"We'll finish the Mass. I've been through this before."

He nodded hesitantly, supported my back with his arm, and lowered his head. Tears edged his deep brown eyes. At the end of Mass Father invited all mothers, including those who were pregnant, to stand for a blessing. With hunched shoulders, I remained seated. Russ rubbed my hand. The pain crippled me. We left Mass without a Mother's Day plant. We carried, instead, the knowledge of our six dead children. Jesus, have mercy.

~

My prayer had become a constant drone, even to my own ears. "How do I handle this pain, Lord?" The answer came more slowly this time but with more certainty than any other answer in all my life. I discerned that I was to write down the various means of prayer and supplication I had turned to during the twelve years since my many illnesses had begun.

I listed and categorized some of the spiritual remedies that helped me get through the valleys of death. I was amazed as I realized each one of them is found inside my Catholic Church. If it weren't for the Lord's help, for my Catholic faith, and for the saints, there is no way I could have gotten through all the suffering I experienced. I know I would have gone insane or committed suicide by now.

These seven remedies, or recommendations, have been birthed from the depths of my own faith experience: prayer, repentance, sacrificial suffering, forgiveness and healing, fasting, bodily reparation, and eucharistic adoration. I still turn to them in times of need.

1) *Prayer:* During intense suffering I pray Saint Faustina's Chaplet of Divine Mercy. Prayed on ordinary rosary beads, the Chaplet of Divine Mercy is an intercessory prayer that extends the offering of the Eucharist, so it is especially appropriate after receiving Communion at Mass. Its brief, heartfelt pleas occupy my mind and take my focus away from my own physicality. Through it I try to discipline my mind to drift above my pain.

2) *Repentance:* The book *Fire Within* by Father Thomas Dubay, S.M., is a powerful book about prayer. The book examines the writings of Saint Teresa of Avila, who taught that everyone is called to contemplative prayer and purification.

Saint Teresa compares our relationship with God to a mansion. The mansion consists of seven circles, or areas in the soul, with the exterior area being chamber number one and the center, heaven, being chamber number seven, the highest level. Saint Teresa describes the traits and sins of souls found within each chamber and advises readers how to improve their spiritual lives.

Before entering heaven, everyone, whether on earth or in purgatory, will be freed from sin and its effects. My entire will must be given to God for His use and reconstruction. To purify me, God burns away the areas where I have built poor character. Then He rebuilds my character to a level that can withstand the purifying fires of this life and even the afterlife. When we suffer, our true character is revealed. Once revealed to us, and once we admit our weaknesses, we can experience repentance. In repentance we turn from sin and accept God's purifying forgiveness.

3) *Sacrificial Suffering:* Because all Christians—including those in heaven, in purgatory, and on earth—are connected to one another through baptism, we can pray and offer our sufferings as sacrifices for each other. When I offer sacrifices for people, I do so in three stages.

a) *Accept: I choose an attitude that accepts suffering versus one that fights it.* I embrace the suffering and offer it up by a commitment of my will. I make the suffering a gift to God and to the members of His body. I have come to see that, just because someone offers this pain, it does not mean the pain will go away. Christ's suffering was not alleviated because He offered Himself for us. He accepted every moment of His passion. So I decide to do something with the suffering instead of letting it be wasted.

When I meditate on the fact that Christ is leading me through these valleys of death, peace emerges in my heart and soul. If I did not give these sufferings greater value and meaning, I would experience, as many people do, a deep depression. But Christ saves me from this by allowing me to join my sufferings to His own suffering and thus give them supernatural meaning.

b) *Offer: I especially offer up my sufferings for those in purgatory.* My frequent prayer is: "Lord, I offer this up for the reparation of my sins, the sins of my family, of the world, and of the poor souls in purgatory." Because the souls in purgatory are being purified and are thus in a passive state (versus those in heaven and earth who are active), the Church says it is a great act of charity—and even a Christian responsibility —to pray for these souls. The second book of Maccabees (verses 12:44–46) affirms this teaching when it reveals that it is a good and wholesome deed to pray for the dead so they "might be loosed from their sins." Offering my sufferings for these poor souls gives tremendous meaning and value to the crosses that I am given.

We can also apply our prayers and sufferings for those who will not make reparation for their sins, who do not know how to do so, or who do not know that they should. This has also become one of my offerings to the world. And even though my offering may be small in and of itself, God can surely magnify this effort for great good.

In the world's eyes I may seem rather useless at times because I can't hold a full-time job nor even produce art in a speedy manner because of my ailments. Yet I have learned that I can be an effective member of the body of Christ through my prayers for the rest of the body. My worth doesn't lie in the image I have created for myself; I have worth because I am made in God's image.

c) *Fruit: I ask God to show me the fruits of my suffering.* When I see the fruits of my sacrificial sufferings, I know God has answered my prayer. My "Miracle Log" has the evidence of God's faithfulness. This log is a daily prayer register that I have kept for the past four years. On the left column of a given page I note the date and the specific prayer request that I have made, such as becoming a more effective teacher, acting with more patience, ending immorality in the movie industry, or the conversion of a friend. In the right column I list God's answers to my request. God's answers are revealed sometimes within a few minutes, sometimes over a few months or years. Sometimes they are revealed only after the person I prayed for has died. I have learned that God's time is not our time.

By moving through these three steps, I give greater meaning to suffering, something the world often thinks is meaningless. And when I do so on a regular basis, a greater trust in God develops.

4) *Forgiveness and Healing:* A fourth concept that has helped me is found in Father Robert DeGrandis' books on healing and forgiveness. An internationally known priest with a gift of healing, Father DeGrandis has noted that often a person who forgives others (including his own self) can experience physical healing himself. While not all physical suffering is due to unforgiveness in one's own heart, some of it is caused by these unresolved resentments.

Father DeGrandis authored a "Forgiveness Prayer" that encompasses all areas and stages of life, including the pain caused by family, friends, teachers, classmates, public officials, etc. He recommends praying it daily for at least a month and prior to confession. Since we tend to dwell on or "re-play" the pain caused by others, he explains, it takes a similar repetition to rid ourselves of any unforgiveness that remains in our hearts.

5) *Fasting:* I often fast from food or other pleasures on days when my health is good. I have learned that fasting builds self-control and helps develop strength to resist temptation. Fasting is a spiritual boot camp. When fasting, I remind myself that heaven contains the good things I have given up for Christ while on earth. I also ask for a specific gift or virtue. For example, lately I have been requesting prudence, which is the ability to use reason to know the truth,

to distinguish good from evil, and to seek only what pleases God. Imagine obtaining such a virtue!

6) *Bodily Reparation:* This is a practice wherein I use my whole body as a prayer. I offer a specific suffering in a part of my body in reparation for sins related to that body part. I let my pain trigger my prayer. For example, if my head hurts, I offer up my suffering in reparation for sins of the mind, such as unkind, lustful, or untrue thoughts. I offer up an earache in reparation for unholy music, impure jokes, or gossip. Sore throats are offered up for lying, gossip, or harsh words. A sore uterus is offered for fornication, birth control, divorce, homosexuality, adultery, and abortion. Every body part can be used for reparation.

God the Father, the Creator, promised that He will re-create us in His image if we repent and make reparation. He will repair the damage that sin has done to all of us. He will send forth His Spirit and renew the face of the earth!

7) *Eucharistic Adoration:* In this special time when Jesus is exposed sacramentally to us, I ask Him to hold me close as I listen to His heartbeat. In this sacred time, Jesus directs, reproves, and strengthens me.

~

My physical condition had greatly degenerated by 2001.

"How did it go with your new doctor?" Denise, my sister, asked.

"My blood tests uncovered the worst mercury poisoning my doctor has ever seen," I said. "The poisoning seems to have come from some of my red pastels, paints, dyes, and glazes. Also, small amounts may have built up through eating fish from the Great Lakes, having metal dental fillings, and getting childhood immunizations that were preserved in a mercury solution.

"The poisoning accumulated for twelve years and may be removed in six months to three years of chelation therapy. My doctor can not predict how fully my organs will heal, but some healing should occur within a year after treatments are completed. My treatment resembles debt reduction. Eliminate the smallest problem first, and then apply the freed immune resources to the next problem.

"I have many damaged organs. My hypothalamus ineffectively controls sleep, fertility hormones, and digestive enzyme production. My thyroid doesn't produce or convert thyroid hormone. My pancreas produces too much insulin. My stomach produces too few enzymes. My ovaries produce too little progesterone. My upper muscles in my left leg have temporary nerve damage and numbness. There is a growth on my tailbone, and the C.A.T. scan shows impacted sinuses, infection, and three headache-causing cysts. Holes in my intestines allow candidiasis [an infection] to invade my bloodstream.

"And I am allergic to sixteen foods." I took a deep breath.

"Oh, is that *all?*" she gulped.

"Actually, the worst part is my diet. It allows for no yeast; no dairy; no vinegar (no ketchup, mustard, mayonnaise, soy sauce, salad dressing, etc.); no fruit for three and a half months (it contains too much sugar for my pancreas); no lemon juice or tomatoes (they have too much acid); nothing fermented; no refined flour (I have poor digestion); no wheat or white rice (gluten destroys intestinal cilia); no sugar or honey (sugar feeds candidiasis); no artificial sweeteners (my immune system can't remove the toxins); no peanuts or brazil nuts; and nothing to drink except for water or tea and a quarter cup of orange juice with my supplements. Oh, and I should limit citrus fruits; animal fat (it stimulates estrogen production, which stimulates endometriosis growth); and meat (I can only eat meat without pesticide toxins or added hormones that harm ovaries). Plus, I can not eat the foods I am allergic to, and the foods I do eat must be rotated on a four-day cycle to avoid new allergy formation."

"Deb, what *can* you eat?"

"I have no idea."

"How long?"

I sighed, "Maybe eight months, maybe two years, maybe my entire life—it all depends on my progress."

~

You would think that after twelve years of fruitless wanderings looking for the "ailment culprit," I would have been elated to discover that the real root was mercury poisoning. You would think that I would immediately thank God for protecting me from taking birth control pills. If I had taken them, I wouldn't have discovered the real cause of my illness, because the birth control pill would have masked some of my pain and I wouldn't have continued searching for a doctor, like the one who eventually discovered my toxic level of mercury.

Instead worry bit at me. *How will I live without eating green beans, not to mention chocolate malt ball ice cream? I love them!* Why couldn't I have been allergic to kale or seaweed instead? At least then it would appear that I had developed some temperance!

How will I reconcile the fact that the one joy I am tempted to put above my love for God—my love for creating art—is what poisoned me? How will I forgive so many doctors for such poor advice? Will I ever be able to have children? And with all my limping, could I even make it up the steps quickly enough to comfort their cries? Do I want to continue living? If I do, where will I find the strength?

~

"Heavenly Father, I have prayed and asked my family and friends to pray. I have received the sacraments. What else can I do?"

I heard no answer.

I said aloud, "Holy Trinity, I went to confession. I still can not get rid of this despair!"

Defeated, my face in my hands, I cried. I was angry. I was mean. And I could not get out of it. For weeks vicious, self-pitying thoughts swarmed and hovered and choked away my joy. Finally the answer came.

God whispered to my soul, *Invoke all the saints you can think of. Name them, one at a time.*

So at that moment I began to beg the saints to pray unceasingly for my soul. I felt a circle of sacred wind rush in. And I felt their holiness surround me like pillars of stone.

I prayed: "Shield me from this sin of despair, Lord! I am too small and weak to overcome it. I do not know how. Your witnesses are here with me. Grant their prayer request. They are holy in Your presence. Hear them, by the merit of the Paschal Lamb's Eucharist I just received. Lord, I am not worthy to receive You, but only say the word and I shall be healed! Lamb of God, take away the sin of my soul. Lamb of God, take away the sin of my soul. Lamb of God, take away the sin of my soul!"

Then, bit by bit, the bitterness was pulled from me. My breathing slowed down. In stillness I sat, stunned. I learned that God listens to canonized saints because He has purified them. How small I was. How insufficient was my power against the evil one. How grateful I was for the Trinity's strength. I realized that God alone sustains me.

~

I glanced sideways at my friend Stacy and declared, "I am going to confession." Then the jovial, red-cheeked priest walked past me and gently chided, "Remember, only mortal sins must be confessed before Mass. All you 'venials' can take a seat if you want." I knew he was right, but I really wanted a clear conscience before attending the healing Mass to which Stacy and her husband, Rob, had invited Russ and me. So I stood in the long line and waited.

"What did you ask for?" Russ quietly inquired after Mass.

"First, for an illumination of my conscience and an increase of prudence. I want to see my soul as God sees it. Second, I told God that if it's His will, I'm ready for a physical healing. But if more grace can occur through my present sacrificial suffering, then I will accept that. It is in His hands."

"Were you physically healed?" Russ hoped aloud.

"No, but I had my best examination of conscience ever!"

God did not grant me physical healing that night, but He did heal my soul. He reminded me that holy actions such as going to Mass or sculpting a religious object, even if they are used simply as distractions from the pain, are essential and accepted as sacrifices by Our Lord.

~

On that frigid winter night in December of 2001, I eventually opened my mouth and dropped in the Chemet pill. The cold water stung my cankerous mouth as the bitter pill went down, and then the Holy Spirit cradled me—as He always does. I now know I have to go through the sorrowful mysteries of the rosary before I can reach the glorious ones! I have come to learn that this is actually the pattern that most people experience in life—we have to go through "the bad" before we can fully appreciate "the good."

Russ and I have nine children, and we have never rocked them to sleep, never heard them speak; we have never received their smiles. This is an unspeakable pain at times. When you lose a child through miscarriage, a piece of your soul goes with that child. Only in heaven will this piece be restored.

One good that has come with my great loss has been a much deeper respect for human life. Although I was pro-life prior to my miscarriages, and even prayed outside abortion clinics and spoke out against abortion, my commitment to proclaim the pro-life message has greatly increased. I am not sure if I would have reached my new level of commitment without experiencing the wounds that come from miscarriage.

Also, during my first few pregnancies I prayed and longed for healthy children. As I lost more and more, my prayer changed. I just prayed and longed for life, regardless of its form. This is a lesson that much of our society needs to learn. Too often we value life based on its utility, whereas God values all human life.

And then there is the issue of "controlling" birth. Prior to my miscarriages, I was faithful to the Church's teaching that we not stifle God's life-giving power by using artificial contraception, but my heart was not fully into it. I simply never took the time to really explore the issue. In the loss of my nine children, I have come to understand more. I have come to see that there are no guarantees in life except, of course, death.

Being an artist, I tend to live in my mind. I spend a lot of time imagining. Prior to marriage, I imagined what my life with Russ would be like. I imagined a beautiful life, a nice home, a satisfying career, and our raising five kids.

When my reality did not match my ideals, I began to doubt God's love for me. Because I kept praying for Him to remove the problems from our lives, and the problems only increased, I did not think I could trust Him. It took a long time for me to learn to pray differently.

Now I realize that problems will inevitably arise. Hardships should be expected in this life, since we are called to model ourselves after our Savior, who endured His cross even though He did not deserve it. I sometimes still complain about my crosses, but now I am better equipped to handle them.

Eventually I ask God to teach me all I can learn within the problem. Soon enough I see evidence of His presence, which increases my trust in His love for me. I try to see problems as blessings, because I know that God can use them to change my character into something better than it is now. God is bigger than my problems.

I try to let God's truth conquer my fear. I often succeed, but I often fail. I have definitely not graduated from God's "School of Obedience and Repentance" yet, but I will continue to try. Christ fell three times; I have fallen three thousand times. But He got up, and with His grace I have gotten up too. I pray that I will always continue do so.

Yes, grace is free, but it can also extract a heavy price. In the case of Saint Maximilian Kolbe, the price was his very body. He gave his life to save the life of a father and husband, to ensure the children were protected and raised in discipline. He is a patron of all families, even limited families like mine. Although I could not have known it at the time, I think this is why Providence had me choose him as my confirmation saint.

The blessings from paying the price that grace often extracts are immeasurable. They mostly come in the form of peace—a peace in knowing that I am living for and obeying God, and a peace in knowing that these sufferings on earth will be short compared to the eternal glory the faithful will receive for all eternity. This is a prize that I want to pursue, regardless of the cost.

> *May the Lord accept this sacrifice at your hands*
> *For the praise and glory of His name,*
> *For our good,*
> *And the good of all His Church.*
> *Amen.*

Eyes of Faith

Joan Ulicny

I have no memory of the accident that almost killed me at the age of twenty-nine, and only vague recollections of the weeks and months that followed it. My doctors have said that I will never remember it. God did a wonderful thing by blocking my mind from the horrific pain and trauma that I experienced.

My story is not one of tragedy—at least not to me—but of triumph. I was headed for a life of spiritual destruction when I experienced near bodily destruction on a chilly December day in 1986.

According to police records, eyewitnesses, and my parents' recollections, I left my parents' home outside of Pittsburgh, Pennsylvania, at 7:30 A.M. in my sporty white Honda Prelude, after visiting them over the Thanksgiving holiday. I faced an eight-hour drive back to my home near Poughkeepsie, New York. Because I was a young, successful corporate executive, I usually flew everywhere, but not this time. I drove because I brought my dog, Peanut, with me.

Two hours later, while cruising the speed limit on I-80 near Clarion, Pennsylvania, I moved into the passing lane, after signaling, to pass a large truck. The driver changed lanes quickly, without any warning or signal. His truck bumped my car very hard. This forced me off the road and into an immediate out-of-control spin.

I ended up in the lane of an oncoming eighteen-wheeler. The driver of this truck began pumping the brakes as he watched me spin ahead of him. He related in a distraught call to my father the next day that he was afraid of locking his brakes, jackknifing, and crushing my car. My Prelude was hardly a match for his eighteen-wheeler when we collided head-on.

It took more than an hour for an emergency crew to extract me from my car. The driver of the truck that hit me said that I was awake at the scene. But I lost consciousness on my way to Clarion Hospital. The emergency staff at Clarion immediately decided that my injuries were too severe for their facilities. Their records show that I stopped breathing, one clear indication of brain injury. I was revived and taken by ambulance to the nearest trauma unit, Allegheny General Hospital in Pittsburgh.

By the time I arrived at Allegheny, I had a breathing tube in place. I had extensive bruises, and my pupils were not equal, another sign of a brain injury. I responded only to pain, a third sign of a severe head injury.

My parents arrived at Allegheny General Hospital around 2:45 P.M., but they were only allowed to see me for a few minutes before I was taken into surgery to set my broken right femur. My leg was so badly broken, the surgeon commented, that he was amazed the bone had not come through the flesh.

I can only imagine my parents' horror at the sight of their daughter, totally incapacitated. I was attached to a heart monitor, a respirator/ventilator, and life-support. I was also undergoing blood transfusions. My mom said later that the imprint of my car shoulder strap looked as if it had been painted across my chest.

A lot of medical and legal information was presented quickly to my parents. There was no time for detailed discussion or explanation in the trauma unit, where time is a critical factor in saving lives. The initial C.A.T. scan provided an indication of brain damage, but no one discussed specific damage or its results with my parents at that time.

The doctors suspected there might be a problem with the arteries in my neck, which carry blood and oxygen to the brain. They told my parents that they wanted to do an angiogram. The procedure carried some risk because my brain had undergone such tremendous trauma. Injecting any additional substance into my body could add increased pressure to the brain and thus kill me. But without this procedure, the neurosurgeon told my father, I would surely die. My parents consented.

What the angiogram showed astonished the trauma team doctors. It revealed that all four arteries in my neck were clotted. One artery was completely occluded. One clot had already gone to my brain, where it had apparently caused a stroke. My entire left side was paralyzed.

My injury was the first of its kind ever recorded. The doctors told my family that, based on their experience, a person with two clotted arteries did not survive. Yet I lay in a coma, somehow still alive, with clots in all four arteries.

Although the doctors opted for the alternative that seemed the least risky—trying to thin my blood—they said there was no way to prevent another clot from causing further damage or even death. Prayer was all that was left. My family placed their trust in God, knowing that the phone call might come any time notifying them of my death.

My sole sibling, Jeanie, would later write: "Upon seeing you, the only thing I could liken it to was one of our older relatives who had died and was laid out in one of those horrible funeral homes. I was afraid to touch you, afraid that you might be cold, just like the corpses of those old relatives. Grandpap was there, crying; it was the first time I had ever seen him cry. Mom was in shock, racing around like she always does, in perpetual motion. Dad was shell-shocked and simply going through the motions. I felt compelled to keep composure—they needed me to be strong, and so I was."

Sister (Mary) Agnes McCormick, who served at my parents' parish, Holy Trinity Catholic Church in Robinson Township, learned of my accident and came to the hospital. I would later come to see how much of a godsend Sister Agnes was to my family in those early months. She brought along two priests, Fathers Bob Hermann and Andy Fischer, to pray over me. Sister Agnes later wrote, "When they finished [praying], I bent down over her, cupped her face in my hands and asked the Blessed Mother to help her. At that moment Joan's eyes fluttered! I brought this to the attention of both priests. I attribute this sign to their priestly blessing. When we got home, I called Mr. Ulicny [my father] to let him know that we had gone to see Joan and to tell him what had happened. The next day when Mr. and Mrs. Ulicny went to see Joan, the nurse informed them that Joan was showing initial signs of awakening from the coma. We still marvel to this day at this miraculous occurrence."

I would not fully awake from the coma for eighteen days. This time was emotionally draining for my family. They came every day to the trauma unit to hold my hand and talk with me, although I was not responsive. The doctors kept saying that a case such as mine had never been registered. They stated that my neck must have gone back and forth a hundred times in severe whiplash, yet my neck was not broken. My right leg had been crushed and surgically put together with a pin and screws. If I ever walked again, my parents were told, I would only do so with a cane.

My parents were warned that the doctors did not expect me to live. Yet I did. I later came to believe that my survival was through the intercession of Mary, the mother of Jesus.

She wanted to lead me back to her Son, whom I had ignored in the years after high school and leading up to the accident.

As I began to emerge from the coma, it was clear to everyone around me that I had lost much—for how long, my family was not sure. According to my parents, I could recognize and respond to my family, but I could not speak clearly, and my short-term memory was damaged. I had some movement on the right side of my body and less on the left side, which had been affected by the stroke. I was conscious and aware of my surroundings, but my memory was extensively damaged. As I began a program of physical and cognitive rehabilitation, my spiritual rehabilitation was the furthest thing from my mind. Yet I would soon see that this is what I needed most.

I was transferred to the Harmarville Rehabilitation Center on December 20, 1986. There I would spend nearly a year and a half in the brain injury unit, including five months as an inpatient. The glamorous, fast-paced life of Joan Ulicny, the girl from Pittsburgh who fought hard and "wowed" them at IBM, had ended. Gone were the days of "power meetings," of cutting-edge presentations in Argentina, Brazil, Canada, Mexico, and Japan, and of the excitement of business.

I would mourn that Joan Ulicny for a very long time.

Four years earlier, in the summer of 1982, I had landed a coveted international trade position with IBM in Poughkeepsie. I had recently received my master's degree from American University in Washington, D.C., in international affairs, with a concentration in international business. I aggressively pursued the IBM position and was ecstatic to get it. My life as a corporate woman of the world had begun in earnest.

Just two years later I would take even greater strides with the company, which had a worldwide reputation for management expertise, when I was promoted to management at just twenty-six years of age. This was a rare occurrence for someone with so little time with the company. I would manage a department of twelve people. I was recognized at a company banquet, held at Windows on the World, at the top of the former World Trade Center, for being the division's youngest manager.

Just as I had hoped, my new career brought me international travel, material rewards, and prestige. I was a quintessential urban woman of the 1980s, conditioned to fight like a man and shun anything that would hold me back.

But back in the summer of 1982, just weeks before I would begin my IBM career, something threatened to hold me back. I found out that I was pregnant. Shock and horror set in when the doctor told me the news.

"How could this happen? It couldn't possibly be true," I told the doctor.

But it was. I slowly walked out of her office, my feet somehow placing themselves, one in front of the other. I was numb, disconnected from the reality of the event. I felt upset that something foreign was growing within me, something that needed to be removed from my body and my life.

Steve[1] and I had been friends for two years prior to the time we started dating. He lived in the house next door to the one where I lived while I attended American University. During the year after I graduated from American, I was waitressing at night so I could keep my days open for job hunting. It was a terribly frustrating time. I had done everything right—I got my degree, and I hit the streets every day looking for work—yet no firm or government agency wanted me. Steve, on the other hand, did want me, and so

---

[1] Name has been changed.

we started dating. I grew to deeply love and trust him. He would be the first man with whom I was physically intimate.

It was also around this time that I jettisoned much of the faith of my youth. I had always been a bit of a rebel, resenting any individual or organization that attempted to dictate my personal life. I disagreed with the Church on more than a few issues, and I had more or less become one of those "cafeteria Catholics," picking and choosing from Church doctrine what I would adhere to and what I would reject. Finally I stopped attending Mass.

This combination of a lack of deep faith and the excitement of romance led me to make some very bad choices.

After the doctor's appointment I met with Steve. He asked what I intended to do. I did not answer. Instead I asked him, "Are you ready to be a father?" His silence was my answer. I was not ready to be a mother, I told him, not now—just when my big opportunity had come. The timing was all off, I convinced myself. A baby did not fit into my life right now. Steve did not protest. And so the abortion was scheduled and carried out within two weeks.

I blocked out much of my memory of that day. I do remember sitting with Steve in a large, brightly lit waiting room filled with other women and a few men. I did not let my eyes focus on anyone or anything. I could not meet their eyes, because I was certain that my fear would be reflected back to me. The chair's cushions gently pressed against my back. Steve held my hand; we hardly spoke.

The procedure went quickly. As I lay on the table, the only sound was the ominous noise of the suction instrument performing one of the most brutal of acts.

"This was my decision," I told myself. "I have the right to choose."

Soon after the abortion I left Washington, D.C., and Steve. I was headed for New York and an international corporate life. I boxed up my feelings about the abortion, labeled them as a regrettable choice that had to be made, and buried them in the back of my memory. I felt that I had accepted what I had done with responsibility and maturity, and it was time to move on. I threw myself into my career—my new love.

Adjusting to life in the business world was not difficult for me. I was hungry for its challenges. I excelled at my job, gaining confidence daily and looking constantly for ways to improve my performance for the overall benefit of the company. I was truly living my dream. The older daughter of Joseph and Rita Ulicny from the small Pittsburgh neighborhood of Crafton Heights had made it—until that fateful day when everything came to a halt.

On January 9, 1987—almost five weeks after my accident—my vision was retested. The doctors examined my color vision, hand-eye coordination, object and face recognition, and peripheral vision. There were also tests in word problemsolving and in following commands using my right and left limbs.

I had improved in all areas except my vision. The doctors, therapists, and some friends and family members began talking to me about accepting and learning to deal with my handicaps. I resisted their efforts to move me toward acceptance, focusing on one goal instead: the restoration of my eyesight. I could not imagine much promise for my future, only a life of dependency without it. I was petrified. They (correctly) interpreted my search for full recovery as a refusal to accept my reality.

A week later I went home to my parents on a weekend pass. As soon as I was taken inside their home, a small creamcolored ball of fur jumped up excitedly and licked my face repeatedly. From what I could see, it certainly looked and acted like Peanut, and he seemed to recognize me, but I still could not be sure because of my poor vision. I kept looking at him, wondering if this was a replacement my parents had bought. They teased me, amused that I thought they might try to fool me with a new dog.

Even if I could not see well, I felt warm and safe in my parents' home, something I had not felt in a very long time in the cold rehab. Sleeping in my own room, in my own bed (a bed without cold steel retaining bars), without waking to the loud voices of other people in pain, was a gift. For the first time since my accident I felt truly grateful.

It took me a long time to accept the fact that this accident had happened to me. My emotions vacillated between a desperate fear and a raging anger unlike any I had ever known. I was not comfortable with either emotion, nor with the dependency I was forced to accept. My pride prevented me from accepting that this was something I could not handle alone. I wanted desperately to be in control, and I was frustrated because I knew I was not.

As I assessed my situation, the extent of my injuries became increasingly frightening. With the exception of a broken leg, all my injuries were brain-related. I had trouble thinking of words, and putting a simple sentence together was a struggle. The standard I.Q. tests administered to all brain-injured patients showed that I had the intelligence of a third-grade student. I was confined to a wheelchair, my left arm paralyzed. There was something seriously wrong with my eyesight. I could see light and shapes roughly, but I could not see clearly at all, and I could not distinguish between different colors any more.

I progressed slowly in my therapies—too slowly to take much satisfaction from them. While I did my best to maintain some outward appearance of calm, inside I was an emotional tangle of knots and cried out unceasing questions to God.

"What have I done to deserve this?" I asked Him repeatedly. "Why have you forgotten me? Why do You hate me? What could You possibly want from me that justified sparing my life?" Sometimes I cried out, "Why didn't you just let me die? This is too hard, Lord. You picked the wrong person for this one."

It did not seem to matter whether I yelled or just cried softly. God did not seem to hear me or care. I felt so alone. Nobody understood what I was going through, how petrified I was of not seeing, how frightened of being dependent for life.

I had no answers. Instead of listening and searching, I rationalized, creating my own answer: Obviously I had done something terribly wrong to deserve this. I saw my situation as punishment for neglecting God, for the many years of lip service I had paid Him. I had much to learn about how God works and about His infinite mercy.

Spiritually I was dead. I did not readily offer any thanks for the fact that I was still among the living. Caught between self-pity and self-hate daily, I did not feel alive; I merely went through the motions. Nor did I consider the idea that I had been given a second chance at a spiritual life. I was too consumed by my emotional pain to feel any joy. Overwhelmed by my injuries and the realization that this horrible accident had happened, I was paralyzed with a fear greater than any I had ever known.

As my fear grew, I saw that it could incapacitate me, so I began to battle back. I fought to regain the life I had once known and cherished, a life I had worked diligently to attain and that was unjustly taken from me. Yet deep within me, I knew my life would never be the same, that *I* would never be the same.

I was given strength and courage to fight back, a strength and courage that, I recognize now, was not born of myself. It was a gift from my Creator. When I cried out for something to hold onto in my despair, He heard my cries, saw my fear, and in time answered me. First I had to learn patience, that all things come in God's time, not mine—a difficult lesson for a young woman who thought she controlled so much.

Between my rage and my tears, I came to terms with the truth: Although my legal blindness resulted directly from the accident, my spiritual blindness had begun many years before. I learned that God moves a person's heart to seek change in accordance with His will. I learned to let Him lead.

I let others in only slowly, as I learned to trust again and make myself vulnerable. I became aware of my dependence and neediness but still did not trust that others would accept me. I did not want their pity, and I did not want anyone to feel that they had to accept me as I was, damaged; it seemed far too much to ask.

Pride is an awful thing. I was so ashamed of myself, and so enveloped in my own emotional pain, that I could not reach out to others or let them reach out to me. I avoided them before they could reject me.

On February 25, 1987, I turned thirty years old. I told God again that it would have been better to let me die. I was angry, I was scared, and I blamed God. I saw no promise for my future, and I felt no joy or thanks in my heart.

I was formally released as an inpatient from Harmarville that April 15. (How different this "tax day" was from those in recent years!) I had mixed emotions about my dismissal; I was happy to go home, eager for the freedom of a non-institutional environment, but I was anxious. I was leaving without having recovered my eyesight.

I was also leaving with my "spiritual sight" weak. I still believed God was on an active campaign to make my life miserable. I could not pray; I was too hurt and too angry. Any conversation I initiated with God was a one-sided shouting match.

Six months after my accident my progress was far slower than I had hoped. Yet I looked at every accomplishment as my own, born of my own endeavors. I did not credit the One responsible for permitting all my achievements.

Externally, nothing really changed. I continued my out-patient therapy at Harmarville and the neuropsychologist's home program. But finally, instead of questioning why He had not let me die, I began asking why God had permitted me to live. I found myself telling God that I needed His help in learning to trust Him in what I knew would be difficult months ahead.

Then one day in January of 1988 (about thirteen months after my accident), my father read to me a newspaper article about a remote village in the former Yugoslavia, called Medjugorje. Six young people claimed that Mary had been appearing to them there on a daily basis since 1981.[2] Although the Church was still investigating these claims, pilgrimages were permitted. Little did I know that the events said to be taking place in this faraway village—whether they were ultimately true or not—would become the catalyst in resurrecting and recharging my faith.

---

[2] The alleged apparitions of Medjugorje are claims to private revelation. Private revelations are not offered or held by the Church as an article of faith—there is no obligation to believe them, even if the events should some day be judged by the Church to be of supernatural origin. The references to these alleged apparitions in this book are not to be viewed as an affirmation of their validity on the part of the publisher. As with all matters of faith and morals, we should give our assent to the Magisterium of the Church, which Christ established to teach and govern in His name.

The article told of a woman from the Pittsburgh area named Rita Klaus who, after suffering for twenty years, had been healed of multiple sclerosis (MS) in a well-documented case. Klaus attributed her recovery to these reported apparitions of the Blessed Virgin Mary. I told my father that I believed miracles of physical healing could happen, but that Mrs. Klaus—who had studied to be a nun but received a dispensation from her vows when she was diagnosed with MS—must have been very special to God for choosing this vocation. He must have loved her very much. I was certainly no candidate for the same kind of grace.

The next month Sister Agnes called to tell me that on Valentine's Day, Rita Klaus would be one of two speakers at a nearby church. She asked if my father and I would like to go.

Rita began her talk with much of the same material that had been included in the article. As her handicaps and despondency had increased, she said, she became increasingly bitter, and she thought God no longer loved her. She was so angry with God and with herself that she could no longer pray. My attention perked up after hearing this statement. She too had felt abandoned by God, and she had felt that He no longer loved her. *She really is a normal person*, I thought to myself. *She thought God had quit on her too.*

As she described the healing in her life, Rita seemed to shy away from the word miracle. Instead she described what happened to her as a "beautiful grace from God." I thought to myself, *How can I get some of that grace?*

I vaguely remembered my early religion classes and that little blue catechism book, which said that one way to attain grace was to receive the sacraments. Although lately I had received Communion at Mass on Sundays, I realized that I had not received it with a pure heart. I had not been to confession in years. Before my accident, I just did not care.

After my accident, I had been too angry with God to examine my relationship with Him.

As I listened to Rita, I felt perhaps I needed to look at my relationship with God more closely, with something other than my anger. If understanding my life and God's plan for it was possible, it would have to begin with a renewed relationship between us. Shortly after attending her talk, I went to confession. For the first time I was aware that I needed to be reconciled with God.

After more than a year I returned to my apartment near Poughkeepsie with my mother for a visit and to find my passport, which would be needed for the pilgrimage I now resolved to make. It took a long time to muster up the will to visit my apartment because I saw this visit as a public statement that I was never going back to IBM. The apartment represented so much to me. It was *my* apartment. It symbolized my freedom from the confines of my adolescent life, from my family, from my blue-collar upbringing where the fear of layoffs was so prevalent in the 1970s.

Walking through my apartment, I considered a future radically different from the one I had planned. With my health gone and my intellect impaired, I was left rootless. How would I support myself? What could I do with my life?

I always thought that the strongest people were the ones who clearly defined just what they wanted and then went after it. I knew in my heart that I would now live a life of dependence, which I always had thought was a sign of weakness. What I did not realize then was that I would never learn to depend on God until I first learned to rely on others.

But there was still great anger in my heart. I remember saying to God one day, "You knew exactly what to take from me to defeat me, didn't You, Lord? I could have come out of the accident without an arm or leg or even confined to a wheelchair, and then I could have gone on with my life, but You made me dependent by not healing my blindness."

Before we left the apartment, I went to the drawer where I kept my passport. When I opened the drawer, I noticed something strange: My pearl rosary (which I had bought many years before) was lying on top of the passport. I did not recall praying the rosary in the months prior to the accident, but there it was. Although I still felt aimless, I had a strange feeling that, through this "sign," God was somehow blessing the venture I was about to begin.

When I returned to Pittsburgh, I contacted a Father Vincent Cvitkovic, a Franciscan priest from the area, at the prompting of a friend. In that first call Father listened as I spoke of my fears about my handicaps, my anger, and my confusion about why God had allowed this terrible thing to happen to me. Father Vincent responded with empathy. He spoke simply and with a self-assurance I did not possess. Before we hung up the phone he said: "You will see things you would never have seen before the accident."

I continued to hear more about healings that were supposedly taking place in Medjugorje. Cancer, deafness, multiple sclerosis, even blindness were said to have been cured. Again, I thought I had found a way to overcome my blindness.

It has happened for others, I thought, *maybe the Blessed Mother would ask her Son to heal me too.* I wanted to see again; that was my primary goal in wanting to travel halfway around the world to a place I had heard of only two and a half months earlier. At IBM I was trained to identify the source of a problem and then aggressively seek its solution. This is how I viewed the pilgrimage first and foremost. It offered a solution to my blindness.

My trip was really a means to an end—to receive a gift of physical healing and to see clearly once again—versus a means for spiritual renewal. I also harbored doubts about whether Mary would intercede and help me directly. She knew very well how long I had been away from my faith. Perhaps she would see me as a hypocrite, turning to her only in my time of great need. I did not want to be a hypocrite, but I needed help, and I did believe that her Son could heal me. Although I knew I was not worthy of such a gift, I felt compelled to go and ask.

After a long string of coincidences and serendipitous connections, my mother and I left for Yugoslavia on April 6, 1988 —six months earlier than originally planned. Before we left, I found out that several people from our church, including Sister Agnes, would be there at the same time.

I believe I was called there by Mary, but what I actually found there was her Son. There I reacquainted myself with Christ and His teachings, and I gained an understanding of what I could and would do for Him—not just what He could do for me.

One morning we visited Vicka, one of the alleged visionaries. Through a translator I told her my story. When I finished, Vicka looked intently at me. Then the translator shared with me her response: "Vicka says that God has given you this cross, Joan, because He loves you and because He wants something from you, something that only you can give Him. She says that you should continue to pray much and fast much, and most importantly, you must believe."

Vicka's words were now a second prophecy about my future. These two statements made me think more about the possibility that my life was going to have meaning. Maybe something would come from the tragedy.

While climbing the Hill of Apparitions later that week, the hill designated by the six young people as the spot where they first saw the Mother of God, I was startled to run into Sister Agnes and Father Hermann, one of the priests who had prayed over me while I lay near death at Allegheny General Hospital. Sister Agnes excitedly announced that she wanted to take a picture of me placing my left hand on the cross that marked the spot where Mary allegedly first appeared. Sister knew I had no feeling in that hand due to the stroke I had suffered.

As I awkwardly touched the cross, I found myself saying out loud, "God, forgive the man who did this to me."

I was stunned, as was my mother, who was standing beside me.

"Joanie, where did that come from?" my mom asked me.

"I do not know . . ."

Until that moment I had vowed that I would never forgive the man who had caused my accident and had left me to die. I did not know it then, but forgiving the driver was a necessary and much needed grace. My cold heart was starting to heal.

I did not return physically changed or healed. I was still legally blind, and I still had limited use of my left hand. But a spiritual healing that I could only dimly sense was growing within me, calling me to a closer relationship with God. Now I felt I could pray for spiritual change, for patience, for faith, and for the courage to let God dictate those changes, rather than only begging to have my old life restored. I returned home with a new sense of hope, a desire to know God better, and the intention to be open to God's plan for me. I knew it would not be easy to relinquish control over my life to Him, but I promised to try.

I quickly became aware that my concentration on the mysteries of the rosary was more focused than ever before. I was not just following the words; instead I could meditate on the lives of Christ and Mary as I prayed. As I meditated on the sorrowful mysteries, it occurred to me that Christ and

Mary had been human too. They had suffered, and they understood my suffering. This realization comforted me as nothing else had.

"They understand," I repeated to myself. I asked God to help me trust in Him, as He wanted me to do.

In time I discovered that real strength—real character—did not come from within but only in the realization that we are reliant on God for all our needs; it comes when we acknowledge that there is a Higher Power who is ready to give guidance and direction, if we are willing to allow Him. Only God knows what is best for us, what it is that we lack, and what we really need.

It would be months after my return from the pilgrimage before the inspiration to start writing took a hold of me. One day I simply announced to my parents, "I will write my story and call it *A Greater Vision*." And so I did, eventually writing about the trauma of my accident, the intensive rehabilitation, and my horror at all that had been inflicted upon me. I held nothing back, convinced that I was writing only for myself.

I finished writing my story a year later, in 1989. But something about the manuscript felt incomplete, so I set it aside for the next two years, without knowing why.

In 1991 I learned of the Saint Louis de Montfort consecration, a thirty-three-day prayer exercise that culminates with one consecrating (or entrusting) one's life to Jesus through His mother Mary. I was intrigued and felt compelled to make this consecration, knowing in my heart that Our Lady's intercession was the only reason I was alive. This consecration was the turning point in my spiritual life. Nothing could have prepared me for the changes that came after I made it. The consecration is a pledge to be Mary's agent in the world and to be used in whatever way she chooses in order to lead souls to her Son. Mary would soon reveal to me the way in which I was to be used.

By now I had confessed my abortion and thought I had made peace with God. I was growing in strength, physically and spiritually. My balance was better. My speech was better. I was attending Mass almost daily, going to monthly confession, praying my rosary regularly. But after I made the consecration, something happened that would shake me to the core.

In the months leading up this point, memories of my abortion would pop into my mind. They would come while I was at Mass, or driving with my parents, or carrying clothes to the washing machine. I kept these thoughts to myself.

I got up one morning and had just turned on the TV when another flash came to my mind. I had a distinct inner feeling that Our Lady wanted me to write about my abortion in my book. I recoiled at the idea. I fell to my knees in prayer and then asked aloud, "Is that what you want? You want me to write about that? Is that what this is all about?"

I had not told anyone about my abortion. It was my darkest secret, hidden even from my family. How was I now going to write about it in my book, which might then be read by total strangers?

I felt that Our Lady then said to me, *Have you truly given yourself to my Son through me? Let me use this to save souls. I know there will be shame, but will you do this for us?*

I remembered the verse in Saint Luke's Gospel, "Of those to whom much has been given, much will be expected" (Luke 12:48). I had been given much. I was given my life back, and I was given a second chance at a spiritual life. How could I not follow Mary's prompting? I had to sacrifice this secret for the sake of others.

And so, typing with one hand, I found the courage to write my story in its entirety, trusting that God and His mother would use it for good. I wrote of how, as a twenty-four-year-old who did not want to sacrifice an opportunity for a prestigious career, I chose to sacrifice my child through abortion.

Much of my memory is gone because of the brain injury, but I have never forgotten my abortion. I do not believe a woman ever forgets. I have thought about my baby many times over the past twenty years and have even given her a name, Charlotte (I am not sure why, but I have always thought of my child as a girl). With each new year I thought about what she would have been doing: "It is 1985, Charlotte would be a toddler." "It is 1988, Charlotte would have started grade school." "It is the year 2000, Charlotte would have graduated from high school." Mary gave me the courage to take ownership of my child.

One fewer person exists today because of something I chose to do. The reality of what I had done paralyzed me with fear and shame, though I would not admit that to myself for a long, long time. It was my heavenly mother who showed me that I needed to seek God's help and also His forgiveness. I also needed healing. I believe a part of me stopped living when I had my abortion. It was the part that sought out my Creator. I went on living in a body, but had a deadened soul.

I came to see that my healing could not take place apart from Christ. The sacrament of reconciliation was instrumental in the healing process, as God had intended it to be. Great peace came to me after I was reconciled not only with my Creator but with the child I chose to abort so long ago.

I have struggled to answer the question, How does a person come back from abortion? I have learned that one must first accept God's forgiveness and grow daily in the awareness that God's love and mercy are always greater than our sins. This awareness comes only in prayer. We must accept God's forgiveness if we are to ever forgive ourselves.

Coming to know Christ, finding peace in Christ, and finding Christ in the cross: This, I believe, is what Our Lady wanted me to understand when she inspired the words in my heart, *Love your cross, daughter, for it has brought you closer to my Son and to me.* Peace would come only as I surrendered to the cross of Christ. My cross would break me from the evil that held my soul in bondage all the years I chose not to recognize my sin—all the years I rationalized and justified what I had done.

I believe it was Mary who awakened me from the physical coma I lay in immediately after the accident, but more importantly, she helped me awaken from the spiritual coma that had stolen over my soul. She helped me to see myself as God saw me. The shame I felt caused me to look away. I had to come to terms with my past and then choose to not live in it any more. And most importantly, I had to accept the great gift of forgiveness that God had granted me.

I see now that God, in His infinite wisdom, permitted the car accident, though I do not believe He caused it. God permits suffering, I believe, so that we learn to depend not on ourselves but on Him. There is not a suffering that He asks us to endure in which He is not present. I had neglected my soul far too long, and Love came after me.

I am still blind, but I now see with a greater vision, with eyes of faith. People marvel at how I now run marathons and downhill ski despite the fact that I can barely see and was told I would never walk again. These are certainly good, natural accomplishments, but the most glorious part of my story is that my soul was converted to Christ through a tragedy.

God gave me another opportunity to be in heaven with Him—that is the miraculous part of my story. I have been given two chances at physical life—when I was first born and then after my accident—and I have been given two chances at spiritual life—when I was baptized as a baby and now through my adult conversion prompted by my accident. And

God did this for me despite the fact that I took a life, the life of my baby. This is the real miracle.

Although I still yearn for my sight to be restored, I no longer mourn the loss. My blindness, in particular, has been the tool God used to cause me to seek Him in a way I never would have if I could see. What changes a soul to become a lover of God can only, in fact, come from God. It is not what we do but what He does through us. I see my physical blindness as God's gift to me; my total acceptance of this will be my gift back to Him. I trust that God will give me the grace I need to accept whatever crosses might come in the future.

In light of what I have gained from the trials of the past fifteen years, I would not go back to my former "successful" self. In my loss I have gained everything because I have gained Christ. Like the psalmist, "I had to be afflicted so that I may learn God's teachings, so that I may learn God's ways" (Psalm 119). Only through my suffering and trials could God recreate me, refine me, remold me, into what He wanted. And only through His grace could I be sustained.

He can do the same for you or anyone you know who suffers. He can use our sufferings for His glory and then glorify us in the process. We simply need to give Him the opportunity to do so.

Afterword

Power Made Perfect In Weakness

Understanding the meaning of suffering became an urgent personal concern for me not too long ago when I began to develop excruciating pain in my neck. I discovered that the cause was a split disk. While I knew much about the Catholic Church's teaching on redemptive suffering, I did not know how to put those teachings into practice in my life. Furthermore, I did not know why or how suffering could become a spiritually profitable ordeal.

Through this experience I came to see that an academic study of suffering can only go so far. Suffering cannot be completely taught in the objective; suffering is a vocation, a calling that can only be truly understood in the school of suffering. Only by living through it can we more fully understand its redemptive power.

Most of us have unanswered questions about suffering. We wonder how God, if He loves us, could allow us to suffer. Yet throughout salvation history we see that the ways of God are often not the ways of man. Like the pearl fisherman seeking a treasure embedded in the dark heart of the oyster, we too must seek the shining pearls of grace hidden in the darkness of suffering.

When we survey human history, it becomes evident that suffering is simply a given for human beings. It is not a matter of *whether* we will suffer during our lives, but *when*. And more specifically, *how* will we suffer: poorly or well?

When we fail to find meaning in our suffering, we can

easily fall into despair. But once we find meaning in our suffering, it is astounding what we can endure. The key is not the suffering itself, but the meaning found within it.

Would you be willing to endure great agony for six months simply to protect a sparrow? Probably not. You would be hard pressed to find meaning in such suffering. On the other hand, who among us would refuse to endure even years of pain for the sake of a daughter or son? We would be willing and even eager to suffer, because our love for our children would give meaning to such suffering.

In a similar way, the key to understanding suffering is found in the love of God the Father for His Son and for all His children. Our suffering finds meaning in the life, death, and resurrection of Jesus Christ.

When asked, "Why did Jesus come to earth?" people often answer, "He came to die for me." While this is true, there must be more, for if He came only to die, then why couldn't He have simply died as an infant? He was fully God as an infant, so why did He not offer Himself shortly after His birth? As we will see, the mission of Jesus involved more than simply dying. It involved a complete identification with humanity, including human suffering.

The Gospel of Luke tells us how Jesus was walking with two of His disciples on the road to Emmaus shortly after His resurrection, yet somehow they did not recognize Him; in fact, they did not yet know that He had risen from the grave (see Luke 24:13–35). Not surprisingly, then, the men were grieving over Jesus' torturous death. They had thought that He would restore the earthly kingdom of Israel, but He had not. So they were deeply disillusioned as well.

Consider the irony here: Since these men failed to recognize Jesus on their journey, they did not know that they were actually walking with God and talking to God even as they were complaining about God! In the midst of their suffering, these two did not know that the One who suffered for them was staring them in the face. Jesus finally had to say: " 'O foolish men, and slow of heart to believe all that the prophets have spoken! Was it not necessary that the Christ should suffer these things and enter into His glory?' And beginning with Moses and all the prophets, He interpreted to them in all the scriptures the things concerning Himself" (vv. 25–27).

Note what Jesus said about Himself: It was *necessary* that He suffer. In a sense, the question of our suffering begins with a more basic question: Why did God suffer in Christ?

To answer this question we must see the relationship between Adam and Jesus in terms of their relationship to God the Father. The Apostle Paul finds a direct correlation between the fall of Adam and the victory of Christ: "For as in Adam all die, so also in Christ shall all be made alive. . . . Thus it is written, 'The first man Adam became a living being'; the last Adam became a life-giving spirit" (1 Corinthians 15:22, 45).

Shortly after Adam and Eve's creation they underwent a test in the Garden of Eden (see Genesis chapters 2 and 3). Created in the image and likeness of God, Adam and Eve possessed an intellect and a will. In other words, they could know a thing and act on it. So they were given directives and a choice.

Would they use their intellect and will to obey their Creator? This test, if successful, would complete their creation by giving them the opportunity to enter fully into the life of the Trinity through obedience and sacrifice.

Adam was given two commands by God: to till and keep the garden and to refrain from eating from the tree of the knowledge of good and evil (see Genesis 2:8-9, 15–17). If Adam ate from the tree of the knowledge of good and evil, the consequences would be death. Shortly after God gave these commands to Adam, He fashioned Eve from Adam, creating a spousal relationship between the man and woman. It is implied in the biblical text that Adam, as husband, would communicate God's commands to Eve.

The Hebrew word translated here as "keep" (Genesis 2:15) loses some of its impact in English versions of the text. The term is *shamar* and means literally "to guard." Adam was told to *guard* the garden and cultivate it.

At this point in the account, we might well ask, "Guard against what?" But as we read on in the third chapter of Genesis, the answer to that question becomes clear.

> Now the serpent was more subtle than any other wild creature that the LORD God had made. He said to the woman, "Did God say, 'You shall not eat of any tree of the garden'?" And the woman said to the serpent, "We may eat of the fruit of the trees of the garden; but God said, 'You shall not eat of the fruit of the tree which is in the midst of the garden, neither shall you touch it, lest you die.'" But the serpent said to the woman, "You will not die. For God knows that when you eat of it your eyes will be opened, and you will be like God, knowing good and evil" (Genesis 3:1–5).

So often when people read about the serpent in Eden their mind goes back to children's Bibles that depict it as a small snake slyly staring at Eve. However, the Hebrew word for "serpent" is *nahash*, translated as "dragon" in Isaiah 27:1 and "sea monster" in Job 26:13. Clearly this was an imposing foe that did not have Adam and Eve's wellbeing in mind.

We must understand here that the serpent's point of attack was not to tempt the woman to doubt the existence of God. Rather, he raised in her mind doubt about whether she could *trust* God. Here was the test Adam and Eve faced: Created to participate in the life of the Trinity, would they fully enter into the life of the Trinity by imitating the self-giving communion of the Godhead? In short, would our original parents trust God?

From Adam's perspective, the serpent's statement could even have been interpreted as a veiled threat. They would not die if they ate the fruit—but if they refused to do so, the serpent himself might kill them.

Adam and Eve thus faced several choices: Would they entrust themselves to their Father, would they enter into combat with the enemy and guard the garden, would Adam defend his bride? Would Adam risk his life in a self-sacrificing offering? Or would Adam succumb to pride and rely upon his own resources, preserving his natural life?

Of course, we know the outcome of the test: Adam and Eve failed. Their disobedience resulted in their death. They had sought to preserve their natural life, and in the process they had lost their supernatural life. They lost their relationship to God as His children, and they died spiritually. As a result even their natural life was affected, as sin ate away at their bodies and minds. Suddenly life was quite limited.

But God in His mercy would not give up on mankind. His words are the first announcement of the Gospel, the good news foretelling the day when the Messiah would crush the head of the enemy by self-giving sacrifice: "I will put enmity between you and the woman, and between your seed and her seed; he shall bruise your head, and you shall bruise his heel" (Genesis 3:15). Even so, we should note that this initial declaration of the good news warned of a bruising—or in other words, *suffering*.

Adam was given the opportunity to imitate the self-giving, life-giving love of the Trinity, but he failed. The result was a curse.

> To the woman God said, "I will greatly multiply your pain in childbearing; in pain you shall bring forth children, yet

your desire shall be for your husband, and he shall rule over you." And to Adam he said, "Because you have listened to the voice of your wife, and have eaten of the tree of which I commanded you, 'You shall not eat of it,' cursed is the ground because of you; in toil you shall eat of it all the days of your life; thorns and thistles it shall bring forth to you; and you shall eat the plants of the field. In the sweat of your face you shall eat bread till you return to the ground, for out of it you were taken; you are dust, and to dust you shall return" (Genesis 3:16–19).

The consequences of Adam and Eve's sin, while appearing to be quite bad, would actually double as a remedial lesson, showing them that good fruit can come out of suffering. Eve would give herself to her husband, resulting in the pain of childbirth. But the cries of childbirth would soon turn to tears of joy as both parents celebrated the wonder of parenthood. Adam's suffering through toil had good fruit as well: the food he would bring forth from the earth.

As salvation history developed, God made successive covenants with Noah, Abraham, Moses, and David. But in every case man fell short of completely offering himself to God, as Adam should have done. If the love of the Trinity were to be imitated in man, God would have to become a Man and face the trial that Adam faced.

The promised Messiah, Jesus Christ, became a Man two thousand years ago and fulfilled the law by loving the world through the ultimate sacrifice of His life (see Romans 13:10). Saint Paul calls Jesus the "last Adam" (1 Corinthians 15:45) because He laid down His life "as a ransom for many" (Mark 10:45).

Jesus conquered death by taking on human nature, "that through death He might destroy him who has the power of death, that is, the Devil" (Hebrews 2:14). Christ loved by freely offering Himself for you and me, and in the process

He not only purchased us but set an example to show us how to love as He loves.

The serpent in the Garden of Eden suggested to Adam and Eve that there was an easier way to fulfill their destiny: to grasp power by eating of the tree of the knowledge of good and evil. The serpent's remarks implied that they could be like God without self-giving love. This was of course a lie, but Adam and Eve bought it.

Thousands of years later Jesus faced a similar challenge when the enemy suggested to Him that fulfilling His destiny could be done without completely offering Himself up. After giving the keys of the kingdom to Saint Peter (see Matthew 16:19), Jesus announced that He was going to Jerusalem to suffer many things and be killed. Peter reacted to Jesus' announcement of suffering and death with the same spirit conveyed by the serpent in the Garden of Eden: "God forbid, Lord! This shall never happen to you."

But Jesus recognized the false solution to the grave predicament of mankind. He responded: "Get behind me, Satan! You are a hindrance to me; for you are not on the side of God, but of men" (16:21–23).

As Jesus, the last Adam, began to move toward the Garden of Gethsemane, Satan entered Judas (see Luke 22:3). Jesus entered the garden (Matthew 26:36), and then Judas entered the garden (v. 47), setting up a scenario parallel to what had taken place in the Garden of Eden. We see such parallels as well in the description of Jesus' passion: His sweat became like great drops of blood (see Luke 22:44) and He bore the crown of thorns (see John 19:5), reminders of the consequences of Adam's failed ordeal (see Genesis 3:18–19).

When Jesus faced His ordeal, however, He did not fail. Jesus did what Adam should have done: "In the days of his flesh, Jesus offered up prayers and supplications, with loud cries and tears, to him who was able to save him from death, and he was heard for his godly fear. Although he was a Son, he learned obedience through what he suffered; being made perfect he became the source of eternal salvation to all who obey him" (Hebrews 5:7–9).

Though Jesus was in the form of God, He "did not count equality with God a thing to be grasped, but emptied himself, taking the form of a servant, being born in the likeness of men. And being found in human form he humbled himself and became obedient unto death, even death on a cross" (Philippians 2:5–8). Jesus completely emptied Himself and demonstrated the love of God in all its fullness.

The good news is that He rose from the dead, defeating death, hell, and the grave. Indeed, Jesus answered the question first raised in the Garden of Eden—"Can we trust God?"—with a resounding *yes!* Unlike Adam, Jesus obeyed the Father and poured out His life for His bride. When we realize that the bride of Christ is the Church, and Jesus loved us this much, it is almost too much to take in. Oh, how we are loved!

But now—what about us and our suffering? Didn't Jesus suffer and die so that we would not have to? No doubt Jesus suffered and died that we might become a part of the family of God, spiritually healed and sharing in His nature. But He did not eliminate suffering.

The work of Christ does not guarantee an escape from suffering. No—instead, He has changed the meaning of suffering. We are now joined through baptism with Christ in His death and resurrection, and we have become intimately **joined to Him, so much so that we are His Body. Because** of our union with Christ, even our suffering is changed; it becomes redemptive.

Pope John Paul II said in his Apostolic Letter "On the Christian Meaning of Human Suffering" that "in the cross of Christ not only is the redemption accomplished through suffering, but also human suffering itself has been redeemed" (*Salvifici Doloris*, 19). In other words, suffering is worth something if it is in union with Christ.

If the weakness of the Cross—the point at which Jesus was emptied and lifted up—was confirmed by the Resurrection, then our weakness is capable of being infused with the same power manifested in the cross of Christ. Saint Paul experienced much weakness and suffering, but when he prayed about it, Christ answered: "My grace is sufficient for you, for my power is made perfect in weakness." As a result, the apostle could proclaim, "I will all the more gladly boast of my weaknesses, that the power of Christ may rest upon me" (see 2 Corinthians 12:7–9).

Saint Paul understood that our life is a cooperation with the work of Christ when he wrote: "Now I rejoice in my sufferings for your sake, and in my flesh I complete what is lacking in Christ's afflictions for the sake of his body, that is, the Church" (Colossians 1:24). Think about that: Paul said that something is lacking in Christ's afflictions. What could possibly be lacking in Christ's afflictions? Our part!

Our part may be miniscule compared to His. Nevertheless, as Pope John Paul II has said, our sufferings are "a very special particle of the infinite treasure of the world's Redemption" (*Salvifici Doloris*, 27). This is how our suffering can take on meaning: When joined to Christ, suffering is changed and actually becomes redemptive. We participate with Christ in redeeming the world.

Today, Jesus tells us that if we are to follow Him we must deny ourselves and take up our cross daily (see Luke 9:23). Our lives become an imitation of and participation in the love of the Trinity when we offer up our complete lives in union with Christ. As Saint Paul put it:

We are afflicted in every way, but not crushed; perplexed, but not driven to despair; persecuted, but not forsaken; struck down, but not destroyed; always carrying in the body the death of Jesus, so that the life of Jesus may also be manifested in our bodies. For while we live we are always being given up to death for Jesus' sake, so that the life of Jesus may be manifested in our mortal flesh. knowing that he who raised the Lord Jesus will raise us also with Jesus and bring us with you into his presence" (2 Corinthians 4:8–11, 14).

The resurrection is our guarantee that we can trust our heavenly Father. We can participate in the life-giving love of the Trinity by laying down our lives for the sake of His kingdom. The fruit of our suffering is raised to a supernatural level; it becomes eternal in nature.

It is in the midst of suffering that we experience most deeply the love of God. We enter the very heart of the Trinity, and it is there that we come to know God. Christ allows us to participate in His cross because that is His means of allowing us to share in the very inner life of God.

This is why sometimes "bad things happen to good people." Remember Mary, the mother of Jesus, who said yes to God prior to the Incarnation. This *yes*, her *fiat*, would result in great pain; as Simeon told her: "A sword will pierce through your own soul also" (Luke 2:35). But what was the fruit of Mary's suffering? Life for the entire world.

The fact that Jesus suffered and died does not mean that we will not suffer. In fact, we are told that we can expect some suffering if we follow Him (see Matthew 16:24). Jesus does not remove all suffering from us; He changes our suffering and makes it redemptive. Jesus empowers us with His life and enables us to love as He loves by offering our lives in union with Him.

Are you suffering now? Do not despair. This is your opportunity to draw close to Christ and entrust yourself to God (see 1 Peter 2:23; 4:19). It is by taking up your cross and following Christ that you come to know that indeed "all things work for good for those who love God, who are called according to his purpose" (Romans 8:28).

What is the worst thing that has ever happened on earth? Deicide, the murder of God on the Cross. What was its result? The salvation of the world. If out of the worst thing resulted the best thing, then imagine what God can bring out of your situation.

You have read in this book the true stories of people who entrusted themselves to God in the midst of intense suffering. When life hit them "square between the eyes," they picked themselves up from the ground, pursued the Lord, and discovered a treasure, a joy in the midst of their pain. They embraced their suffering and learned about love in the midst of it.

How did these people respond to adversity? They joined their will to the will of Christ. They entrusted their hearts to their heavenly Father. They went to Mass as often as possible, the best place to "offer up" their pain. They spent time in prayer by adoring the Lord in the Blessed Sacrament. They took the focus off themselves and remained faithful in their earthly affairs. They kept an eternal perspective, understanding that one day there will be no more pain or tears, and the fruit of their suffering will have had eternal benefits.

Pope John Paul II sums up best the profound reality they knew: "Down through the centuries and generations it has been seen that in suffering there is concealed a particular power that draws a person interiorly close to Christ, a special grace" (*Salvifici Doloris* 26). In the compelling stories of those who have learned to join their suffering to Christ's, we come to see more clearly how truly amazing that grace can be!

Editor & Contributor Contact Information

To reach one of the editors or contributors by mail, please write to:

(Name of Writer)
c/o Ascension Press
P.O. Box 1990
West Chester, PA 19380
AmazingGrace@AscensionPress.com

Editors:

Jeff Cavins
jcavins@attbi.com
P.O. Box 1533
Maple Grove, MN 55311

Matthew Pinto
mpinto@ascensionpress.com
P.O. Box 1990
West Chester, PA 19380

Contributors:

Mike & Kathie Clarey
AmazingGrace@ascensionpress.com
(c/o Mike Clarey)

Carl Cleveland
tulaneanimal@aol.com

Dr. Kim Hardey
sbhardy@bellsouth.net

Debbie Harding
hardingfive@cs.com

Deb Headworth
credoart@hotmail.com

Thomas Howard
xerxesth@aol.com

Grace MacKinnon
grace@deargrace.com

Janet Moylan
jkmoylan@cox.net

Peggy Stoks
peggystoks@netscape.net

Joan Ulicny
Joangv1@Juno.com

About the Editors

Jeff Cavins served as a Protestant minister for twelve years before returning to the Catholic faith. He is best known as the host of the popular television program "Life on the Rock" and will soon host a live, nationally syndicated radio program on the Starboard Broadcasting Radio Network.

Jeff is the creator of "The Great Adventure," a Bible time-line study system, and the author of *My Life on the Rock*, his autobiography. He has worked in partnership with Dr. Scott Hahn on the popular television series "Our Father's Plan."

Jeff and his wife, Emily, reside in Minnesota with their three daughters.

Matthew Pinto is the author of the best-selling book *Did Adam & Eve Have Belly Buttons? ... and 199 other questions from Catholic teenagers*, and creator and co-author of the *Friendly Defenders Catholic Flash Cards*.

Matt has founded and co-founded several Catholic apostolates, including CatholicExchange.com and *Envoy* magazine. He is also a former staff member of Catholic Answers.

Matt appears regularly on Catholic radio and television programs and conducts seminars throughout the country on a variety of Catholic issues. A native of suburban Philadelphia, Matt and his wife, Maryanne, reside in West Chester, Pennsylvania and are the parents of three boys.

To order additional copies of
Amazing Grace for Those Who Suffer,
or for bulk discounts,
please call Ascension Press
(800) 376-0520.

––––––––––

Please visit
www.AmazingGraceOnline.net
to find out more about the
Amazing Grace Series.

––––––––––

Also visit
www.AscensionPress.com
for information about
other Ascension Press titles.